Theology in Service
to the Church

Theology in Service
to the Church

Global and Ecumenical Perspectives

Edited by
ALLAN HUGH COLE JR.

CASCADE *Books* • Eugene, Oregon

THEOLOGY IN SERVICE TO THE CHURCH
Global and Ecumenical Perspectives

Cascade Books
An Imprint of Wipf and Stock Publishers
199 W. 8th Ave., Suite 3
Eugene, OR 97401

www.wipfandstock.com

ISBN 13: 978-1-62032-587-2

Cataloging-in-Publication data:

Theology in service to the church : global and ecumenical perspectives / edited by Allan Hugh Cole Jr.

224 p. ; cm. —Includes bibliographical references.

ISBN 13: 978-1-62032-587-2

1. Ecumenical movement. 2. Theology, Doctrinal. 3. Theology, Practical. I. Title.

BX9 .T48 2014

Manufactured in the U.S.A.

For Ted Wardlaw,
theologian in service to the church

How very good and pleasant it is when kindred live together in unity.

—Psalm 133:1

Contents

Contributors

Allan Hugh Cole Jr. is Academic Dean and Professor in the Nancy Taylor Williamson Distinguished Chair of Pastoral Care at Austin Presbyterian Theological Seminary, Austin, Texas. He has been a scholar in residence at the Center of Theological Inquiry in Princeton, New Jersey, and currently serves on the Research and Development Task Force of the Presbyterian Church (U.S.A.)'s Committee on Theological Education (COTE). His publications include *Fathers in Faith: Reflections on Parenthood and a Christian Life* (Cascade); *The Faith and Friendships of Teenage Boys,* with Robert C. Dykstra and Donald Capps (Westminster John Knox); *A Spiritual Life: Perspectives from Poets, Prophets, and Preachers* (Westminster John Knox); *The Life of Prayer: Mind, Body, and Soul* (Westminster John Knox); *Good Mourning: Getting through Your Grief* (Westminster John Knox); *Be Not Anxious: Pastoral Care of Disquieted Souls* (Eerdmans); *From Midterms to Ministry: Practical Theologians on Pastoral Beginnings* (Eerdmans); and *Losers, Loners, and Rebels: The Spiritual Struggles of Boys,* with Robert C. Dykstra and Donald Capps (Westminster John Knox).

Deborah van Deusen Hunsinger is Charlotte W. Newcombe Professor of Pastoral Theology at Princeton Theological Seminary. An ordained Presbyterian minister, she is interested in educating clergy and laypeople to offer theologically sound, psychologically informed, and contextually sensitive pastoral care in the church. She is author of numerous articles as well as author, coauthor, or coeditor of five books: *Transforming Church Conflict: Compassionate Leadership in Action,* with Theresa F. Latini (Westminster John Knox); *Healing Wisdom: Depth Psychology and the Pastoral*

Ministry, with Kathleen Greider and Felicity Kelcourse (Eerdmans); *Pray Without Ceasing: Revitalizing Pastoral Care* (Eerdmans); *The New Dictionary of Pastoral Studies,* edited by Wesley Carr et al. (Eerdmans); and *Theology and Pastoral Counseling: A New Interdisciplinary Approach* (Eerdmans).

George Hunsinger is Hazel Thompson McCord Professor of Systematic Theology at Princeton Theological Seminary. He is a delegate to the official Reformed/Roman Catholic International Dialogue (2011–17), and in 2006 he founded the National Religious Campaign Against Torture. His publications include *The Eucharist and Ecumenism* (Cambridge University Press); *Evangelical, Catholic and Reformed: Essays on Barth and Other Themes,* 2 vols. (Eerdmans); *Torture Is a Moral Issue: Christians, Jews, Muslims and People of Conscience Speak Out* (Eerdmans); *For the Sake of the World: Karl Barth and the Future of Ecclesial History* (Eerdmans); *Disruptive Grace: Studies in the Theology of Karl Barth* (Eerdmans); and *How to Read Karl Barth: The Shape of His Theology* (Oxford University Press). He is a member of the Center of Theological Inquiry in Princeton, New Jersey, and his research focuses on the history and theology of the Reformed tradition and the work of Karl Barth. In 2010 he received the Karl Barth Prize awarded by the Union of Evangelical Churches in Germany.

David H. Jensen is Professor in the Clarence N. and Betty B. Frierson Distinguished Chair of Reformed Theology and Associate Dean for Academic Programs at Austin Presbyterian Theological Seminary, Austin, Texas. His research explores the interconnections between Christian theology and everyday life. His publications include *God, Desire, and a Theology of Human Sexuality* (Westminster John Knox); *Flourishing Desire: A Theology of Human Sexuality* (Westminster John Knox); *Parenting* (Fortress); *Living Hope: The Future and Christian Faith* (Westminster John Knox); *The Lord and Giver of Life: Perspectives on Constructive Pneumatology* (Westminster John Knox); *Responsive Labor: A Theology of Work* (Westminster John Knox); *Graced Vulnerability: A Theology of Childhood* (Pilgrim); and *In the Company of Others: A Dialogical Christology* (Pilgrim). He is currently writing a theological commentary on 1 and 2 Samuel. He is also editor of a book series titled Compass (Fortress) that encourages theological reflection on everyday practices such as eating, shopping, playing, and working.

Nico Koopman is Professor of Systematic Theology, Director of the Beyers Naudé Centre for Public Theology, and Dean of the Faculty of Theology at the University of Stellenbosch in South Africa. He is also an ordained pastor in the Uniting Reformed Church in Southern Africa. His research focuses on the meaning of religious faith for public life. He has published widely on themes in the field of public theology, including a book with Robert Vosloo, *Die Ligtheid van Lig. Oor morele oriëntasie in 'n postmoderne tyd* (*The Lightness of Light: On Moral Orientation in Postmodern Times*), which was awarded the Andrew Murray Prize for theological literature. He has been a scholar in residence at the Center of Theological Inquiry in Princeton, New Jersey, and was also the first chairperson of the Global Network for Public Theology. As an academic, public speaker, and writer he plays a leading role in public theological discourses in the academy, churches, and broader society, in South Africa and internationally.

Paul Lakeland is the Aloysius P. Kelley SJ Professor of Catholic Studies and the Director of the Center for Catholic Studies at Fairfield University in Connecticut, where has taught religious studies, Catholic theology, and ecclesiology since 1981. He was educated at Heythrop Pontifical Athenaeum, Oxford University, the University of London, and Vanderbilt University, where he received the PhD in 1981. His most recent books include *Church: Living Communion* (Liturgical) and *Yves Congar: Essential Writings* (Orbis). His latest book, to commemorate the fiftieth anniversary of Vatican II's document on the Church, *Lumen Gentium,* will be published by Liturgical Press as *A Council That Will Never End:* Lumen Gentium *and the Church Today.* He is a member of the American Academy of Religion, the American Theological Society, and the Catholic Theological Society of America. In the fall of 2010 he was the Alan Richardson Fellow at Durham University in the United Kingdom.

Arie L. Molendijk is Professor of the History of Christianity and Professor of the Philosophy of Religion at the University of Groningen in the Netherlands. He was a Humboldt Fellow at the Ludwig-Maximilian University in Munich (1992–93), a member scholar at the Center of Theological Inquiry in Princeton, New Jersey, in the spring of 2008, and a senior fellow at the International Consortium for Research in the Humanities' "Dynamics in the History of Religions between Asia and Europe" in Bochum (2010–11). He has published extensively in the history of ideas, in particular of nineteenth- and twentieth-century theology, religious studies, and philosophy. His publications include a book on the theologian and sociologist Ernst Troeltsch, *Zwischen Theologie und Soziologie. Ernst Troeltsch's Typen der christlichen Gemeinschaftsbildung: Kirche, Sekte, Mystik,* (Gütersloher); a monograph, *The Emergence of the Science of Religion in the Netherlands* (Brill); and the coedited volumes *Exploring the Postsecular: The Religious, the Political, and the Urban* (Brill), *Holy Ground: Re-inventing Ritual Space in Modern Western Culture* (Peeters), and *Sacred Places in Modern Western Culture* (Peeters). Presently he is a fellow at the Netherlands Institute of Advanced Study and is working on a new book about Max Müller's mega-edition of the *Sacred Books of the East* (http://www.sacred-texts.com/sbe/index.htm).

Amy Plantinga Pauw is Henry P. Mobley Jr. Professor of Doctrinal Theology at Louisville Presbyterian Theological Seminary. Her publications include *The Supreme Harmony of All: The Trinitarian Theology of Jonathan Edwards* (Eerdmans); *Making Time for God: Daily Devotions for Children and Families to Share,* with Susan Garrett (Baker); and *Essays in Reformed Feminist and Womanist Dogmatics,* coauthored with Serene Jones (Westminster John Knox). She is the senior editor of *Belief,* a thirty-six volume theological commentary published by Westminster John Knox, and also serves on the board of the Louisville Institute. She received a Henry Luce III Fellowship in Theology for 2012–13 for a project on Wisdom Ecclesiology.

Marcus Plested is Associate Professor in Greek Patristic and Byzantine Theology, Marquette University. He was formerly Vice-Principal and Academic Director, Institute for Orthodox Christian Studies (Cambridge Theological Federation) and Affiliated Lecturer, Faculty of Divinity, University of Cambridge, England. He is a member of the Center of Theological Inquiry in Princeton, New Jersey, and has taught, lectured, and published widely in the field of Orthodox Christian studies. His publications include *Orthodox Readings of Aquinas* (Oxford University Press) and *The Macarian Legacy: The Place of Macarius-Symeon in the Eastern Christian Tradition* (Oxford University Press). Other research interests include the understanding of wisdom in the Christian tradition and the interaction between Western and Eastern theological traditions.

Cynthia L. Rigby is W. C. Brown Professor of Theology at Austin Presbyterian Theological Seminary, Austin, Texas, where she has been teaching since 1995. He publications include *The Promotion of Social Righteousness* (Witherspoon); *Blessed One: Protestant Perspectives on Mary,* with Beverly Roberts Gaventa (Westminster John Knox); and *Power, Powerlessness, and the Divine* (Duke University Press). A weekly writer for the *Dallas Morning News* blog *Texas Faith,* she is currently completing a book titled *Renewing*

Grace (Westminster John Knox). She is active in the American Academy of Religion and is an ordained minister in the Presbyterian Church (U.S.A.).

David Tombs is Assistant Professor of Conflict Resolution and Reconciliation at the Irish School of Ecumenics, Trinity College, Dublin, Ireland. His primary research focus is on religion, ethics, and reconciliation, and his areas of expertise include conflict and conflict resolution in Northern Ireland, post-conflict justice and truth commissions in Latin America, and political and contextual Christian theologies in a global perspective. His publications include *Explorations in Reconciliation: New Directions for Theology*, with Joseph Liechty (Ashgate); *Latin American Liberation Theology* (Brill); *Truth and Memory: The Church and Human Rights in El Salvador and Guatemala*, with Michael A. Hayes (Gracewing); and *Rights and Righteousness: Religious Pluralism and Human Rights* (Northern Ireland Human Rights Commission). In addition to Northern Ireland he has carried out research in El Salvador, South Africa, Sri Lanka, and Israel/Palestine, and has been a scholar in residence at the Center of Theological Inquiry in Princeton, New Jersey. His current research is focused on gender violence and torture practices and their implications for theology. He is currently writing a book on crucifixion as an instrument of torture and sexualized violence.

Olli-Pekka Vainio is a theologian and Research Fellow of Philosophical Psychology, Morality, and Politics, Research Unit of the Academy of Finland at the Faculty of Theology, University of Helsinki, Finland. He is a member of the Center of Theological Inquiry in Princeton, New Jersey. His research interests include the history of philosophy and theology, and contemporary philosophy of religion. His publications include *Beyond Fideism: Negotiable Religious Identities* (Ashgate); *Engaging Luther: A (New) Theological Assessment* (Cascade); and *Justification and Participation in Christ: The Development of the Lutheran Doctrine of Justification from Luther to the Formula of Concord* (Brill).

Hetty Zock is Professor of Psychology of Religion and Spiritual Care, and KSGV Professor of Religion and Mental Health at the University of Groningen, the Netherlands. She earned the MDiv and PhD degrees at the University of Leiden and worked for ten years as a minister in the Dutch Reformed Church. She has been teaching psychology of religion since 1994 and spiritual care since 2000. She is a member of the Center of Theological Inquiry in Princeton, New Jersey. Her publications include *Religious Voices in Self-Narratives: Making Sense of Life in Times of Transition* (de Gruyter);

At the Crossroads of Art and Religion (Peeters); and *A Psychology of Ultimate Concern* (Rodopi).

Preface

CHRISTIANITY IS A GLOBAL religion with growing numbers of expressions. As such, it calls for deepening relationships across varying traditions while also formulating collaborative visions. The latter requires providing for diverse perspectives that remain conversant with both tradition and contemporary movements. Christianity without tradition proves episodic, if not narcissistic. Christianity without contemporary sensibilities proves stale, if not irrelevant. Of course, Christians have always spoken with a range of voices. Yet the current global religious context, marked by differences and pluralism, behooves us to speak with more intention, clarity, and unity across our diversity. Moreover, Christians must be facile not only when speaking with persons who embrace other religions—for example, Jews, Muslims, Hindus, or Buddhists—but also when speaking with one another, that is, with the panoply of persons who follow Jesus in the twenty-first century. A thriving church will require Christians from various traditions and on varying trajectories to become familiar with one another, appreciate one another, and work in a common service to God in Jesus Christ.

In 2012, a group of distinguished scholars from around the world representing a range of Orthodox, Catholic, and Protestant perspectives gathered at Austin Presbyterian Theological Seminary in Austin, Texas. Our goal was to deepen our relationships and to share our visions, especially as regards how theological reflection may, indeed must, serve the church. The occasion was the Williamson Distinguished Scholars Conference, a biennial event made possible by Hugh and Nan Williamson, longtime friends of Austin Seminary. The conference theme, "Global and Ecumenical Perspectives on Theology in Service to the Church," brought together thirteen scholars representing a range of expertise. The group presented their essays related to the conference theme, received feedback from participants, argued with one another in constructive ways, discussed numerous salient matters facing the global church, and ultimately produced the essays in this volume.

This conference, intentionally global and ecumenical in representation, modeled what may be accomplished in ecumenical conversations on theology in service to the church. Conference discussions, like the essays you will read in this book, were substantive, thoughtful, challenging, constructive, and hopeful. In my judgment, the church ecumenical needs its scholars to do more of the kind of work evident in this book. Perhaps such work will inform more unity across diversity among those who seek to be faithful to Jesus Christ.

Acknowledgments

THIS BOOK WAS MADE possible through the generosity of Hugh and Nancy Williamson, faithful friends and supporters of Austin Presbyterian Theological Seminary, where I am privileged to serve. The Williamsons care deeply about theological education and the church, and their witness and generosity continues to enrich both. I am grateful for their friendship and presence in my life.

I give thanks as well for the Austin Seminary community, including its Board of Trustees, administration, faculty, staff, students, and alums. A school of the church, the Austin Seminary community embodies both a commitment to rigorous intellectual pursuit and a passion for Christian ministry and service. This community provides me and so many others the opportunity to live out our vocations thoughtfully and in earnest, with excitement and joy. I am especially grateful for the Seminary's president, Ted Wardlaw, whose leadership, vision, faithful support, encouragement, sense of humor, and love for the church offers me, and others, so much. I am grateful, too, for Alison Riemersma, my assistant in the dean's office, whose copyediting skills made this book better and whose hard work and support consistently buoy Austin Seminary, me, and my own work.

It has been a pleasure working with the fine people at Cascade Books on this project. I appreciate the contributions of my editor, Rodney Clapp, and copy editor, Jacob Martin, both of whom helped make this book better. I remain grateful as well for the ongoing support of K. C. Hanson, editor-in-chief, Matthew Wimer, assistant managing editor, and James Stock, marketing director, all of whom demonstrate a refreshing hospitality and grace.

Acknowledgments

Most of all, I am grateful for my family, who support and nurture me vocationally and otherwise. My parents, Allan and Jeri Cole, introduced me to God's love and the arms of the church at a young age, as much through their examples as through their words. Their lives continue to demonstrate that parental love can bear the image of godly love. My wife, Tracey, and our daughters, Meredith and Holly, show me a depth of love—both human and divine—and bring me experiences of joy and gratitude beyond what my own words can express. In the words of the psalmist, "the boundary lines have fallen for me in pleasant places" (Ps 16:6).

Historical, Doctrinal, and Philosophical Theology

1

Reflections on the Reception of the Church Fathers in the Contemporary Context

—Marcus Plested

THIS PAPER BRINGS TOGETHER various thoughts relating to the reception of the Fathers that have arisen in my research and teaching over the last few years. It argues for the ongoing relevance of the patristic matrix for any form of theological endeavor that seeks to serve the church. Indeed, I contend that the Fathers provide us with a model for scriptural engagement and gospel proclamation, doctrinal articulation, and pastoral practice that should be regarded as normative. But this recognition of the normative character of the patristic witness does not amount to any sort of static or culture-bound notion of authority, nor does it suggest that the Fathers were infallible or superhumanly prescient—able to offer pat answers to the problems and burning issues of our own time. The pattern of patristic reception I am proposing may be illustrated (and I use the word advisedly) through a number of visual considerations relating the above to the Orthodox icon.

TEACHING PATRISTIC PASTORAL THEOLOGY

Let me begin with some considerations arising from a postgraduate class on patristic pastoral theology and pastoral practice. This class, "Texts and Practices in the Early Church," is a seminar-based course that was developed for the master of arts in pastoral theology offered by the Cambridge Theological Federation. One of the course materials, designed to help students conceptualize and articulate their understandings of the weight and import of the patristic witness, was a set of seven models of reception and reappropriation. There is nothing especially binding about the number seven in this context (indeed an earlier sketch worked with only five models), but seven is, as we all know, a most attractive number for a theologian.

SEVEN MODELS OF PATRISTIC RECEPTION AND REAPPROPRIATION

1. **Imitative**
   According to this model, it suffices to do what the Fathers did and to re-say what they said. The Fathers, in this view, have all the answers to today's questions.

2. **Normative**
   In this model, the church fathers are seen to provide a *paradigm* of pastoral theology and practice that we are called on to "translate" to our own specific contexts—preferably within the context of a living tradition, a continuum of faith.

3. **Reconstitutive**
   According to this model, the churches have lost their way and have become severed from their past. We must, therefore, start over again with a return to the Fathers, reappropriating and recreating the patristic tradition in our own context.

4. **Recollective**
   In the recollective model, the experience of the early church is there to be remembered, recalled, and recontextualized. The patristic tradition represents a somewhat distant, almost utopic, reality which we may invoke with respect and attempt somehow to relate to our own contexts.

5. **Imaginative**

   According to the imaginative model, the Fathers give us a rich vein of material and experience that we may freely draw upon for inspiration, or reject, as we see fit. We are in no way bound by the Fathers but see them as a colorful and potentially instructive resource.

6. **Connective**

   Here, the patristic experience allows us to make connections between then and now, as we see need. The patristic experience may, on occasion, illumine contemporary practice and reflection but has no intrinsic authority or interest beyond the historical. "They did it like this, we do it like that."

7. **Reactive**

   The reactive model rejects the Fathers, regarding the patristic approach to pastoral ministry as an example of how *not* to do it. The patristic witness is seen as irredeemably dated, irrelevant, outmoded, patriarchal, culture-bound, useless, et cetera.

Naturally, these models have very permeable boundaries. Roughly speaking, recognition of the authority and relevance of the patristic matrix diminishes as one descends down the list. These models have proved to be of some use for students in this particular course. Indeed it has been striking to see how positively students respond to patristic material. Even with classes of very mixed backgrounds, including many of a broadly liberal theological persuasion, the church fathers remain an inexhaustible treasury.[1] I have yet to meet anyone who has plumped for model 7 as their model of choice.

Introducing theological students to the pastoral theology of the early church is not always a straightforward affair. There is a great imaginative leap required, not to mention a high degree of hermeneutical sophistication. Texts are necessarily the principal means of entry into the pastoral theory and practice of the early church and the first task has been to encourage students to immerse themselves into the life and thought of the early church through close study and critical discussion of some key texts. But issues of reception and reappropriation in an ecumenical context have

---

1. As the French Oratorian Louis Thomassin put it, "inexhaustum est penu Theologiae Patrum." *Dogmatum theologicorum* 1, preface, §xx. This was a remark enthusiastically embraced (if slightly misquoted) by Fr. Georges Florovsky, the herald of a thoroughgoing patristic revival in twentieth-century Orthodox theology. See his "Patristic Theology and the Ethos of the Orthodox Church," 22.

always been to the fore of class discussion. The early church is indubitably a key source and pivotal point of reference for all our various ecclesial traditions. This does not, of course, mean that it is necessarily normative for all these traditions or beyond critical evaluation and discussion. Responses to it have certainly not been uniform—and this has made for some lively discussion in class.

PATRISTIC THEOLOGY: SOME KEY CONSIDERATIONS

Study of the approach to theology in the early church is deeply salutary for any form of theological endeavor today. The church fathers did not produce "pastoral theology" as such, nor did they compose systematic treatises on Trinitarian theology, Christology, or ecclesiology. Their theology was necessarily pastoral and ecclesial—written in and for the church. In our own woefully divided and compartmentalized theological sphere, this holistic approach has much to commend itself.

Mention of the pastoral and ecclesial context brings us to the central problem of tradition, tradition understood not as the dead weight of the past but as the living community of faith in which the gospel is both received and transmitted. This process of reception and transmission is pre-eminently one of education and formation. Patristic theology, as I say, is best understood not as a series of more or less disconnected reflections upon discrete sub-disciplines, but as an attempt to teach and communicate and inculcate the revelation of God in Christ, "and him crucified" (1 Cor 2:22).

To theologize in this context is not to write "about" God but to recognize and proclaim God, and to consider the consequences of that recognition and proclamation. St. John the Evangelist has the title "the theologian" in the Eastern Orthodox tradition not because of his intellectual skills but because he proclaims, more emphatically than the other evangelists, that the Word in Christ is indeed God, that the *logos* is indeed *theos*. The other figure to have the title "the theologian" is St. Gregory of Nazianzus. In his case, the title again recognizes not so much his theological erudition as his peerless defense of the equal and identical divinity of Father, Son, and Holy Spirit. Theology, at least as understood by the Fathers, is thus inseparably bound up with the life of the church. It loses its essential ecclesiality at its peril.

Two definitions may help flesh out what I am trying to say about the patristic conception of theology. The first is the familiar declaration by St. Irenaeus of Lyons, that "the glory of God is a living human being." Humankind is the pinnacle of God's creation, the summation of God's purposes. A human being living an authentically human life is God's glory, God's self-revelation in the world. And "the life of the human being," Irenaeus continues, "is the vision of God."[2] In other words, our life makes sense only in relation to the vision, the love, and experience of God—in relation, that is, to theology. The other definition comes from St. Gregory the Theologian, who defines the human being as "an animal . . . in the process of being deified" (ζῷον θεούμενον).[3] There is no need for us to claim that we are by nature distinct from the animal kingdom, or indeed to deny that the observable processes of evolution (such as they are) may have had some part in producing our current make-up. What is different about us is not so much our nature but our calling, our vocation to share the very life of God. This process of deification—exactly equivalent to St. Irenaeus' "vision of God"—is that which defines and shapes an authentically human life. This is what theology is really about.

Having outlined *some* aspects of the theological enterprise of the early church, let me also outline some other (slightly less elevated) considerations. Many patristic texts represent something of a "counsel of perfection." We must be constantly alive to the gap between theory and practice. Was, for example, the ideal pastor sketched by Gregory in his *Apology for His Flight* ever more than an unattainable ideal?[4] We must also recognize that we have no direct access to the pastoral life of the early church. L. P. Hartley's poignant observation, "The past is a foreign country: they do things differently there," referred to a gap in time of some fifty years.[5] What of a gap of fifteen hundred years or more? It is a great mistake to underestimate the hermeneutical impedimenta surrounding any attempt to understand let alone appropriate the Fathers. We must be also alive to the effect of the various lenses through which we view this period. The Fathers wrote in specific sociocultural and historical contexts. This inevitably has a formative influence on some of their responses to issues such as, *inter*

---

2. Irenaeus, *Against Heresies* 4.20.7 (SC 100).
3. St. Gregory, *Oration* 38.11 (PG 36:324).
4. Ibid., 2 (PG 35:408–513).
5. Hartley, *The Go-Between*, 1.

alia, the status and role of women or the legitimacy of slavery. Again, such considerations must inform our critical response to the sources.

Moving on now to some reception issues that have emerged in my recent research, let me now sketch a number of visual and iconic hermeneutical considerations—beginning with some considerations that emerged in the process of researching and writing my book on *Orthodox Readings of Aquinas*.[6]

Multiple Perspective

The term *reverse perspective* is often used to characterize the visual principles of the Orthodox icon by contrast with the linear perspective that became standard in Western art in the Renaissance. Rather than inveigling the gaze of the viewer to rest on some imagined vanishing point in the distance through the use of convergent sight lines, the perspective of the icon springs outwards, arresting the attention with its sheer immediacy. Conventional notions of distance collapse as certain objects are rendered larger the further away they are. The absence of an outside light source, with attendant effects such as *chiaroscuro*, mitigates against any sense that one is merely a spectator. The light comes, rather, from within the icon. The persons depicted emerge to impress themselves upon the viewer and require a response, whether of veneration or of rejection. *Theoria* (contemplation) in this case, is inescapably participatory, ineluctably relational. The very nature of the icon confounds any attempt to treat it simply as an object. Indeed, as a function of this non-linear perspective, the icon becomes, in a sense, the active subject and the viewer the viewed.[7]

What we call reverse perspective is, however, only one of the ways in which the Orthodox icon operates. Indeed, "reverse perspective" is something of a misnomer in that the technique long predates the linear perspective of which it is supposedly the reverse. Icons also routinely combine a view from above with face-on presentation, use variable dimensionality, or represent interior space with exterior features: there is no single perspective, reverse or otherwise. In the icon, we are also

6. Plested, *Orthodox Readings of Aquinas*. The section on reverse and multiple perspective reproduces and reworks material from chapter 1 of that work.

7. A most useful and perceptive discussion of current research regarding reverse perspective may be found in Antonova, "On the Problem of 'Reverse Perspective'" and *Space, Time, and Presence in the Icon*.

prompted to question our received notions of time as non-simultaneous events are depicted on the same plane. In the icon it is always "now." In short, the icon operates on what we should call a multiple perspective, in both spatial and temporal terms.

The notion of multiple perspective is a most useful one for any undertaking that involves the reading of texts. If the study of reception history has taught us anything it is that texts are never received as neutral archival material. When one author reads another, there is always an ongoing and very present dynamic of interpretation, negotiation, and dialogue. We do well to be aware of this interactive and synchronic dynamic in our encounter with church tradition. We should be under no illusion that we are somehow outside the picture, capable of purely objective analysis of what we observe in the past. We are, rather, part of the picture, responding and relating to tradition within a rich and ever-expanding vista of possibilities.

This is the primary benefit of a multiple perspective: the realization that patristic sources are not simply inanimate objects from the past to be observed and pronounced upon from some lofty height of supposed impartiality. Our sources are as much active subjects as objects of investigation—better approached, in other words, as icons than as paintings of the conventional Western type.

An Iconic Mode of Reception

We might go further and speak in terms of an *iconic mode of reception*. In Christian history, the Fathers have been used as weapons with depressing regularity, employed as sources of theological artillery with which to confound and dismay one's enemies. Passages from their works have been decontextualized, objectified, and depersonalized: torn from their scriptural foundations and thrown at the enemy with all the subtlety of a sledgehammer. Such an approach manifestly betrays the very nature of the patristic theological enterprise.

I have christened such polemical use of the Fathers "patristics as ballistics." This is a characterization I conceived of as part of my study of the patristic hermeneutic of the Council of Aachen (AD 809)—Charlemagne's attempt to secure the formal adoption of the *filioque*.[8] This council stands as a stark example of "patristics as ballistics" or, to put it another way,

---

8. The section reproduces and reworks sections of Plested, "Patristic Hermeneutic," 130–37.

non-iconic reception. The decree of the this council, the *Decretum Aquis-granense*, represents a departure in patristic reception. Patristic authority had long been appealed to in conciliar settings but the Council of Aachen is unprecedented in the way in which it presents the Fathers as an indiscriminate and univocal force whose authority is both predetermined and incontrovertible—and does so primarily in order to shame and confound those obstinate heretics, the Greeks, in the vexed matter of the *filioque*.

A non-iconic mode of reception, in short, brings the Fathers down to earth, cutting the connection between their works and their persons. Their writings become merely an archive that may be accessed and utilized on demand. For all the reverence given and authority ascribed to them, they are, ultimately, just objects for our use, weapons in our hands.

By contrast, an iconic mode of reception is revealed in the nature of the icon itself. The material becomes a means of manifesting and revealing immaterial realities: "heaven in ordinarie" as that sublime poet, George Herbert, puts it. An iconic approach to the Fathers looks to them as living saints and ecumenical teachers. Such an approach is in essence both personal and relational. An iconic mode of reception is dynamic, not static. In this mode of reception, the Fathers are ultimately subjects, not objects.

If we examine the history of the *filioque* dispute we see that it is the non-iconic mode of reception that has prevailed. Seemingly ever more extensive and invariably partial collections of patristic material are thrown into the ring from the time of Photius onwards. Anselm of Havelberg, in his debate with Nicetas of Nicomedia in 1136, brings to bear Cyril and various Latin Fathers and claims never to have even heard of any *per filium* formula. The Latin delegates to the discussions at Nicaea-Nymphaion in 1234 brought with them a substantial battery of texts on the *filioque* that, so far as they were concerned, brooked no dissent. In the run-up to the re-union council of Lyons (1274), Nicholas of Cotrone adapted and circulated a weighty but highly defective anthology of patristic citations supporting the *filioque* which formed the basis of Thomas Aquinas's *Contra errores grae-corum*. At the reunion council of Ferrara-Florence (1438–39), the Greek delegation was outmaneuvered and flummoxed by much of this material. It had few answers to the sheer volume of patristic material with which it was faced apart from a recurrent charge of interpolation and falsification—a charge it was only able to prove occasionally. Forced to fight on ground not of their choosing and on an uneven playing field, the Byzantines were forced into capitulation.

But what might an iconic mode of reception look like? Photius of Constantinople's answer when presented with reports of patristic support for the *filioque* is instructive. Photius does not expect inerrancy from the Fathers. To err is human and the Fathers are human. If we do encounter teachings inconsistent with the scriptural witness and the proclamations of the Ecumenical Councils in the Latin Fathers, we should hide rather than expose their failings and not emulate Ham in failing to cover the nakedness of his father, Noah.[9] Photius is not working on the basis of any extensive knowledge of the Latin patristic tradition and can come across as unduly dismissive in what he calls, in the *Mystagogia*, "your Fathers." In this respect he can be quite as culturally limited as the Carolingian theologians of the Council of Aachen. Nonetheless, his point on errancy is an important one. Photius also very correctly points out that much of what was expressed as a theological opinion was being taught as dogma by many Latin theologians of his day. This estimation tallies nicely with Augustine's own clear sense of provisionality with respect to his teaching on the *filioque*.

An iconic approach to the Fathers must, therefore, involve a recognition of their capacity for error. As human beings, their works are necessarily imperfect. We need have no obligation to follow Gregory of Nyssa in his universalism or Augustine in his more extreme anti-Pelagian positions. Again, as human beings, the Fathers do not speak with one voice—indeed some would barely speak to one another in their own time.[10] Here we may choose to supplement the notion of iconic reception with the distinction made by some Fathers between the image and the likeness.[11] The image pertaining to human beings by virtue of their creation, the likeness being the gradual process by which the image is realized and perfected. In their earthly lives, the Fathers may be seen as growing into the likeness: approaching perfection but not yet perfect.

This plurivocity is recognized in many of the ablest theologians of East and West. St. Maximus the Confessor and St. John of Damascus allow for a *per filium* formula precisely so as to embrace both the Latin and the Greek perspectives on the Trinity. St. Gregory Palamas frankly confronts certain differences between various Fathers but sees no underlying disharmony in their chorus. Although he squarely rejects the *filioque* doctrine

9. Photius, *Mystagogia* (PG 102:352A).

10. Here we might think of St. Jerome and St. Ambrose or St. Epiphanius and St. John Chrysostom.

11. For example, by St. Irenaeus of Lyons and St. Diadochus of Photice.

(in his *Apodictic Treatises*) he willingly speaks of the Holy Spirit as "common to both" Father and Son, and specifically as the pre-eternal rejoicing of Father and Son.[12] Such formulations arise out of his sympathetic reading of Augustine's *De Trinitate* in the Planoudes translation. Indeed, Palamas uses *filioque* language in the context of the immanent Trinity—but not in respect of origination. It seems to me that this "Orthodox *filioque*" is of considerably greater significance for Orthodox appropriation of the *filioque* tradition than the compromise *per filium* formula.

In the West, John Scotus Eriugena substantially extended the range of Greek sources available in Latin, helping correct the woeful imbalance and limited range evident in the *Decretum Aquisgranense*. He was acutely aware of the growing cultural and theological gap between East and West and to help bridge it he proposed a bold synthesis of Denys and Augustine, one that expressed the underlying harmony of these two very different figures.[13] On the *filioque*, he adopts a distinctively Eastern position emphasizing the causation of the Father but upholding procession through the Son, *per filium*. Eriugena also develops a compelling and dynamic understanding of authority that consists in the continuum of faith instituted by the Word incarnate and transmitted to the apostles and to their successors.[14]

The *Sentences* of Peter Lombard offers a seminal treatment of the fundamental convergence of apparently divergent patristic sources—all under the guiding maxim *non sunt adversi sed diversi*.[15] Thomas Aquinas, for his part, is fully cognizant of the differences that exist among the doctors of the church but is also frank about the possibility of error, for instance through excess of zeal in combating particular heresies.[16] But he is convinced of the underlying harmony of the holy doctors in accordance with both scripture and reason. That said, Thomas will tolerate no disharmony on the matter of the *filioque* in that this is a matter of papal authority. Here, I fear, we are back in the distinctly non-iconic realms of the *Decretum Aquisgranense*.

In the modern period too we can trace a number of promising instances of iconic reception. Speaking just of the Orthodox tradition, the

12. Sinkewicz, *Saint Gregory Palamas*.

13. See D'Onofrio, "The *Concordia*," 115–40.

14. See Marler, "Dialectical Use of Authority," 95–113.

15. On this maxim, see Ghellinck, *Le Mouvement*, 517–23.

16. For the Greek Fathers in Thomas, see Emery, "Note," 193–207. See also Plested, *Orthodox Readings of Aquinas*, 15–21. For the Fathers in general in Thomas, see Elders, "Thomas Aquinas," 337–66.

whole revival of Orthodox theology in the twentieth century is built around the creative reaffirmation of the Fathers: Fr. Georges Florovsky's neo-patristic synthesis stands as a particularly fine example. This reappropriation requires not repetition but a "new creative act." An essentially analogous notion of patristic revival also lies at the center of the extraordinary theological achievement of Fr. Sergius Bulgakov.

I trust this gives some flavor of what I understand iconic reception to be. An iconic approach enables us to engage with the Fathers in a dynamic mode, learning from them as living teachers and saints. It also underlines their historicity, spurring us to explore their *Sitz im Leben*. The iconic mode encourages us to expand our notion of patristics beyond dogmatics and thereby give full credence to the scriptural, liturgical, and mystical dimensions of the Fathers' theological enterprise. It allows for plurivocity, error, and harmony. It precludes an archival proof-text approach and subverts any static or culture-bound notion of authority.

CONCLUDING REMARKS

The Fathers constitute an indispensable resource for any form of theology that seeks to serve the church. Indeed, I would go so far as to suggest that any such theology is bound to adhere to the second of my seven models— the "normative" model. It is also my contention that patristic reception is best conceived of in dynamic and even visual terms. We should not think of patristic reception in terms of the dead weight of the past, still less as furnishing ammunition for own theological predilections. We should, rather, approach the Fathers much as we might approach an icon: treating the patristic tradition as a living and multi-perspectival reality irreducible to system or merely rational analysis. Through such an iconic mode of reception we may ourselves enter into a mode of theologizing that is necessarily pastoral and necessarily ecclesial: theology in the service of the church indeed but also theology born of the church, born of the living continuum of faith which belongs as much to us as to the Fathers.

2

Justification

Ninety-Four Theses

–George Hunsinger

THESES

Christ Imparts His Perfect Righteousness

1. Jesus Christ is our righteousness (1 Cor 1:30).

2. We will never have any other righteousness before God than the righteousness we have in him.

3. He gives us his righteousness by giving us himself, and in giving us himself he gives us his perfect righteousness (John Calvin).

4. His person and his benefits are one. He does not give the one without the other.

5. Union with Christ is therefore the context within which the benefit of his righteousness is imparted to us.

6. It is freely imparted by grace through faith, and it is in virtue of this perfect, imparted righteousness that we are justified before the judgment seat of God.

The Ground of Our Righteousness in Christ

7. The righteousness imparted by Christ is grounded in his perfect obedience, both active and passive, which took place apart from us (*extra nos*) for our sakes and in our place.

8. By his active obedience he perfectly fulfilled the law of love in all its dimensions, while by his passive obedience he perfectly bore, in his passion and death on the cross, the just penalty of the law against sin in order that we might be spared.

9. This, then, is the great exchange (*admirable commercium*), that he takes our sin and death to himself and gives us his righteousness and life.

How Christ's Righteousness Is Given and Received

10. Christ's righteousness is not imparted to us in bits and pieces but whole and entire.

11. It is imparted instantaneously by grace to the faith that unites us with Christ and that makes us members incorporate in his mystical body, the church (*totus Christus*).

12. His perfect righteousness is imparted to faith once for all, in and with our baptism, and then ever anew day by day.

The Meaning of "Passive Righteousness"

13. The perfect righteousness that we receive from Christ, and by which we are justified, is not gradually limited or replaced by a righteousness that takes shape within us and to which we contribute with the assistance of grace.

14. As helpless sinners in ourselves, we do nothing to contribute to, or to constitute, the righteousness by which we are justified.

15. We are passive with respect to its being constituted by the obedience of Christ, but not with respect to receiving it, for the act of reception by which we receive it is the gift of faith.

Justification and Works of Love

16. Works of love are a consequence, not a cause, of the righteousness by which we are justified.

17. They are not a cause, because Christ himself and Christ alone is at once the sufficient cause and content of the righteousness by which we are justified.

18. Works of love are a necessary consequence, however, because when they are absent, faith is dead and Christ's justifying righteousness has not been received.

19. Thus the ground of our justification is not to be found in works of love we might perform, but in Christ's perfect, vicarious obedience, and in particular in his death on the cross, so that we are justified not by works but "by his blood" (Rom 5:9).

Forensic Justification

20. The righteousness by which we are justified does not arise "forensically" from declaration.

21. We are not righteous because we are declared righteous. We are declared righteous because we are righteous (Francis Turretin).

22. It is because we are righteous in Christ by Christ, and not by mere declaration, that we are justified before the judgment seat of God.

Justification and the Eschatology of Righteousness

23. We are more perfectly in Christ than he is in us (Peter Martyr Vermigli).

24. Our righteousness, like our life, is hidden with Christ in God (Col 3:3).

25. It is therefore something real, hidden, and yet to come. It is not a "legal fiction."

26. Our righteousness in Christ is not any less real because it remains hidden, nor any less valid before God because we look for it with eager expectation to be revealed in its final, glorious, and unsurpassable form.

27. The reality of our righteousness in Christ is therefore thoroughly eschatological.

28. We have it here and now only in the tension between the "already" and the "not yet."

29. We have it, that is, only in the tension between what has already been imparted to us and what has yet to be actualized and revealed in us.

Justification and the Eschatology of Sin

30. In the time between the times our status as sinners is also thoroughly eschatological.

31. Although the power of sin is broken so that sin no longer has dominion over us, we are still truly sinners who must pray for forgiveness every day.

32. The gift of righteousness in Christ covers all our sins, past, present and future, even though our sinfulness in itself would make us worthy of divine condemnation, not only before baptism but after it.

Simul Iustus et Peccator

33. In the time between the times we are therefore *simul iustus et peccator* (Luther).

34. On the one hand, in Christ and because of Christ, we are completely righteous in God's sight, being clothed in Christ's perfect righteousness.

35. Yet on the other hand, because sin still clings so closely, we remain sinners in ourselves, not partially but totally, even after baptism.

Sin and Righteousness Are Essentially Categorical

36. Although sin and righteousness admit of degrees, they are essentially categorical before God and are therefore mutually exclusive.

37. Their overlap in the time between the times, as determining factors of our spiritual lives, is an eschatological mystery.

38. The tension will be resolved at last when Christ appears in glory and we shall be like him—righteous as he is righteous, alive in glory as he is alive—because we shall see him as he is, and ourselves as he has

made us to be in union and communion with him (1 John 3:2; 1 Cor 15:52; Phil 3:21).

39. The transition in us (*in nobis*) from sin to righteousness, and from death to life, is finally more like resurrection from the dead than it is like a gradual progression from illness to health.

40. Although there is indeed continuity between renewal as we experience it in this life and its glorious fulfillment in the life to come, it is a matter of continuity in the midst of radical discontinuity (1 Cor 15:51; 13:12).

Justification and the Holy Spirit

41. The principal work of the Holy Spirit is to give us the gift of faith by bringing Christ to us (objectively) and us to Christ (subjectively) in order to make us one with him (John Calvin).

42. It is therefore in and through the Holy Spirit that we are in Christ by Christ, for the Holy Spirit is always in the Son and does not operate without him (Athanasius).

43. The Holy Spirit may be described, more particularly, as the "subjective possibility" of justification, even as Jesus Christ may be described as the "objective possibility" of justification.

44. Jesus Christ is justification's "objective possibility," because without his vicarious obedience and saving death apart from us (*extra nos*), we could have no righteousness before God and would be eternally lost.

45. The Holy Spirit, on the other hand, is justification's "subjective possibility," because without the Holy Spirit's working in our lives (*in nobis*) through Word and Sacrament, the grace of justification could be neither known nor received.

46. The Holy Spirit is also justification's "subjective reality," because in and through the Spirit, again by means of Word and Sacrament, the "objective reality" of justification—as accomplished apart from us by Christ alone—is communicated as a finished work to faith.

47. In short, we cannot by our own power or understanding, believe in the Lord Jesus Christ, or come to him, except by the working of the

Spirit, who inspires faith in us, and empowers us for good works, as he wills (Martin Luther).

48. The Holy Spirit, moreover, adds nothing to the finished work of Christ or to his saving righteousness, but rather "applies" it—or better, "actualizes and re-presents" it—to faith by grace.

49. The Holy Spirit actualizes and re-presents Christ's saving righteousness here and now in three main ways: (a) once for all, (b) again and again, (c) more and more.

50. The Holy Spirit actualizes and re-presents Christ's saving righteousness "once for all," because Christ's perfect righteousness, whole and entire, is given to faith as a gift in a way that is irrevocable, unrepeatable and binding.

51. This "once for all" aspect corresponds to baptism—through which justification is effectively signified, sealed, communicated, and fulfilled—because baptism is also something irrevocable, unrepeatable and binding.

52. Moreover, the Holy Spirit actualizes and re-presents Christ's saving righteousness "again and again," because the Spirit encounters, teaches, and encourages us in a way that is new each morning.

53. This "again and again" aspect corresponds to our dying and rising with Christ as whole persons each day.

54. Finally, the Holy Spirit actualizes and re-presents Christ's saving righteousness by grace "more and more," because over the course of time the Spirit makes us to increase and abound in love.

55. The "once for all" and the "again and again" aspects both pertain especially (if not exclusively) to justification, because they concern the gift of Christ's perfect righteousness as something given to faith freely and sufficiently apart from any merit or good works.

56. The "more and more" aspect pertains especially (if not exclusively) to sanctification, because it concerns the Spirit's work of gradual renewal through which we learn to perform deeds of repentance, justice, and love.

57. All three aspects—and each in its own way—arise from the Spirit's incomparable gift of making us one with Christ.

Justification and Sanctification

58. The entire life of faith is a life of continual repentance.

59. In repentance we turn again each day from the old self that was put to death with Christ (*peccator*) to the new self that has been raised up with him (*iustus*).

60. It is as Christ sanctifies us through the gift of his Spirit that we turn from the old self to the new.

61. Sanctification takes place mainly in two ways, first through works of love and justice (*vivificatio*) and second through acts of confession, contrition, and rectification (*mortificatio*) (John Calvin).

62. Through sanctification we are brought into conformity with Christ, who died on the cross for all in order that the faithful might live no longer for themselves but for him, and therefore for the world that he loves (2 Cor 5:15).

63. The sanctifying power of the Holy Spirit in our lives belongs entirely to God and not to us.

64. God rewards our works of love and acts of repentance as his gifts, but this reward pertains only to degrees of glory, and not to the free gift of eternal life itself (1 Cor 15:40–41).

Justification and Eternal Life

65. Justification and eternal life are inseparable gifts. We do not have the one without the other.

66. The gift of eternal life is given immediately to faith in union with Christ, in and with baptism, through the impartation of Christ's perfect righteousness, and so through the gift of our justification before God.

67. Eternal life is not something that can be merited in any way, for, like our justification, it is solely the free gift of grace.

68. Eternal life is given freely by grace through faith, in and with baptism. The baptized are not only those who in themselves are unworthy, but even more they are those who, apart from grace, have deserved God's just condemnation (*iustificatio impii*).

Eternal Life Does Not Need to Be Earned

69. We are not loved by God because we are worthy. We are worthy because God loves us (Martin Luther).

70. The motivation for doing good works, whether works of love or acts of repentance, is not to attain eternal life.

71. What motivates them is simply gratitude for the inestimable gift of God's grace.

72. Works of love are either gratuitous, seeking nothing in return, or else they are not works of love.

73. Likewise, acts of repentance are either undertaken freely for their own sakes, in love and obedience to God, with no ulterior motives, or else they are not acts of repentance.

Even Our Best Works Are Tainted

74. All our good works are tainted by sin, and so are not pleasing in themselves in God's sight (Isa 54:6).

75. They are made acceptable by God's mercy alone, through which they are justified and sanctified by grace.

76. The justification of works depends on the justification of the person.

Assurance of Faith

77. The gifts and promises of God are irrevocable (Rom 11:29).

78. The gift of faith includes the assurance of salvation so that faith without assurance is deficient or confused.

79. Assurance is not based primarily on anything in ourselves—whether faith, works, or evidence of the Holy Spirit—but supremely on Christ and the promises of God.

80. If the faithful were to dwell upon their sins as they persist after baptism, they would only despair.

81. If, on the other hand, the faithful were to place excessive confidence in their good works or their untroubled consciences, they might easily fall into the sins of presumption and pride.

82. It is therefore incumbent upon them, as part of their ongoing repentance and sanctification, that they should look continually away from themselves to Christ, clinging solely to his promises.

Perseverance

83. The grace of justification includes the gift of perseverance.

84. The perseverance of the faithful is grounded objectively in their eternal election in Christ and subjectively in their confidence that the God who has begun a good work in them will not fail to bring it to completion (Eph 1:4; Phil 1:6).

85. If anyone should fall away from Christ into apostasy or dissolute living, making a shipwreck of their faith, it would seem that such a person did not have faith to begin with (1 Tim 1:19).

86. Lapses into sin, even serious sin, are not beyond the infinite mercy of Christ, whose grace restores the fallen by moving them to contrition and repentance.

87. Those who persevere to the end, and who call upon the name of the Lord, will be saved, not by their own power but by the grace of God working within them (Matt 24:13; Acts 2:21; Col 1:10–12).

Justification and Justice

88. Justification means the removal of injustice, the prevailing of mercy, the restitution of the sinner, and the imperative to seek justice for the oppressed.

89. It means that all our disorders are rectified and that the world is reconciled to God.

90. It means that in the time between the times, the church, in love and witness to Christ, is called to stand against all social disorders, and for justice, freedom, and peace in the world.

91. Most especially, it means solidarity with the victims of social disorder and opposition to systems of social and economic injustice.

92. We cannot be conformed to Christ, whose heart was moved to look upon our sin as our misery, without seeking to alleviate the misery of those most in need at the bottom of society.

93. To establish justice on earth for the poor, the miserable, and the oppressed, God always stands on this and only on this side, always against the exalted and for the lowly, always against those who already have rights and for those from whom they are robbed and taken away (Karl Barth).

94. Justification and justice, salvation in Christ, and social responsibility are therefore inseparable.

ANSWERS TO QUESTIONS BY A REFORMED THEOLOGIAN

Question 1

It has been a central feature of the classical tradition, emphasized by both Thomas Aquinas and John Calvin, that justification is the forgiveness of sins. I notice that you do not link the two in any way. Are you concerned that forgiveness is a declarative act and therefore quite different from justification?

No, I think that forgiveness and justification, while not identical in every respect, are essentially the same. I would see justification as a specifically juridical or forensic interpretation of the meaning of forgiveness. I would therefore give forgiveness a certain priority over justification, even while giving justification a certain weight in understanding what forgiveness looks like in the face of divine judgment. Justification spells out the conditions that make it possible for us to be forgiven and to withstand the judgment of God. We are clothed in the gift of an alien righteousness that we played no part, and were thus "passive," in producing.

Question 2

You have followed Reformed tradition in emphasizing the active and passive obedience of Christ. Do you have any concern that the New Testament gives so little emphasis to the atoning significance of Jesus' active obedience? (Romans 5 points to a single act rather than a lifetime of obedience.)

I think I read Romans 5 differently than you do. I would see Christ's "act of righteousness" (Rom 5:18) as encompassing his whole life of obedience, and as culminating supremely in his saving death. There is, moreover, only one obedience of Christ but it entails both active and passive aspects, at every point (not sequentially) and in various ways (not inflexibly). I think the standard Reformation tradition (Lutheran and Reformed) is right about this matter.

Question 3

Some recent Reformed New Testament scholarship has been less confident than Luther in equating the "righteousness of God" in Paul's exposition of justification with the "righteousness of Christ." Do you see the two as totally equivalent or is some nuancing required?

Calvin had to deal with something like this question in his critique of Andreas Osiander.[1] The righteousness of Christ, he argued, is the form in which we are made righteous by the righteousness of God, but it is a human righteousness grounded in Christ's human obedience. It is "that righteousness which has been acquired for us by Christ's obedience and sacrificial death."[2]

Question 4

Calvin was very careful to explain that although the death of Christ was the grounds for the reward of eternal life, good works are "a kind of cause" because they are a necessary step in the "ordo salutis." Would you concede this?

Causal language is always difficult. There can be no secondary cause or ground for the reward of eternal life alongside and independent of faith alone. Good works are a necessary condition for the validity of faith, because without them faith would be dead. But they are not grounds for the reward of eternal life in any strict sense of the term *grounds*. With respect to sanctification, it is promised that believers will do the good works that they were appointed to walk in. The reward given to these works is not properly to be thought of as eternal life itself, but rather as pertaining instead to degrees of glory within eternal life. Reward must at all costs be kept distinct from the inadmissible idea of "merit." The rewards that believers receive in

1. Calvin, *Institutes*, III.11.5.
2. Ibid.

eternal life are in no sense owed to them or caused by them. God crowns nothing other than his gifts when he crowns our good works with his rewards. The difference between Reformed and Catholic understanding on the status of good works, by the way, seems to come down to the difference between thinking that grace gives us the mere possibility of consenting (meritoriously) to it when doing good works (the Catholic view) as opposed to thinking that we are actually moved to give this consent by grace alone in doing good works (the Reformed view). Thomas seems to allow for something like the Reformed view when discussing "initial" justification but then retreats from it when considering meritorious good works and acts of penitence, both of which are seen as "a kind of cause" of the reward of eternal life itself, and which when lacking can lead to eternal life as actually being forfeit, or at least as necessitating being sentenced to purgatory. The Reformed would do well to eschew all such notions.

Question 5

I am not wholly sure what is intended by the subjective/objective distinction in justification. Are those without a faith inspired by the Holy Spirit objectively justified but not subjectively justified? And what would be the ultimate implication of this?

In discussing justification Calvin sometimes seems to conflate justification with the idea of reconciliation. For example, with reference to 2 Corinthians 5:21, he states of Paul, "Doubtless, he means by the word 'reconciled' nothing but 'justified.'"[3] I take "reconciliation" to pertain mainly to the objective aspect of the salvation accomplished for us by Christ (2 Cor 5:19). If so, then following Calvin's lead, it would seem to follow that justification itself has an objective aspect. In fact, like everything pertaining to salvation in Christ, justification can be seen to have both an objective and a subjective aspect. The objective is the precondition of the subjective (*extra nos*), and the subjective is the appointed fulfillment of the objective (*in nobis*). If Christ's saving work is universal in scope in its objective aspect (e.g., 2 Cor 5:14), then those without faith may be seen to exist under the sign of eschatological hope. The ultimate implication with regard to understanding the destiny of unbelievers would be to adopt a stance of reverent agnosticism that is nonetheless filled with hope (cf. Rom 11:32).

3. Ibid., III.11.4.

3

Theology Unbound

The Fading Away of a Classical Discipline[1]

–Arie L. Molendijk

INTRODUCTION

AS RELIGION FLOURISHES NOWADAYS, theology—especially in its classical form—is having a hard time. Dogmatical theology is losing
its authority in late modernity. To a great extent This is a consequence of
changing dialectics between professionals and lay people. Many Christians—including theologians—think they do not need this academic stuff,
or even that it is detrimental to their belief. Also in liberal theology, where
I come from, there is quite some distrust of the field of systematic theology,
in particular of the branch of dogmatics or *Glaubenslehre*,[2] as the field is

1. The substance of this contribution is taken from an earlier article I wrote: Molendijk, "'Non-Binding Talk': The Fate of Schleiermacher's Concept of Historical-Empirical
Dogmatics." I thank Walter de Gruyter Publishing House for the permission to republish
this material.

2. I take "dogmatics" as the (authoritative) exposition of the teachings of a specific
church (denomination) at a specific time in history. In this sense it has to be distinguished from the "theology" of a particular theologian, who has more liberty to develop
his or her own views.

often called after the ground-breaking work of Friedrich Schleiermacher, the "church father" of the nineteenth century. The great church historian and liberal theologian Adolf von Harnack (1851–1930) allegedly said, rearranging his library, "we place the [books of] dogmatical theologians in the literary section [*schönen Literatur*]," thereby disclaiming the scholarly pretensions of his colleagues.[3]

In this essay I investigate the fate of dogmatical theology from a European perspective, focusing on two towering figures: the German systematic theologians Friedrich Schleiermacher and Ernst Troeltsch. I shall concentrate on those elements in their conceptions of dogmatical theology that may help explain the problems that its practitioners are presently facing. In this way I hope to shed new light on the fading away of the field, or—if you think this is putting it too crudely—at least on its loss of significance. This has been a long process, as will become clear in the course of this paper. To make it more palpable (and also to give my contribution a more local flavor) I will give some Dutch examples too, although it has to be kept in mind that the Netherlands is an extreme example of the process of de-Christianization that is taking place in parts of Western Europe.

HISTORICAL PRELUDE

Allard Pierson (1831–1896) is doubtless a remarkable figure in Dutch intellectual history. Born in 1831 into a wealthy Pietist family, he resigned as a Protestant minister at the age of 34, unable to reconcile his own views with those of the church, taught afterwards (from 1870–1874) at the Heidelberg Theological Faculty,[4] and went on to occupy the first Dutch chair of Aesthetics, Art History, and Modern Languages established at the University of Amsterdam.[5] In 1876, Pierson published a nearly 150-page discussion of two works in dogmatics in what was then the leading Dutch intellectual journal. The review, titled "A Funeral," is one of the most devastating critiques in the history of Dutch theology. In the same spirit with which the Dutch once fought Catholicism, Pierson declared that we now have to uncover the sophisms and the utter ineptitude of traditional Protestant dogmatics in any possible form.[6]

3. Zahn-Harnack, *Adolf von Harnack*, 115.

4. Pierson, "Heidelberg."

5. Molendijk, "Abschied vom Christentum."

6. Pierson, "Ter Uitvaart," esp. 496.

The year 1876, in which the most important reorganization of modern Dutch higher education took place, including the Faculties of Theology,[7] was not (as Pierson probably had hoped) the end of theological dogmatics as an academic discipline. Notwithstanding several ups and downs, the field did, however, become more and more marginalized over the course of the twentieth century. In 2008, the recently appointed dogmatician of the Amsterdam Free University organized on the occasion of his inaugural address a colloquium that challenged the negative image of the field.[8] Even within theological departments, it seems, the relevance of dogmatic theology is doubted.

SCHLEIERMACHER'S CONCEPT OF *GLAUBENSLEHRE*

Schleiermacher's treatment of dogmatics as part of the historical division of the encyclopedia of theology is often hailed as a major innovation. Schleiermacher himself was conscious of the fact that he differed in this respect from previous theologians and claimed that the justification for this relocation of the field can only be found in its exposition.[9] Both church statistics and dogmatics are discussed in Schleiermacher's *Brief Outline of the Study of Theology* under the heading "The Historical Knowledge of the Present Condition of Christianity." Dogmatic theology is defined in the *Glaubenslehre* as the science of the coherence of the teachings of a specific church at a specific stage of history.[10] The term *systematic theology*, which is also used in this context, has, according to Schleiermacher, the advantage that it points to the (necessity of a) coherent exposition of a body of teachings, but the term obscures both the historical character of the discipline and its orientation toward the leadership of the church.[11] Schleiermacher's view that dogmatics must be beneficial for the guidance of the church fits well with his overall conception of theology as a positive science, which

7. Molendijk, *Emergence of Science of Religion*, chap. 3, sect. 4.

8. Anonymous, "Pleidooi voor herwaardering dogmatiek."

9. My discussion is based on the second edition of Schleiermacher's theological encyclopedia, *Kurze Darstellung des theologischen Studiums*, and the second edition of his *Glaubenslehre—Der Christliche Glaube nach den Grundsätzen der evangelischen Kirche im Zusammenhange dargestellt*. Henceforth cited as *KD* and *CG*, respectively. Here see *KD* §195.

10. "Dogmatische Theologie ist die Wissenschaft von dem Zusammenhang der in einer christlichen Kirchengesellschaft zu einer gegeben Zeit geltenden Lehre" (*CG* §19).

11. *KD* §97.

implies above all that it is necessarily related to a specific way of belief, practice, and (ecclesial) community.[12]

Two elements in this concept of dogmatics are of special importance for our discussion. First, dogmatics is not a mere description of, or report on, the current teachings of a church community; individual conviction on the part of the theologian is a prerequisite. Second, it is not necessary that different dogmatics pertaining to the same church and time period be equivalent or in agreement (*unter sich übereinstimmen*).[13] As far as the first issue is concerned, Schleiermacher did not deny the possibility of a description of the teachings that were (presumed to be) valid in a certain period. He argued, however, that the coherence or systematic connection of the teachings current in a church can only be demonstrated by someone who is convinced of their value and truth. Neither an idiosyncratic exposition of heterodox teachings nor a purely irenic collection of those convictions that no one disputes will suffice. Rather, the dogmatician must take a stance in the struggle of diverging views in order to come to a precise, trustworthy, and convincing exposition. He must show how the dominant religious and ecclesial "principle" of the current age has developed so as to be able, in turn, to outline the possibilities for improvement that are consonant with that principle. What comes from a previous period is likely to be ecclesiastically fixed, whereas the future course of doctrinal development will have to be "presaged" by the individual.[14]

This means that the dogmatician not only needs a clear overview of the current dogma, but must be sure about his or her own point of view as well.[15] This observation has an important consequence: Schleiermacher's stress on the individual *Ansicht* and judgment of the dogmatician implies that there can be a variety of dogmatics. This variety is reinforced by his claim that even if one agrees about the dominant principle, it can be conceived in different ways. Varying dogmatics may all have an equal claim to churchliness (*Kirchlichkeit*).[16] In Protestant churches there is no need for complete conformity and agreement. Different views can be current and to some degree accepted, as long as they are not officially (*amtlich*)

---

12. Ibid., §1.
13. Ibid., §196; cf. §97.
14. Ibid., §199; cf. §202.
15. Ibid., §202.
16. Ibid., §200.

contested by the church leadership.[17] So Schleiermacher accepted in principle a plurality of dogmatics, even within one particular church. Two basic presuppositions, however, hold this pluralism in check. First, on this view, dogmatics is oriented toward a particular church, acknowledges this church's authority, and seeks mutual understanding within its community. Second, the church's teachings are considered to evolve in an organic way, which makes it possible for the dogmatician to detect a guiding principle. But the gate to pluralism was opened further still by another basic feature of the *Glaubenslehre*: its discussion of dogmatic statements and principles of faith (*Glaubenssätze*) as articulations of pious states of mind (*fromme Gemütszustände*).[18] This could be and has been interpreted (somewhat against Schleiermacher's own intentions) as a move down the road toward a highly individualized expression of the faith of religious communities.

Schleiermacher characterized dogmatics as the learned and didactic exposition (*darstellend belehrend*) of the Christian faith. Next to the other two main forms of transmission—the poetic and the rhetorical (*der dichterische und rednerische Ausdruck*)—the didactic (sometimes called the logical or dialectical) way of exposition is especially helpful for clarifying the structure and coherence of the Christian faith. Dogmatics aims at the highest degree of precision and seeks to overcome disagreement and seeming contradictions among utterances expressed in the other forms of communication. Schleiermacher also recognized that there are religious communities that do not develop a dogmatics at all. The dogmatic approach presupposes, he argued, both a culture in which scholarship has gained an independent status (separate from the arts and commerce) *and* a religious community in which scholarship is valued and accepted as an aid for guiding the expression of the pious self-consciousness.[19] The implicit corollary of this observation is, of course, that the significance of dogmatics can also dwindle in Christian communities. At present, there are doubtless many Christians all over the globe who have a rather low opinion of dogmatics (or theology in general) and some of them even regard it as a threat to their belief.

17. Ibid., §196.
18. *CG* §15.
19. Ibid., §16.

HISTORICIZING DOGMATICS

Schleiermacher's view was clearly important for Ernst Troeltsch's understanding of dogmatics. Although it has been claimed that Troeltsch overstated the similarities between their conceptions,[20] it is evident that, like Schleiermacher, he considered dogmatics to be a *Glaubenslehre*, that is, an exposition of the Christian faith at a certain moment of history. Troeltsch's own concept and execution of dogmatics is somewhat unclear, and Walter Wyman is probably right when he points to the tension between Troeltsch's view of dogmatics as historical theology and his actual practice, which must ultimately be characterized as philosophical theology.[21] Troeltsch's own *Glaubenslehre* was not historical to the end, but turned speculative and even metaphysical at the very moment that he introduced the dichotomy between historical-religious and actual-religious elements of faith.[22]

What interests me most here, however, is not the way Troeltsch developed his own theology and dogmatics (and the possible inconsistencies accompanying this venture), but his view of dogmatics as a theological discipline. It comes as no surprise that his view on this matter is also thoroughly historical. The entries pertaining to dogmatic themes that he wrote for the first edition of the encyclopedia *Die Religion in Geschichte und Gegenwart* are all structured along a historical pattern. The entry on dogmatics itself, for instance, starts with a general discussion of the phenomenon among various religions, and then treats in chronological order the Catholic, Old-Protestant, and New-Protestant conceptions of dogmatics. Such an approach makes the reader aware of the transformations of dogma and the discipline itself during the course of the history of (Western) Christianity.

Troeltsch nicely summarized the general tendency to historicize dogmatics in the following observation taken from his 1908 survey of the preceding half-century of theology: "Dogmatics has everywhere abandoned the demonstration of scientifically valid general truths in favor of personal, subjective convictions of a confessional sort, and seeks to harmonise these with the church's dominant tradition and forms of expression."[23] It loses its authoritative character and becomes a confessional expression of the in-

---

20. Birkner, "Glaubenslehre und Modernitätserfahrung," 336–37.

21. Wyman, *Concept of Glaubenslehre*, 161–67, 193; cf. Molendijk, *Zwischen Theologie und Soziologie*, 158ff.

22. Troeltsch, *Glaubenslehre*, 72.

23. Troeltsch, "Half a Century of Theology," 58.

dividual appropriations of the Christian substance of life.[24] Of course, one may try to stick to a fixed confessional creed and a traditional dogmatics, but it is more sensible to admit that religious life just does not conform to any official, prescribed standards.[25] This transformation of the task of dogmatics follows, according to Troeltsch, from a renewed understanding of the church. This new understanding again leads not only to tolerance, but also to relativism and subjectivism in the churches themselves. To convey this view, Troeltsch pointed to examples of an extreme variety of opinions even within the leadership of one particular Protestant congregation.[26] Troeltsch admitted that within a particular church community, a specific traditional form of the Christian spirit (*überlieferte Formung des christlichen Geistes*) can be fundamental and authoritative (*verbindlich*), but for Protestants generally this binding tie (*Bindung*) has become very loose.[27] Karl Barth's verdict on Troeltsch's *Glaubenslehre* as "non-binding talk" is not completely beside the point, since this type of dogmatics seems to have hardly any authoritative character at all.

Troeltsch's view of the field, of course, has been severely criticized as individualistic, relativistic, and even anarchistic, and a large part of the twentieth century has indeed been dominated by a counter-movement that allegedly preferred stable dogmas to individualized faith. However, if we take a closer look at what is actually happening at the moment in many of the Western, mainline churches—and to some extent also in evangelical and charismatic churches—can we then simply dismiss Troeltsch's view? Must we not admit that, to a large extent, he was correct in his analysis of church life and in his diagnosis of the loss of (ecclesiastical) authority? Recall how Troeltsch himself reacted to critiques of the individualized, less binding, and less authoritative modes of religiosity and forms of Protestant community. In his important article "The Dogmatics of the 'Religionsgeschichtliche Schule'"—written, incidentally, for the University of Chicago Divinity School's *American Journal of Theology*—Troeltsch not only proposed his own view, but also addressed possible objections:

> It may be said that such a dogmatics is individualistic and anarchistic, and that it is not suited for a social religious life and for preaching in the church. The first assertion is certainly not true. A

24. Troeltsch, *Glaubenslehre*, 4.

25. Ibid., 16–17.

26. Ibid., 16.

27. Ibid., 4.

dogmatics of this kind, rather, strives constantly to make the closest possible connection with the living power of historical Christianity. . . . But, on the other hand, it presupposes an individual diversity among different dogmatic theologies in a church, and to that extent renounces the unyielding power of a dogma to which all alike must be subject [*entbehrt der festen Kraft eines gleichen, alle bindenden Dogmas*]. . . . [I]t is the duty of the churches, if they are to meet the needs of life itself, to guarantee individual freedom. Hence a dogmatics such as we have indicated can meet the needs of many believers, while the needs of different groups will be met by a different sort of dogmatics. If the churches are not able or willing to exercise this broad-mindedness, they will inevitably fall more and more into the background. They must understand that a new epoch in the spiritual development of humanity must be able to find expression in the churches or else it will pass the churches by [*oder die Kirchen beiseite schieben*]. If they cannot actually do justice to the movement, they are essentially defeated [*innerlich überwunden*] and must content themselves with dominion over a narrow circle of reactionary [*rückständig*] believers.[28]

Such an outcome, of course, has to be avoided in Troeltsch's view, and the churches must therefore be transformed into flexible institutions offering a large degree of freedom to their members.

In this citation, there are many crucial words, two of them being "needs" and "freedom." Troeltsch's view of what dogmatics can and ought to be is to a great extent determined by his view of what is going on in the intellectual and spiritual world of his time. He is not only looking back at what once was, but is looking ahead as well. Even for interpreters who are sympathetic to him, this can be hard to swallow. In a very nice essay, Hans-Joachim Birkner, for example, discusses Troeltsch's view of dogmatics in terms of a loss of meaning and complete privatization of the field,[29] which goes explicitly against Troeltsch's intention to strengthen community as far as possible. One may fear, of course, that dogmatics will go down the road to complete subjectivization and thus become obsolete because of its sheer lack of relevance for a broader church community, but that is not what Troeltsch meant. He did not mourn losses, but called for a transformation of dogmatics, so that it could help ministers preach and serve the needs of their congregations in the tradition of the Christian faith, thereby making "it possible for the community as a whole to retain a sense

28. Troeltsch, "Dogmatics of the History-of-Religions School," 101–2.
29. Birkner, "Glaubenslehre und Modernitätserfahrung," 331, 337.

of historic continuity and to come to an understanding with conservative dogmatic treatises."[30] Troeltsch's adversaries have claimed that this is the end of dogmatics, but the pluralization of points of view and the fact that the Protestant churches have lost the authority to prescribe their views to the believers are developments that must be taken into account—at least by liberal theologians. What this transformation actually implies depends to a great extent on how one sees the field, but for proponents of dogmatics as *Glaubenslehre* such as Troeltsch, it was evidently not the end of dogmatics.

POSTSCRIPT

In this last section I want to extend my discussion to the contemporary theological landscape and make some remarks concerning the present state of the art of dogmatics. This is a hazardous undertaking, given that the situation seems to be somewhat unclear. Since the posthumous appearance of Troeltsch's *Glaubenslehre*, there has doubtless been a vast production of dogmatic work, and the massive volumes of Karl Barth's *Church Dogmatics* made an especially lasting impression on generations of theologians until the 1970s and 1980s. Presently, though, it is much harder to survey and judge the situation. Dogmatic treatises do still appear, and vacancies for dogmaticians are still filled, but most observers would be hesitant to say that the discipline is flourishing at the moment.

It seems very hard nowadays to produce a full-fledged dogmatics, and those scholars who nevertheless try their hand at it scale down their claims in at least two respects. First, it is seldom claimed that the whole traditional ground of the field is covered. An older and even more influential *Glaubenslehre* such as one first published in 1973 by the Leiden dogmatician Hendrikus Berkhof explicitly leaves out elements that were treated in older works, because these are deemed to be no longer relevant to present-day believers.[31] Second, the claim to present a normative overview that binds one's own church community is either significantly weakened or altogether dropped. The most influential Dutch dogmatician of the last quarter of the twentieth century, Harry Kuitert, published a book about the Christian faith under the title *The Generally Doubted Christian Belief: A Revision*, in which he explained his own beliefs. Most of his readers will have missed

---

30. Troeltsch, "Dogmatics of the History-of-Religions School," 100.

31. Berkhof, *Christelijk Geloof*, xviii–xix. The English translation, *Christian Faith*, appeared in 1979.

the allusion in the title to the "general and undoubted Christian belief"[32] of the Apostolic Creed, but the book was a bestseller, and in later publications Kuitert went even further, stripping down the Christian faith to an utter minimum. Finally, he arrived at what could be nicely summarized as an "atheistic shade of religion," an expression already used in the nineteenth century, denoting a form of "Christian belief" that made Allard Pierson feel sad and melancholic.

The example of Kuitert shows very clearly that there is a market for theological and spiritual literature, at least in the Netherlands, but that the dogmatic approach—which Schleiermacher had characterized as the learned and didactic mode of expression—seems not to be the most popular one. Other modes of Christian communication, such as the inspirational, poetical, witnessing, and biographical, seem to resonate much more easily and are increasingly practiced by learned theologians. Even if we acknowledge the existence of mixed forms of presentation,[33] the systematic exposition of Christian teachings seems to hold little attraction to writers no more than readers and the heyday of dogmatics or, for that matter, *Glaubenslehre* seems to lie behind us. In general, our age does not seem to be the age of full-fledged systematics in any form and traditional dogmatics, of course, aims at a systematic and comprehensive coverage of the Christian faith. Establishing a special chair for specific loci such as Sin or Justification to make things easier for the Ordinarius in dogmatics does not seem to be a great help, since the point of the discipline is to provide a full and integrated picture, not an amalgam of fragments.

A more fundamental reason for the decline of dogmatics (already mentioned by Troeltsch) is that the (Protestant) churches have changed from authoritative and even compulsory institutions to associations with a high degree of freedom. Ordinary believers no longer accept traditional beliefs in the way they were authoritatively handed down by the church leaders, but decide for themselves to a much greater degree than in past centuries. This explains how thirty percent of the members of the main Dutch Protestant Church presently believe, if statistics can be trusted, in reincarnation. Especially since the 1960s, the old structures of authority have been significantly challenged, and this has had repercussions for the

---

32. "[O]ns algemeen, onbetwijfeld christelijk geloof." Kuitert, *Het algemeen betwijfeld christelijk geloof*.

33. An example of what I have in mind here is Friedrich Wilhelm Graf, *Moses Vermächtnis*.

churches and the religious field as such. "Theology unbound" is a way to capture this development, which may be evaluated in contrary ways—in terms of loss (of structure and content) as well as in terms of gain (of individual autonomy and freedom). It may lead to more individualized and proper ways of believing and piety *and* at the same time to kinds of popular Christian religion that shock schooled theologians (and not only them), because the Christian message is, for instance, downsized to one of personal well-being, instrumentalizing God for personal benefits.

To summarize the trend as I see it, one could say that the transformation of dogmatics into a *Glaubenslehre* is a token of a changing religious climate, in which lived religion in its many varieties becomes the basis for theologies that can no longer be defined and prescribed merely by a small elite cadre of church leaders. Doubtless, Schleiermacher had the life of the church and the reigning beliefs in mind when he wrote his dogmatics, but as the variety of church life grew in the course of history and the factual religious freedom and pluralism were acknowledged and even accepted, it became ever more difficult to maintain "the unity of the heterogeneous" (Troeltsch). Thus, dogmatics was transformed into an exposition of the Christian faith (or parts of it) according to the personal belief of a professional theologian with a view of what would be convincing to the broader church community. As the diversity grew still more and the autonomy and authenticity of personal belief were valued more deeply, it became harder and harder to present a normative view, let alone "force" this view upon church members or theology students.

One might object that I exaggerate and that the loss of authority is perhaps not so obvious as I suggest. Perhaps, but as the dialectic between professionals and lay people and between authority and autonomy—especially in the religious domain—has changed, it will hardly be possible to restore or enforce an authoritative view of Christian faith that is somehow binding. A modern *Glaubenslehre* may invite people to rethink their belief, but it is no longer an offer that cannot be refused. It can take into account the existing religious and dogmatic variety within a church community by becoming even more historical-empirical, but—as both Schleiermacher and Troeltsch rightly stressed—dogmatics cannot be reduced to simply taking stock of what is going on. It must offer a view of its own and present at least a guiding principle to invite its readers to follow this particular track—being aware of other possible tracks, wherever they may lead, and, even without really knowing where we are heading on this particular track, simply trusting that in the end things will be alright. This may be a far cry from the authoritative exposition of the Christian faith that dogmatics was supposed to supply in the old days, but it may be the final consequence of the historical turn of a field that is becoming modest about what it can achieve in the radically pluralized worlds of late modern Christian faith(s).

4

Understanding Religious Disagreements

–Olli-Pekka Vainio

WILLIAM FAULKNER ONCE STATED, "The last sound on the worthless earth will be two human beings trying to launch a homemade spaceship and already quarreling about where they are going next."[1] Disagreement seems to be something genuinely human and a necessary part of our existence. The miserable repercussions of eating from the tree of knowledge appear as an ability to define "knowledge," "right," and "wrong" in ways that mutually contradict each other. It is possible for us to disagree about almost everything; even the nature of disagreement itself is open to questioning. More precisely, the most important areas of disagreement can be characterized as follows:

- philosophical disagreements
- scientific disagreements
- political disagreements
- moral disagreements
- religious disagreements
- aesthetic disagreements

1. Speech to UNESCO Commission, quoted in *The New York Times*, October 3, 1959.

Concentrating on religious disagreements, I will first offer a simple overview of some psychological and philosophical constraints that produce disagreement. Special attention is paid to the heuristics and biases that form the background machinery for human belief formation procedures, and I discuss possibilities to mitigate these occasionally harmful biases. The purpose of this is not to reduce disagreements to different biases because that would entail global skepticism. Instead, I think it is worthwhile to acknowledge the factors that have an effect on our belief formation procedures, so that we may approach truth. Lastly, I will consider how we should frame religious identity and the nature of religious convictions in a way that takes into account the variety of disagreements without lapsing into relativism.

UNDERSTANDING DISAGREEMENTS: PSYCHOLOGICAL ASPECTS

Disagreement typically refers to situations where two or more individuals or parties hold conflicting propositional attitudes, that is, the contents of their beliefs and desires differ to some extent. Sometimes disagreement is due to our limitations. Even if we seek to address the same issue and interpret the same evidence, we come to different conclusions because something limits our access to relevant knowledge. The causes for this can be divided into external and internal limitations.

External
a. Time, location, networks, general limitations of human communication

Internal
a. Personal: intellectual capacities, intellectual virtues, personal narratives and experiences, motivation, moods
b. Pan-human: Heuristics and biases

External limitations are well known to us. Gaining knowledge requires time, correct materials, helpful colleagues, and ways of communication that ensure that we really understand the dilemmas we are facing. Our location in philosophical space and time will affect how we perceive new ideas. Randall Collins and Charles Taylor, among others, have demonstrated the contingent nature of philosophical trends. Collins argues that networks play the central role in how philosophical ideas spread and succeed to convince people. A somewhat pessimistic conclusion is that the ideas that prove to be most influential are not always those that are true but which are made by the most networked individuals and which resonate with the spirit of the times.[2]

Taylor interprets the rise of secularization in Western societies as a result of the possibility to choose one's worldview more freely.[3] For example, the dwindling public presence of religion in some corners of the Western world does not result from the maturity of the human race, as the Enlightenment story would like us to believe, but from mere availability of other options. Therefore, what we hold as knowledge can be just a result of, say, market forces that happen to persuade us to hold on to certain views over others.

We do not need to go so far as some postmodern skeptics and argue for total opacity of language and culture. Yet it would be naïve to deny that language sets boundaries to what and how we can communicate with our peers. Anyone who has followed any public debates recognizes the frustration that results from the feeling that the speakers do not understand each other. It takes time and energy to find common ground, which then enables mutual understanding, although even this does not guarantee agreement over the matter.

In addition to external limitations, we are bound by our own internal limitations. Our intellectual skills are what they happen to be. We may want to improve our thinking in order to become more conscientious, but this is very hard. Against the background of our life narratives, we resonate more with some values than others. Sometimes we feel more motivated to dig deeper, sometimes we just don't give a damn. Even such mundane matters as amount of sleep and the type of food we have consumed can affect our mental processes. Even the movie we just watched may prime us to favor some views over others, and we do not even notice this. These limitations are beyond our grasp and often there is very little we can do about them.

In addition to the aforementioned limitations, our cognitive machinery has certain features that are more ambiguous. Here I want to concentrate on cognitive heuristics and biases that have effects on our reasoning, and which on the one hand help us to reason in the first place, but which, on the other hand, make it hard for us sometimes to find the truth of the matter.[4] To use a simple, but potentially reductive metaphor, our brains are

---

2. Collins, *Sociology of Philosophies*.

3. Taylor, *A Secular Age*.

4. Good introductions to biases are, for example, the following works: Kahneman,

like computers, which need operating systems to function. The operating system consists of simple applications, biases that perform different tasks and make it easy and economical to lead our daily lives. Thus heuristics and biases are an essential part of us, and we are doomed to operate with them without the hope of new updates. It is, however, important to note that biases are not always harmful. Instead, they are essential tools which we need to survive. But herein lies the problem. Biases are not automatically interested in *truth*, but in *survival*.

A short list of our most common biases goes as follows:

Self-Serving Bias: We are harsher towards an out-group than an in-group. A classic study was made by Babcock and Loewenstein, in which they gave the same legal case to two groups for investigation and judgment.[5] The first group was first divided between plaintiffs and defendants, but the second was not. Both groups had the same evidence. The first group interpreted the evidence favoring their randomly selected side, the second group showed more variation in their judgments. If we currently inhabit a clearly defined identity and have well-argued convictions, it is harder for us to take into account the opposing arguments and see their rationale.

Confirmation Bias: We automatically seek to confirm our present beliefs and neglect the conflicting evidence. We read books that confirm our previous views and spend more time in activities that strengthen our current commitments than in activities than could potentially challenge them.[6]

Simplicity Bias: We favor the solutions that are simple. Sometimes "Ockham's razor" is thought to mean that the simplest solution is the correct one, but this is not true. Ockham's razor means only that the simplest solution is the easiest to work with and we should not factor in more causes than necessary. But nothing here is meant to suggest that simplicity is always the indicator of truth. We automatically favor simple solutions because they save time and energy. It is easy to see how propaganda can utilize this cognitive feature. Blaming Jewish people for the misfortunes of 1930s Germany was effective because it conveniently attributed a simple solution to a highly complicated matter.

Thinking, Fast and Slow; Plous, *The Psychology of Judgment and Decision Making*; and Thiele, *The Heart of Judgment.*

5. Babcock and Loewenstein, "Explaining Bargaining Impasse," 109–26.

6. For simplicity, confirmation, and coherence biases, see Harman, "Practical Aspects of Theoretical Reasoning," 45–56.

Coherency Bias (rationalization effect): We aim to maintain equilibrium in our belief system so that phenomena that seem to create an internal conflict are somehow balanced with our previous beliefs. This can mean turning a blind eye to conflicting evidence, or interpreting it in a way that eventually supports our cause. Coherency bias attempts to deal with cognitive dissonance by altering our beliefs to accommodate new information so that our story seems coherent and rational.

Availability/Recognition Heuristic: When faced with a choice among multiple options, we normally choose the one that is most familiar to us. If some idea comes to us easily, we automatically consider it more probable.[7] One day I was walking on a street in London when I saw a banner with the shady picture of a nun on it. There was no name on the banner but I made a guess that the nun was St. Edith Stein, and my guess was correct. When reverse engineering my rationalization, I saw how I had made the choice. I know only two famous nuns, and the nun in the picture was not Mother Teresa; so it *had* to be St. Edith Stein. Of course, the recognition heuristic does not guarantee that the face of an unknown nun always belongs to St. Edith Stein. Recognition heuristics help us to make efficient choices in some situations but can also prevent us from thinking outside the box because we tend to favor the familiar.

Overconfidence Effect: Approximately 70 percent of human beings think that they are smarter than the average. So something is wrong here. But from the strict evolutionary perspective, overconfidence helps. The chances of Admiral Nelson's fleet at Trafalgar would have probably been slimmer if their ships' names had been *Equal Outcome, Ordinary, Run of the Mill, Ephialtes,* and *Peaceful Negotiator* instead of *Victory, Leviathan, Conqueror, Minotaur,* and *Defiance,* etc.

Sadly, people seem to be overconfident when they are not sure what to think and, ironically, when the actual accuracy of beliefs rises over 80 percent, people start to doubt and become less confident. Experts and those who have been trained are often prone to be too confident about their judgments.[8]

Contrast Effect (framing): The context of our perception tends to distort our judgments. An average person looks small when pictured next to a

---

7. Thiele, *Heart of Judgment*, 64. More generally, about the effect of "cognitive ease" to our thinking, see Kahneman, *Thinking*, 59–62.

8. Plous, *Psychology of Judgment*, 219; Thiele, *Heart of Judgment*, 67.

professional basketball player. The breeze can feel warm or cold depending on the temperature to which we were exposed before experiencing the breeze. If an option is presented to us as a "moderate" choice between two "extremes," it is easy to respond to it positively compared to a situation in which the choice is presented without the context. Obviously, choosing the extremes cunningly, one can influence decision-making.[9]

The Out-Group Homogeneity Effect: We think that "they" are more homogenous than "we." It is easier for us to allow more diversity when thinking about the in-group, but we need to picture the out-group as somehow more unified and unitary than the in-group.[10]

Actor/Observer Effect: This is closely related to the out-group homogeneity effect. We think that whenever one of "them" makes a choice, he or she is always acting based on his or her "nature." That is just the way they are, we say. We, on the other hand, never make choices due to our characteristic features. "We" merely make informed judgments based on the careful assessment of the evidence. One result of this is that we think that the others are always more biased than we are (and the others think similarly about us).

Groupthink: Biases can also affect groups. If a significant majority of the group favors a particular solution it is increasingly difficult for individual members to oppose the majority. A typical characteristic of groupthink is the inability to take into account possible hazards or counterarguments. Groupthink can easily take hold of groups that are very homogenous and where members share similar backgrounds and convictions.[11]

If we are relatively normal human beings, we immediately recognize these biases in our daily lives. However, it is always easier to spot biases in other people, and it is very hard spot them in ourselves. Merely being aware of the existence of biases does not help us very much because we do not make misjudgments all the time, but when we do, we do not know that we just made a bad choice until it is too late.

Next, I will look at some ways of mitigating the negative effects of biases.

---

9. I recently attended a seminar in Oxford where experts discussed the ethics of doping. One of the panelists presented his "rational option" between two "extremes" of allowing all kinds of doping and forbidding everything, including caffeine. The "rational" here meant allowing some sort of doping that is controlled and approved by authorities.

10. Thiele, *Heart of Judgment*, 66.

11. Schafer and Crichlow, *Groupthink versus High-Quality Decision Making*.

DEBIASING

Can we fight against our biases? Can a computer fight against its operating system? The task can seem quite hopeless, or even schizophrenic. Luckily humans are not like computers. We can engage in self-criticism and reflect on our actions and decisions critically. This is called *debiasing*.

However, the extent to which we can actually improve our cognitive performance is a matter of debate.[12] Due to the deeply entrenched nature of the biases, we are never absolutely free from their influence. There is always something we can do, but overcoming our biases is not an easy task. One major obstacle is the fact that we often resist debiasing and do not want to hear criticism or insinuations that we are not thinking or acting optimally. When the contested matter is very close to our hearts, we may react aggressively to such allegations. On the other hand, some methods of debiasing are not natural to us and not necessarily available to everybody. Some debiasing methods can also be counterproductive and trigger other biases.[13]

Basic debiasing strategies include the following:

Rewards and Sanctions: If you are offered a prize for thinking conscientiously and punished for carelessness, you surely perform better than without sanctions. Right? Well, no. Sadly, rewards and punishments do not help us if we do not have pre-existing abilities and faculties to perform well in the first place. Rewards may *motivate* us, but they do not make our judgments more balanced. The same holds for using accountability as a motivator. Making people explain to others what they have learned does motivate us, but it may lead to distortions if we know what the others want to hear.[14]

Consider the Opposite: Self-serving biases can be successfully encountered by forcing people to adopt different viewpoints. Of course, this is easier in the laboratory than in real life.[15]

Think with Others: Thinking about the problems in groups can help, but the group needs to be diverse enough and contain enough different perspectives so that there is no particular view that dominates the group. In

---

12. See Larrick, "Debiasing," 316–37; Johnson-Laird, *How We Reason*, 292. It is possible that disagreement has a neurological basis, at least to some extent; see McGilchrist, *The Master and His Emissary*.

13. Larrick, *Debiasing*, 331. For debiasing strategies, see also Kahneman, *Thinking*.

14. Larrick, *Debiasing*, 321–22.

15. See Babcock and Loewenstein, "Explaining Bargaining Impasse."

order to prevent peer pressure and groupthink, it is necessary that the differing ideas and convictions are brought forth simultaneously and without the fear of negative reactions. Again, easier said than done.

Acknowledge Your Biases and Get Educated: It is possible to improve our performance, but not much. People who are good mathematicians tend to perform better in tasks that require statistical precision when given enough time. When time is limited they tend to make the same mistakes as the rest of us. Still, acknowledging our biases can help us to recognize them and prepare in advance when we see that we are drawn into situations where biases are likely to kick in. One of the best in guides in debiasing is Daniel Kahneman's *Thinking, Fast and Slow*, which offers several ways to educate our minds to perform in optimal ways.

The general problem with biases is that they are subconscious and not under our direct voluntary control. This intuitive system takes care of the most of our mental processes, and it is only seldom when we need to resort to deliberative functions. But, alas, even deliberative functions are not free from viruses, as the analytic philosophical discussion on disagreement shows.

UNDERSTANDING DISAGREEMENTS: PHILOSOPHICAL ASPECTS

In recent analytic philosophy, disagreement has become one of the most discussed topics.[16] Within epistemology, there is now a sub-discipline called *the epistemology of disagreement*. Peter van Inwagen was one of the thinkers who initiated this discussion and his seminal essay is worth quoting at length, as it encapsulates some of the crucial points in contemporary discussion:

> I ask again: what could it be that justifies us in rejecting political skepticism? How can I believe that my political beliefs are justified when these beliefs are rejected by people whose qualifications for engaging in political discourse are as impressive as David Lewis's qualifications for engaging in philosophical discourse? These people are aware of (at least) all the evidence and all the arguments that I am aware of, and they are (at least) as good at evaluating evidence and arguments as I. How, then, can I maintain that the evidence and arguments I can adduce in support of my beliefs actually justify these beliefs? If this evidence and these arguments are capable of that, then why aren't they capable of convincing these

16. See, e.g., Feldman and Warfield, *Disagreement*.

other people that these beliefs are correct? Well, as with philosophy, I am inclined to think that I must enjoy some sort of incom-
municable insight that the others, for all their merits, lack. I am
inclined to think that the evidence and arguments I can adduce in
support of my beliefs do not constitute the totality of my justification for these beliefs. But all that I am willing to say for sure is that
something justifies me in rejecting political skepticism, or at least
that it is possible that something does: that it is not a necessary
truth that one is not justified in holding a political belief that is
controverted by intelligent and well-informed political thinkers.[17]

Genuine disagreement entails that *epistemic peers*, who have shared all relevant evidence come to different conclusions regarding the meaning of the
evidence. By epistemic peerage I mean the relation between two persons
who

a. share equal reasoning capabilities;

b. have sufficient degree of intellectual virtues, that is to say, when they
   reason, they reason conscientiously;

c. have equal access to the relevant evidence; and

d. have shared the reasons for their respective position with each other.

It might be worthwhile to add that the persons must be not just intelligent
but very intelligent and well trained in the subject of debate, because disagreement between two totally clueless persons is not philosophically very
interesting, no matter how funny it otherwise might be.

As van Inwagen points out, it is possible that epistemic peers may hold
mutually conflicting beliefs: A thinks that *p* is true while B thinks that *p* is
false. It is the *combination of epistemic peerage and the asymmetry of beliefs*
that causes the philosophical problem of disagreement. If either or both are
missing the situation is not philosophically interesting.

In the literature, there have emerged two basic solutions to the dilemma.
According to the *skeptical view*, if persons A and B are epistemic peers holding
opposing views, they will lose their epistemic rights to their respective views.
Their views cancel each other. But according to the *steadfastist view*, which
van Inwagen favors, both A and B retain rights to their respective beliefs.
Both skeptical and steadfastist views are *general* if their proponents think
that there exists one rule that defines the proper way of conduct in all possible cases of disagreement. What makes the generalist position problematic

17. Van Inwagen, "It Is Wrong," 137–53.

is that we can easily think of particular cases when either the skeptical or steadfastist position seems correct and rational for us to choose.

Think, for example, of simple perceptual beliefs. I see an animal running across the frozen lake, and I say to my friend, "Look, there's a fox." But he answers, "No, it is too big and gray; it must be a wolf." In this case, it does seem rational for us to withhold our beliefs until we see the footprints of the creature.

But let us consider another kind of case. I say, "We need to continue sentencing people to death for committing extreme crimes." And my friend says, "We should not sentence people to death, no matter what their crimes are." In this case it seems rational for me and my friend to stick to our guns because withholding would in effect lead to the automatic victory of the prevailing condition.

Thus it seems that generalism is not the ideal strategy and we need to be more case sensitive. Recognizing this has given rise to a third option, which can be called the *dynamic view*. It is inherently particularistic as it does not subscribe to the generalist thesis. Because there is no general rule for disagreement cases, we need to consider every case as unique.

Nevertheless, it seems that both skeptical and steadfastist views are able to appreciate some genuine intellectual goods, such as critical thinking and persistence. But the problems of these two views are clear: the skeptical view will make skepticism the default philosophical position; steadfastism, in the worst-case scenario, creates intellectual ghettoes and disables dialogue.

Before trying to find some way out of this standoff, we need to take a deeper look at those philosophically crucial factors (which resonate with what was said about human cognitive processes earlier) that generate the problem of disagreement. Graham Oppy has summarized the relevant factors of religious disagreement as follows:

> (1) there are differences in starting points—i.e. differences in prior probabilities, doxastic presuppositions, worldviews, initial assumptions, doxastic frameworks, and the like; (2) there are differences in evidential bases for belief that are not amenable to full disclosure . . . ; (3) there is disagreement on a relatively wide range of topics—i.e. disagreement is not restricted to a relatively small number of related propositions—even though, of course, there is also wide agreement on a massive background of less relevant matters; (4) there is not total transparency of reasons for beliefs about religious matters—i.e. the reasons that one has for holding

> one's beliefs about questions of religion are not fully transparent to oneself, and the reasons that others have for holding the beliefs that they do on questions about religion are not fully transparent to one either; (5) there are hard questions about the extent to which the judgments that one makes about questions of religion are independent of the judgments that other people make about questions of religion; and (6) there is mutual knowledge—prior to any particular religious disagreement between doxastic peers— that there is a very wide spectrum of peer opinion on many questions about religion.[18]

Two additional factors could be added to Oppy's list. The aforementioned problem of neutrality seems to give *prima facie* justification for contested beliefs in the cases where there is no neutral space between two competing options.

Secondly, our ideological relation to the one with whom we disagree limits how we perceive the challenge. When challenged, we are able (because of our biases) to take into consideration only adjacent competing views that require only minor corrections to our currently held views. It is possible that we are massively wrong, but we are unable to consider this as a live possibility. This has two interesting consequences. First, those who are closest to us are our strongest enemies. This is so because we know how they have reached their conclusion, what their presuppositions and authorities are, and that their views are to a considerable extent identical with ours.

For example, if a contemporary Lutheran theologian says that there's something wrong with the doctrine of transubstantiation, a Roman Catholic Christian will take this more seriously, compared to a situation in which the same comment might come from the mouth of Richard Dawkins or his kin. These kinds of disagreements are well known among Christians, and they may have devastating effects on Christian communities.

Second, we are not really able to care about the views of those who are far off. It is easy to dismiss those whose views differ massively from ours as totally irrelevant, and even label them as corrupted or evil. In many cases these two seem to be the only options for a great number of people.

So what should we do when we disagree? Earl Conee, for example, has suggested that it is possible to hold views that are under disagreement in an "instrumental" way. This means that one can "argue for [them] . . . seek

---

18. Oppy, "Disagreement," 197.

further reasons for [them], [and] . . . object to [their] rivals."[19] However, one cannot consider these contested beliefs as justified. This works well within the scientific method where we can expect resolutions in due time and where the debated issues are not existential—but in many cases this seems to demand too much from us. The questions of life do not grant us with an unlimited amount of time. Additionally, most of our action-guiding principles are problematic in this respect, because in order to act upon our beliefs we need a relatively high level of certainty.

Instead of raising the bar of justification so high that almost all our value judgments become unjustified, we could approach the problem from a more relational angle. Among others, Catherine Elgin and Michael Bergmann suggest that in some cases of disagreement it could be possible to recognize the rationality of rival views.[20] Simply put, it is possible that the parties consider the rival view wrong but still rational. In practice, this would entail being able to say something such as, "I understand why you hold the view you do."

Elgin thinks that the best way to make progress in disagreement situations is that both parties stick to their guns and try to demonstrate the superiority of their position. The respective parties need to present their cases as well as possible so that the strengths and weaknesses of each view are manifested. Ideally, this would lead to maximal transparency of each view and its respective background assumptions. This, in turn, helps us to locate the source of disagreement, which quite likely is an axiomatic meta-level conviction, or "control belief."[21] These control beliefs are deeply held convictions, which are very hard to overturn due to their intuitive natures.[22]

People do not hold their control beliefs only in instrumental ways or think that they are only tentatively true. Yet, it is possible to recognize that other control beliefs can be coherent and rational as well. This is not

---

19. Conee, "Peerage," 322.

20. Elgin, "Persistent Disagreement"; Bergmann, "Rational Disagreement," 336–53.

21. Wolterstorff, *Reason within the Bounds of Religion*, 67–68.

22. However, people change their control beliefs when they experience conversions. While I am writing this, the people of the United States are about to choose whether President Barack Obama gets a second chance. In recent weeks, my iPad's Pulse app (which collects the most interesting headlines and stories) has offered several political conversion stories where people reflect their life narratives as journeys away from the Democratic to the Republican party—and vice versa. Sometimes these stories help to locate the meta-level reasons why people see certain political ideologies as more compelling than others.

much of a solution but it is the only way toward reasonable confrontation between conflicting worldviews.

Mutual recognition of rationality of opposing positions will result in pluralism. By pluralism, I mean here merely the descriptive fact that there exist multiple reasonable positions that cannot be easily ruled out, but of which many are probably wrong or at least less right.[23]

If we put this inevitable pluralism together with the previously mentioned psychologically necessary feature to favor our own perspective and those communal problems resulting from our inability to consider far-off views seriously, etc., we are faced with rather bleak prospects.

William Alston argues that in this kind of setting trying to find *one* way to settle once and for all the nature of epistemic justification will only multiply our problems. In addition to disagreeing about particular claims, we disagree about the criteria of how to evaluate those claims. Of course, it would be very nice indeed to have one general criterion for knowledge, but it seems that philosophers disagree so widely about these criteria that it takes a lot of optimism to think that a consensus will be reached anytime soon. Moreover, using only one criterion will, in the cases of disagreement, result almost automatically in skepticism, when the opposing claims annul each other.

Alston gives this advice to epistemologists (and humans in general, I suppose): "We human beings are thrust into a matrix of uncertainty and fallibility, and the better part of wisdom is to recognize that and make the best we can of it, without wasting time yearning for absolute guarantees outside the activity of human inquiry."[24]

Instead of being an attempt to find the perfect criterion for knowledge, real-life knowledge acquisition involves complex processes, time, and will, shaped by necessary features, such as intellectual virtues. In his book *Beyond "Justification"* Alston lists fifteen different epistemic desiderata, some of which are more essential than the others, and most of which locate some genuine epistemic good, such as truth, understanding, reliability, and coherence.

---

23. A part of this view is that our convictions can be "partially defeated." In this case, our level of confidence suffers some kind of damage and we cannot go about our business as if nothing had happened as some versions of steadfastism seem to suggest. However, one persisting problem in the discussion has been the lack of precise formulation of what "the reducing of confidence," or beliefs "having less justification than before," means in practice. For discussion, see Thune, "Partial Defeaters," 358–59.

24. Alston, *Beyond "Justification"*, 239.

This leaves us an "irreducible plurality of epistemic desiderata and forces us to undertake the baffling task of integrating them somehow into a comprehensive epistemology of belief."[25] Alston readily admits that this will lead to a "blossoming of a thousand flowers" (which is not particularly trendy in analytic circles). However, could it be that Alston's multiple desiderata approach might give us grounds for assessing which flowers are worth nurturing?

From the Alstonian perspective it could be possible to recognize *degrees* of rationality of competing claims. It also could help us to recognize the weaknesses in our own position, and the reasons why everybody is not buying our story. Alston's reliabilist framework centers on the idea that beliefs have adequate ground when they have been formed by a reliable belief-forming process.[26] Having adequate ground means in this context that the person has *prima facie* warrant to act upon his or her beliefs as if they were justified. This is what people do anyway: they do not ask the philosopher's permission to believe what they believe and to act according to their beliefs. However, recognizing this irreducible plurality of values and worldviews and meeting it with multiple relevant criteria of evaluation could be seen as a fruitful way to evaluate, communicate, and criticize beliefs; this would prevent the slide to simplistic standoffs and enable the possibility of trans-communal discourse, when the competing parties have multiple epistemic desiderata to choose from and which they recognize as their own. This will not do away with disagreement, but from this perspective disagreement is not necessarily a bad thing. Disagreement can be seen as an enhancing factor in knowledge acquisition, as a necessary means of criticism, and as a boundary against intellectual, political, and religious absolutism.

WHAT DOES THIS MEAN FOR THE INDIVIDUAL BELIEVER?

All that has been said before is rather abstract from the perspective of the normal religious individual. What does lowering the certainty actually mean? Doubting? In fact, doubt has been offered as one means to relate religious identities to the fact of religious pluralism. Accordingly, we should not be too sure about our beliefs because they might be wrong in the end,

25. Ibid., 176.
26. Ibid., 244.

and surely we cannot think that our well-educated and intelligent peers are all wrong while we are right.

For example, Peter Berger and Anton Zijderveld argue that faith communities should accept that doubt has a positive role in religious life. This means that faith communities should be able to make distinctions between core beliefs and more marginal components of their belief systems, and be open to historical scholarship, which helps to bring out the historical roots and contingencies of one's own tradition. Simultaneously, in order to combat postmodern cynicism, the community needs to reject relativism, build empathic relations to the "others," participate in peacemaking and conflict resolution, and, finally, accept that in contemporary Western society, *choosing* one's belief system is morally desirable.[27]

Of course, Berger and Zijderveld's proposal contains an interesting mix of proposed uncertainty and the praise of attitudes that do not square well with uncertainty. I cannot discuss that paradox here but I merely suggest that perhaps using doubt is not as helpful as they may think or that their way of using the concept is not very well characterized.

But if we want proceed with the concept, the first thing to do is to locate what we are actually "doubting." Is it our beliefs, our ways of coming to believe the things we believe and how we hold on to our convictions, or the actual results of those beliefs? I think that it is wise to doubt all of these every now and then, but we should be conscious about what we are actually doing and why. We cannot question all three spheres at the same time. The boat needs to be fixed while we are sailing in it.

The problem, however, about doubt is that if we come to hold beliefs or convictions in a way that leaves us doubtful, we feel less satisfied and more stressed as our working memory keeps on checking for other alternatives.[28] This has serious consequences for religious identity. If we choose, as we sometimes do, to keep our options open, we are not getting the things we usually want from the worldviews we embrace. Choosing an identity that is unstable is something that makes us dissatisfied and regretful. This leads to reversion of our choices and search for a new identity, which in the end may lead to cynicism and relativism.

How then should we understand the nature of religious identity and religious knowledge? The problem with the general concept of "knowledge" is finding a way to define what it means. Like all philosophical questions,

27. Berger and Zijderveld, *In Praise of Doubt*, 116–18.
28. Bullens et al., "Keeping One's Options Open," 800–805.

this is also plagued with disagreements. This leads us easily to think that maybe there is no truth to be had in philosophy and theology. Truth and knowledge should then be reserved for mathematics and some set of natural sciences. Elsewhere we deal only with individual preferences, which do not yield to universal evaluations. Maybe instead of truth, philosophy and theology should seek beauty, for instance. This rather skeptical stance gives a sort of solution to religious disagreements. In the end, they are futile.

This understanding of philosophy and theology is tempting, but for my taste too self-effacing. It simply does not follow from the fact that philosophy is not able to give us fool-proof, knockdown arguments on the big questions that there is no such thing as philosophical, or theological, knowledge.

In his recent meta-philosophical work, Gary Gutting explores the nature of philosophical knowledge and the idea of progress in philosophy. He also touches on religious knowledge and the nature of the arguments that people use either to prove or disprove God's existence. At first, Gutting seem to support the skeptical or agnostic conclusion, when he claims that "for any standard version of [theistic or atheistic] argument . . . there are solid philosophical reasons that show just why the argument fails."[29] Therefore, there is "no generally compelling argumentative basis for accepting or rejecting the existence of God." Does this then lead to holding religious convictions by faith alone, and that there is no room for reason and argument in religion? According to Gutting, this does not follow from the aforementioned impasse. The impasse itself results from serious philosophical work; it is not self-evident. It is a result of philosophical inquiry that in many cases there are several possibilities that are live options. It is very hard to provide knockdown arguments to basic philosophical positions. It might be that there are abstract entities or not. It might be that God exists or that God does not exist. Both are possible and also rational positions to hold.

What role do the arguments themselves play in religious life, then, if they are unable to demonstrate either of the desired conclusions? Gutting adopts a moderate steadfastist position and states,

> This [impasse] does not exclude the possibility that some individuals may be in epistemic situations that entitle them to the premises of valid arguments for or against religious beliefs. If, after careful reflection, it just seems overwhelmingly obvious to me that, say, the universe must have an intelligent cause or that certain

29. Gutting, *What Philosophers Know*, 233.

sorts or amounts of evil are just incompatible with an all-good, all-powerful creator, then I have an intellectual right to accept the conclusions that follow from these premises. But I still have no basis for claiming that others, who see things differently, are not epistemically entitled to their views.[30]

Gutting seems to think that for our beliefs to be justified externalist standards are enough. If we have done our epistemic job conscientiously and still have our convictions, we are entitled to believe them, even in the face of peer disagreement.

Recently, Robert Audi has given a more nuanced account of religious life that is able to accommodate the elements Berger and Zijderveld cherish.[31] Audi makes a relevant point that too often philosophy of religion concentrates on beliefs and evidence when a religious lifestyle consists of several things other than mere propositions. Yet Audi steers away from pure pragmatism and non-cognitivism. Truth and justification are relevant topics in religion but they should not be the only ones. Religion consists of propositional, behavioral, attitudinal, and emotional dimensions: "An overall religious commitment is a commitment to act in certain ways as well as to accept a certain outlook on the world; and it requires doing a certain range of deeds, cultivating or nurturing certain attitudes and emotions, and maintaining an openness to responses from other people."[32]

For Audi, religious life is a balancing act, which is necessarily rather elusive and multiform, and is eloquently illustrated in the following quote:

> Rational religious commitment lies somewhere between a head-long confidence in what we passionately wish to be true and a timid refusal to risk disappointments, between the safety of according to religious beliefs the easy confidence we have in things that bombard the five senses, and the skeptical detachment that comes from suspending judgment on whatever is not plainly evident to all, between a merely aesthetic participation in religious practices and a dogmatic codification of an outlook on the world, between non-cognitivist attenuation of religious texts and tenets and rigid literalism in understanding them, between apathy and conformism, between scepticism and credulity. Rational religious commitment may be elusive; it differs in many

---

30. Ibid., 232–33.

31. Audi, *Rationality and Religious Commitment*. For a similar account, see Cottingham, *Spiritual Dimension*.

32. Audi, *Rationality and Religious Commitment*, xi.

ways from one person to another; and even in single life, it may change much over time, for better or, sometimes, for worse. But if our notion of rationality is not too narrow, if our religious lives are well integrated, if our sense of the mutually enriching interconnections between the religious and the secular is sufficiently keen, and if we do not try to justify needlessly strong cognitive attitudes, we may hope both to construct an adequate theory of rational religious commitment and to progress toward a lasting reconciliation of faith and reason.[33]

This sensibility that tries to balance different elements in one's religious outlook is something that you rarely see examined in academic theology and philosophy. Religious commitment is a "life-choice" rather than just "cognitive choice" and this necessarily rules out all straightforward solutions to demonstrate the truth or falsity of religious (or any) worldviews or convictions, while simultaneously seeing the value of examination and evaluation of these convictions.

In addition to trying to provide general rules of public discourse, Audi seeks to sketch a form of religious cosmopolitanism, which results from integration of relevant dimensions of one's life into a single whole. By integration Audi means that our belief system should be internally coherent, that our beliefs should cohere with our desires and emotions and our actions should be grounded in our beliefs and desires. Integration aims at "theoethical equilibrium," where a person's religious, scientific, ethical, and aesthetic convictions are constantly changing as they react to new challenges but are ideally moving towards greater coherence. This includes also taking into account competing views and cultures. In practice this means sharing resources with them, gaining more understanding and engaging in cooperative practices.

But how does this avoid the problem of keeping one's options open? Audi's answer is theological: "If we are all created by God who is omniscient, omnipotent, and omnibenevolent, and if reason is viewed as given to us for guidance of life, then there is no reason to resist the growth of knowledge and at least some reason to pursue it."[34] In this way, Audi is able to secure good religious grounds for growth in virtues and knowledge without resorting immediately to extra-theological reasons. The crucial thing here is that this move is possible only from a very conscious and strong religious identity.

33. Ibid., 295–96.
34. Ibid., 172.

Constructive and Public Theology

5

Knowing Our Place(s)

The Ecclesial Role(s) of the Theologian

—Paul Lakeland

WHEN I ATTEND ACADEMIC conferences and find myself in the company of theologians and scholars of religion from a variety of different traditions, I usually feel at home and quite relaxed. Much more relaxed, in fact, than I commonly am when speaking in an exclusively Catholic context, even if it were a roomful of Catholic theologians. One would think, I suppose, that the opposite would be true, and that the fact that Catholics among Catholics or Methodists among Methodists could take so much more for granted about the history, traditions, and doctrines they share would mean a more accepting and fruitful context for dialogue. And yet I do not find it to be so. In my own Catholic tradition, apparently, this problem goes to the very top. I was once told on pretty good authority that in the early years of his pontificate John Paul II would host an annual seminar at Castel Gandolfo, his summer residence, where he would sit down and roll up his sleeves to engage the other participants as equals in academic debate. Those invited were always world-renowned scholars, but no Catholics were allowed.

It may be that dialogue within one tradition takes a lot for granted and therefore is focused only on the exploration of differences, whereas ecumenical dialogue takes differences for granted and seeks common ground. It may, on the other hand, be that different ecclesiologies coexist within one tradition, usually unthematized but there nonetheless, and in consequence the dialogue is perhaps not always about what it seems on the surface to be about. Or, again, it might just be that theologians among themselves practice a kind of professional insouciance which, in church circles, they must exchange for at least the appearance of pastoral earnestness. Maybe we are comfortable together because there is no altar call at the American Academy of Religion.

The distinction that first comes to mind when we think about Protestant and Catholic understandings of the role of the theologian has to do with the idea of "vocation," which Edward P. Hahnenberg has so recently written on in extraordinary fashion.[1] The role of theologian is evidently a "calling" in the Protestant sense, and indeed one to which you can be ordained in more than a few traditions. Compared to this, the Catholic tradition is distinctly odd, or at least very different. Traditionally Catholics have unfortunately tended to reserve the term *vocation* for those called to or entering into ordained ministry or religious life. Any relationship between these vocations and the role of theologian is quite accidental and, frankly, not highly correlated. Theologians in the Catholic tradition these days, unlike a generation or two ago, may or may not be ordained, and the majority are not. Bishops, however, who may or may not be good theologians or indeed know very much theology at all, are the official teachers of the faith, and theologians qua theologians have no connection whatsoever to the charism of teaching with authority in the Church. Practically, at any rate, that is the case, though the fact that in the medieval church the *magisterium* was primarily located in theologians might suggest that looking at the question theologically we could come to another conclusion. But for the present the ecclesial understanding of what theologians do is nicely captured in a remark I recall but cannot reference from a book I read long ago, which declared that there are only two ways that Catholics can do theology: with a canonical mission or as a hobby. In other words, theology is done as an officially approved aide to the bishops or as a purely private pursuit of no ecclesial consequence. The relationship of the non-canonically-missioned

---

1. Hahnenberg, *Awakening Vocation*.

theologians to the teaching of the Church would be approximately that of the philatelist to the Postal Service.

So when one begins to think about the roles of theologians vis-à-vis the Church in the categories of vocation or calling, it is almost inevitable that any further taxonomizing will take the form of identifying their roles relative to the Church or tradition to which they adhere. One need not necessarily jump to the categories of faithful or unfaithful, professing or dissenting, pastoral or critical, whether relative to ecclesial or biblical fundamentalism, though there are undoubtedly some who do and it is difficult to employ such terms without at least seeming to be judgmental about one or another alternative. So I will use somewhat less current terms for three different possible relationships theologians might have to the formation of sound teaching, if only to undercut the potential for identifying one or another as more or less valuable. The terms I will use and briefly outline here are *insiders*, *liminals*, and *aliens*. But be warned; while I think terms like these are better terms for avoiding the either-or judgmentalism of the usual pairings, I believe that they too must give way in the end to a more holistic vision of the theological task, which I will explore in the second half of the paper.

It would be a mistake to assume that insiders are necessarily conservative voices. Insiders see their work primarily in relationship to the Church, but whether they are conservative or liberal will depend pretty much on which of Antonio Gramsci's two classes of intellectuals they exemplify. Are they under the impression that their work stands somehow above or outside social and political contexts, or do they see themselves as marked by, even representative of, particular social groups or classes? Are they, in Gramsci's categories, traditional or organic intellectuals?[2] The key to distinguishing theologians in this way is not ideological so much as political. What are their relationships to the forces of production, as Walter Benjamin might ask, and indeed did in his essay exploring the role of the writer in a revolutionary society.[3] Nor, of course, should one assume that insiders are somehow more conventional or less moral than others; or less conventional or more moral. It is simply that insider theologians conceive of their professional responsibility in terms of apologetics, broadly understood. They are either traditional intellectuals, who mostly do not recognize or may even reject the role of context and history in the way theology is done, or

2. Gramsci, *Prison Notebooks*, esp. 3–23.

3. Benjamin, "The Author as Producer," in *Reflections*, 220–38.

they are organic intellectuals who understand quite consciously that their work is expressive of a relationship to the church conceived institutionally.[4] But, conservative or liberal, they work in close relationship to the forces of production, to the Church as institution, and are therefore—honorably and sometimes quite critically—somehow or other negotiating the relationship between faith and the institution in such a way as to satisfy the powers behind the forces of production. Some are comfortable with this position, some less so, but all of them are realists about the powers that be.

Liminals, as the word suggests, are those individuals who work on the threshold between the Church and the secular world, or perhaps between the church and other major world religions. These too might in principle appear in both more "progressive" and more "traditional" guises. However, in the present-day more conservative ethos of institutional Catholicism the traditional liminals become indistinguishable from insiders, and disappear from sight. In any guise, liminals are driven by a more hortatory and less coolly rational rhetorical style. They may seem more choleric, where the insider is inclined to be phlegmatic, though frankly both have their choleric and phlegmatic moments when things seem to be going in the wrong direction. They may be thought more foolhardy, in danger of throwing out the baby with the bathwater, though they would probably defend themselves by saying that the baby has already gone off to join an ashram and the bathwater is cold and uninviting. They are more anxious and perhaps, in the end, more puritanical. They expect more from the Church and when it does not come, they forgive less. But they bring an edge to theological debate that complements the solidity of insider theology. They too are organic intellectuals, but their self-understanding is more proletarian than the first groups. They identify with "the Christian masses," however technical or, indeed, frankly abstruse their work may sometimes seem.[5] Theology cannot afford to be edgy all the time, but a little attitude can be refreshing. Sometimes, however, their independence of the forces of production can be perilous, especially if their ecclesiastical position locates them within the forces of

4. They are as different as Avery Dulles and Rick Gaillardetz, Robert Imbelli and Yves Congar, Sarah Butler and James Alison, John McDade and Nicholas Lash, Paul Murray and Gerard Mannion. As befits my Catholic focus, these names are all of Catholic theologians.

5. We need our Beth Johnson and Michel de Certeau, Roger Haight and Ada Maria Isazi-Diaz, Mark Jordan and Shawn Copeland. Just as, if the face of Catholicism were like the more liberal postonciliar era, we would need those who would then have seemed liminal, like George Weigel or the late Richard John Neuhaus.

production. At that point the forces of production can sometimes treat them as a species of class traitor and threaten to expel them.[6]

And then there are the aliens, by which I mean the voices from outside the tradition whose work enriches and challenges that of both insiders and liminals. Here the list is almost endless, from Foucault to Bourdieu, from Hitchens to Eagleton, from A to Žižek. The work of the aliens is not always or even often theological in character, unless we broaden the meaning of the word to the point of irrelevance. But it is the intellectual face of secularity, it is the place where Christian theology can engage what Karl Rahner calls the concupiscence of the world, the trial-and-error, unguided, sin-and-grace-filled hunger for the transcendent. Inevitably, it is the liminal theologians who will most likely seek to engage the aliens. The insiders, not at all illegitimately, will want to use them for their own apologetic purposes.

Well, this is a parlor game we could go on with endlessly. Somewhere in the space between taxonomy and the roman à clef we are all of us curious to know just where we are being placed, if only because even if we are put in the wrong place there is an undoubted *frisson* to hearing our names mentioned at all. But I want to terminate this exercise because, though it is entertaining and open to a thousand challenges and corrections, it is my conviction that this kind of taxonomy is ultimately antithetical to the spirit of the gospel and unproductive for the Christian community.

The problem with the typical divisions among theologians such as those I have sketched above, or even the more obvious taxonomy of liberals, moderates and conservatives, always ranks theologians relative to "the Church" understood as "the forces of production." But the Church is not the institution, above all—perhaps surprisingly—not in the Catholic tradition where spirituality is so communal, even to a fault. Catholics, contrary to some caricatures, are not saved by membership in the institutional structures of the Church but by membership in the community of faith. While the communal rather than individual orientation of soteriology in the Catholic tradition seems to separate Catholics from Protestant sensibilities, in fact the distinction between the Catholic community of faith and the human structures that have grown up within it makes space for a more

---

6. I'm sure that Roger Haight will not mind my using him as a classic example of this problematic. *His* challenging but legitimate theological interests led not only to his removal from a teaching position at Weston Jesuit School of Theology in Cambridge, Massachusetts, but eventually—in an unprecedented move—to his being forbidden to teach even at Union Theological Seminary in New York City. Only someone with clerical status can be treated in such fashion.

ecumenically valuable approach to the work of the theologian. What happens, in other words, if we can conceive of the role of theologian in categories that sidestep the question of the relation to the institutional Church?

Those readers who are not Catholics will perhaps have noticed that all the insider and liminal theologians I have listed in my footnotes are, or at least purport to be, Catholic. This, if not deliberate, was almost inevitable. I am sure that if I were sufficiently familiar with the ecclesial terrain of the Orthodox, the Episcopalian, or maybe even the Southern Baptist tradition, I could have done something similar to the outline I just provided. But such an outline requires a centripetal community of faith, if not always a high ecclesiology. I use the term *centripetal* here to refer to traditions in which the relationship to the church or community of faith looms large in the task of the individual Christian, professional theologian or otherwise. More evangelical or Pentecostal traditions have only a minimal centripetal component and are much more focused upon mission and evangelization, the "centrifugal" component of Christian praxis. So the theologian in the centripetally concerned church is far more likely to be taken up with issues of ecclesiology, liturgy, or sacramental life than with questions of evangelization or even mission. My assumption is that in a more centrifugally oriented community of faith the opposite would be the case.

So here is my thesis: the work of the theologian is not valuable relative to the demands or understandings of the institutional church, but relative to the needs of the community of faith. This means that theologians should not be valued or disvalued for their political or ideological leanings, but for the contribution they make to the enrichment of the faith-life of the community. In other words, the question is not are they progressive or are they liberal, but are they conscientiously seeking the good of the faith community?

I would like to suggest that, following Bernard Lonergan, the good theologian is the one who is open to religious, moral and intellectual conversion, and that s/he sees the ultimate role of the theologian, at however far a remove, to be the promotion of an environment of conversion for the whole church. But what is "the church" and what constitutes conversion? In his seminal essays in *A Second Collection*,[7] which mark a significant shift in his thinking, Lonergan argues that religion and theology have moved from a classical into an empirical model. In our world, says the Canadian Jesuit, the human being is no longer understood in terms of some fixed

7. Lonergan, *A Second Collection*.

conception of human nature, but as an "incarnate subject." Just so, perhaps even more so, one might extend Lonergan's model to the whole community of faith and argue that today it is best understood as a "collective incarnate subject," both buffeted and constituted by the many cultural and intellectual currents of (post)modernity. One of the ecclesiological problems for centripetal communities of faith like that of the Catholic Church today is the tension between a body of believers who are largely at home in the (post)modern secular world and an institution that continues to think in classical rather than empirical categories.

Lonergan's account of the new theological paradigm in which the human person is seen as an incarnate subject, adapted to an ecclesial context where the Church is a collective incarnate subject is inherent in ecclesial imagery from Vatican II such as People of God or pilgrim, but is also present in the idea of the Church as the Mystical Body. The model of the Church as the Mystical Body of Christ, which came to real prominence only in the first half of the twentieth century, is in so many ways the parent to the more recently developed models for the Church.[8] In ecclesiology today as in Christian anthropology, the rigidity of the soul/body dualism gives way to much more complex understandings of the relationship between what can change and what abides. In the neoscholastic ecclesiology of the Church as a perfect society, the shape of the Church as we know it in history is part of its essence, is permanent, is that without which we would not be Church. But at Vatican II and beyond, the Church is always growing and changing in ways we cannot predict and that will surprise us. There is a core, a permanent reality, of course, but this permanent reality is located in the community of the faithful throughout history who, in the power of the Spirit, have the responsibility to preserve the tradition and to grow with the times.

In order to arrive at the possibility of conversion, Lonergan argues that the individual must somehow actualize the "four transcendental precepts." These are: "be attentive, be intelligent, be reasonable, be responsible." Later he modifies this to "be attentive, be intelligent, be responsible, be loving and, if necessary, change." In Lonergan's view all genuine knowing has to follow this path, and it does not take much thought to realize that this set of precepts clearly articulates an experientially based path to knowledge. Actualizing the transcendental precepts in one's life is the

---

8. The work of Emile Mersch was crucial in bringing this theological model before the academic community; see especially *The Whole Christ*.

route to conversion in Lonergan's view, at each of the three levels at which he says conversion can occur: religious, moral, and intellectual. Perhaps, after all, there is then only one ecclesial role for the theologian, to aid in the intellectual, moral, and religious conversion of the Church. And if so, there is little possibility that the theologian can do much to help this if s/he is not already well along in the process of conversion, so perhaps we should explore this latest thought a little by examining the process of conversion as Lonergan understands it.

To summarize very briefly the notion of conversion as Lonergan understands it, we have to begin with religious conversion. This is a "being grasped by love" that is in essence religious, since it requires openness to transcendence, though it is not necessarily recognized by the one who experiences it *as* religious. Hence, Lonergan sometimes calls it affective conversion. From it follows, logically and perhaps even sometimes chronologically, both moral and intellectual conversion. Moral conversion involves a shift from satisfactions to values, while intellectual conversion is the process of becoming aware of what knowing really is, that is, defined by acts of meaning, not just "looking." The deeper the religious conversion, the more far-reaching the moral conversion, while the intellectual conversion is a more difficult process, one not attained, he thinks, in any great measure by the majority of people.

If we follow the logic of the process of conversion as Lonergan outlines it, it seems pretty clear that while a theologian is going to have to be someone who reaches the third, intellectual level of conversion, her or his service to the community of faith will in large part relate more to the level of religious conversion. There is an obvious taxonomy of theological activity implied in the threefold process of conversion; there are pastoral theologians, moral theologians, and systematic/foundational theologians. Those at the furthest remove from everyday religious practice, the third category of systematic/foundational theologians, acquire their authenticity, however, only as a consequence of their religious conversion, and their service to the community of faith, even when their scholarship is at its most abstract or theoretical, is only as good as the religious conversion upon which it must ultimately rest. It is the "being grasped by love" that is the essential starting point, even for the theologian.

This set of considerations might bring us back again to the threefold division of theologians I suggested earlier, of insiders, liminals, and aliens, but now considered relative to their roles in promoting religious conversion rather than relative to the institutional Church. If religious conversion is a "being grasped by love" that is religious though not always understood in religious categories, then any thinker whose work leads us closer to self-transcending love might qualify as a theologian. Someone as edgy or liminal as Simone Weil or Michel de Certeau might be good examples. "Aliens" like Julia Kristeva or Friedrich Nietzsche or George Orwell might be others. Where self-transcendence is furthered, we might say in more traditional terms, the grace of God is at work. If nothing more, this is one good reason why Church theologians might want to attend to at least some secular thinkers. By the same standard it is also why non-religious thinkers who promote ethics (moral conversion) and clear thinking about thinking (intellectual conversion) might be encouraged to consider the self-transcendence (love) that these intellectual movements of the spirit rest upon. What's missing among the new atheists is not moral probity or intellectual acuity but love.

While, then, the ecclesial role of the theologian may be most directly a matter of thinking about thinking (systematic and foundational theology) or of the promotion of values (moral theology), it is always in the end pastoral because it has its *raison d'être* and its foundation in the experience of being grasped by love. This, to recap, is evident in Lonergan's four transcendental precepts that he believes guide all responsible thinking, whatever the discipline. One must be attentive (or read the signs of the times and one's own experience), be intelligent (in the analysis of these signs), be responsible (in drawing appropriate conclusions and courses of action), be loving, and if necessary, change.

This approach to the theological task also allows us to revisit and perhaps appropriate Benjamin's remarks about the creative artist and the relationship to the forces of production, though in a fashion that may make at least some "insider" theologians uncomfortable. Whatever the theologian's immediate task, be it the exegesis of Romans, the explication of Irenaeus or constructing an apologia for Modernism, the ultimate task is enriching the capacity of the community of faith for self-transcendence. In this sense we are all church theologians, though perhaps not Church theologians. But it is tempting to point out that the community of faith is to the institution as the proletariat is to the forces of production. If we take this strictly and admit that the theologian, like any responsible "intellectual worker," needs to be an organic intellectual—that is, someone aware that s/he represents a particular "class"—then no theologian worth her or his salt will be able to settle for being a Church theologian. Such a relation to the forces of production divides the attention of the one whose calling it is to help the community grow in love. On the other hand, the theologian who is a church theologian writes not so much out of class consciousness as from the perspective of the community of faith, which is a "class of the whole." The important thing is to do so independently of the forces of production. Strangely enough, then, for those whose theological work is done in centripetal traditions like the Catholic Church, academia is a wonderful enabler. The freedom it brings makes possible, though it does not guarantee, the process of religious, moral, and intellectual conversion that too close a relationship to the forces of production precludes.

I realize that the position I am maintaining here is open to being attacked as cynical or merely jaundiced in its estimation of the Church as an institution. Not to mention that it may smack to some of warmed over Marxism. Obviously, the institution too has the responsibility to be a school of love for the community of faith. The problem is that all institutions have an inbuilt inclination to want to preserve themselves in their current form. This is a glaringly obvious problem in my own Catholic tradition; just as the Church is entering hospice care, to borrow Bryan Massingale's striking image, Church leadership enters into denial.[9] One mark of this denial, though by no means the only one or perhaps even the most important, is the institutional disregard for all theological work that is not that of the most traditional of traditional intellectuals.[10]

So to reject the notion of Church theologian is not to abandon the commitment to being a church theologian. Theology, as Ghislain Lafont has written, is a charism that "has a life of its own." "It is more supple and more precise," he continues, "more diverse than the episcopal charism that in its turn is tied to governing a Church as a body while observing 'the rule of faith.'"[11] Moreover, the verification of the charism of the theologian, he says, is fourfold. First, perseverance in truth is a gift of God granted to those who pursue inquiry in a spirit of humility, just so long as "the theologian keeps his or her spirit and heart centered on the Mystery he or she seeks to investigate, to speak about and to understand."

9. Massingale, "See, I Am Doing Something New!"

10. Anyone who is at all familiar with the recent critique of Elizabeth Johnson by the U.S. Bishops' Committee on Doctrine will know exactly what I mean. The documentary history of this particularly painful episode in American Catholicism is now available in Gaillardetz, *When the Magisterium Intervenes.*

11. Lafont, *Imagining the Catholic Church.*

We find shades of Lonergan here. Second, the charism is kept faithful by the collective character of theological inquiry today, as "it ceaselessly corrects itself." This insight is one that the Catholic magisterium of current times frequently overlooks when it "investigates" the work of this or that theologian. Third, the sense of faith of the Church makes its contribution through the phenomenon of reception. If it is of the Spirit it cannot in the end be withstood, and if not it will fade away; which leads to the fourth and final verification, the action of time.

Magisterial interventions cause more problems than they solve, thinks Lafont. They are too often motivated by "a preoccupation with the need for intellectual security rather than . . . a jealous love of the Word of God," they seem to be insufficiently patient with the slow pace of some developments, they fail to grasp the new because of commitment to categories already at hand, and they even contribute to the theologian who feels misunderstood or underappreciated engaging in "a kind of 'research without self-investment'" that may be disconnected from active involvement with the meaning of the faith of the People of God. They may, in other words, push theologians away from a relationship to the community of faith by failing to recognize the distinction between institution and community. In our terminology rather than that of Lafont, one might say that the more the institution insists upon the closeness of the theologian's task to apologetics narrowly construed, the more likely that task is to miss out on the "being grasped by love" that is the essential component in conversion.

I am not going to apologize for how Catholic this paper is. Its Catholic character is accidental, but its inductive nature is essential. Whether one accepts the remark of Jon Sobrino that "true theology begins with indignation"[12] or Gustavo Gutiérrez's well-known phrase that as reflection on praxis, "theology comes after,"[13] it is increasingly clear to me that sound theology must be inductive. And to be inductive it has to be contextual. I think that Ada Maria Isasi-Diaz got it exactly right when she described the theologian as "the professional insider."[14] To be a theologian one has to have the skills and training to bring knowledge of the tradition in which one lives to the process of reflection on praxis. But one has also to be located concretely within that tradition.

12. From a private conversation with the author, London, 1975.

13. Gutiérrez, *Theology of Liberation*, xxxiv.

14. Isasi-Diaz, *En la Lucha*, 87–89.

One of the good things about the inductive method is that if it is employed correctly it eventually results in generalizable conclusions, though these must always be placed in dialogue with the wisdom derived from other theologians in other locations. Hence, after all this Catholic ecclesiology, it is possible to see that there is considerable ecumenical advantage to pursuing an understanding of the role of the theologian along the lines suggested by Lonergan. Just as the individual Christian's primary responsibility is to conscience, so the theologian's is to the transcendental precepts. Any theologian works out of the intellectual inheritance of her or his own tradition, Catholic or Baptist, Orthodox or Anglican, but each is surely motivated by a sense of being grasped by love, or s/he cannot engage fully in the theological task. Moreover, each must surely be ready to stand at a critical distance from the home tradition on that unhappy day when it fails to be supportive of that experience of "being grasped by love" that is both the necessary beginning and the ultimate end of conversion. More importantly, a commitment to the transcendental precepts and the work of religious, moral and intellectual conversion that they entail provides a far more solid background awareness for ecumenical dialogue than does the wary jockeying for position that it used, at least, to entail. Ecumenical theologians today sometimes explain that the debate about the meaning or merits of particular doctrines in traditions in dialogue has been replaced by the painstaking exploration of how seemingly different beliefs are both faithful to the apostolic tradition. Analogously, the real dialogue that is only possible when we are ready in principle to be changed and corrected by the wisdom of the other is enormously facilitated by focusing on the clarification of our common commitment to clear thinking (the transcendental precepts) and the process of conversion.

The *saving* presence of the Church in the world is to be found in the Church as the community of believers and in the lives and witness of individual believers, not in the Church as Church, which as what James Alison has called "the regime and discipline of signs" can only be effective in and through the ways in which believers enflesh these signs in history, signs "aimed at summoning forth certain shapes of human desire, interpretation, and living together, rather than coercing people into sacred structures."[15] The challenge to the Church qua Church is to rid itself of everything which impedes its sign value; the challenge for the baptized is to act in history in faithful witness to the sign that is the Church, both the

15. Alison, "Sacrifice, Law and the Catholic Faith."

sign of the Cross and the sign of the Reign of God. The Church is always present as the regime of signs, but the sign becomes sacrament only in the lives of Christians. The temptation of the Church, always needing to be countered by the praxis of believers, is to see itself as a system of goodness and thus to place law and ethics ahead of the nourishment of faith in the gospel. The role of the theologian is to correct this imbalance. And, unfortunately for my own Catholic tradition at least, too many of our energies today must go into pointing to the failure of the institution to allow the being-grasped-by-love to proceed. Only the theologian who is grasped by love can aid in that healing process.

6

Earthen Vessels

Theological Reflections on North American Denominationalism

–Amy Plantinga Pauw

T HERE ARE MANY WAYS to be church, and Christians have been trying for two thousand years to find the perfect recipe for organizing their communal life. The perennial Christian strategy, as Lutheran ethicist Larry Rasmussen has noted, is to gather the folks, break the bread, and tell the stories.[1] From New Testament times onward, Christian communities have struggled to figure out how people gather and who gets to break the bread and tell the stories. That is, the church always has polity, that is to say, *political*, questions to address. Christians are always faced with decisions about how power is to be distributed in their life together, to the end of establishing an enduring, cooperative form of communal life that both assures the sustenance of the church's vital ministries and is in some way transparent to their convictions about God.

---

1. Rasmussen, "Shaping Communities," 119. I am grateful to the members of the 2012 Williamson Distinguished Scholars Conference, and especially to Paul Lakeland, for helpful feedback on an earlier version of this essay.

Communal Christian negotiations around polity are never carried out in isolation from other forms of political life. Over the centuries, Christians have been inveterate borrowers and scavengers, appropriating and adapting various models of human organization that were available in the larger society—the empire, the nation state, the corporation, the shopping mall, the political caucus, the regulatory agency. Church structures, in turn, have made contributions to the development of political life on a larger scale.[2] Church governance is thus never only about the regulation of the church's internal life: governance models also reflect how Christian communities relate to the larger social order. Since both church life and the larger social order are dynamic and evolving, this historical embeddedness also means that church polity is always to some degree contingent and provisional. Even in traditions whose basic polity has remained unchanged for centuries, alterations in the social order, both large and small, often prompt shifts in form and emphasis in church governance. In North America, for example, past and present advancements in the social status of women and gay and lesbian persons have provided contexts for several Protestant churches to reconsider the appropriate role of these groups in church leadership. Likewise, democratic sensibilities among North American Roman Catholics, combined with a drastic priest shortage, have encouraged burgeoning lay leadership in Catholic parishes, as ecclesial lay ministers, both male and female, carry out many tasks once reserved for ordained priests.

These historical observations about the interdependence of church structures and the larger social order do not contradict or undermine theological affirmations about the divine institution of the church, or about the ongoing guidance of the Holy Spirit in the church's life. Instead, they are a reminder that the church is a creaturely reality. As creature, the church is intrinsically oriented toward God, the source and sustainer of all life. As creature, the church is also materially and socially dependent on other

---

2. For example, as historian Brian Tierney notes, "When medieval thinkers reflected on the right ordering of the church they did not hesitate to call on the secular wisdom of the world. But the secular ideas that they borrowed, first from Roman law then from Aristotle, were not simply repeated parrot-like; they were transformed and given back to the world charged with a new significance. The church both learned from secular law and political thought and contributed significantly to their future development. The theory and practice of representation in general councils contributed to the later development of secular representative assemblies; the idea that natural law limited the power of monarchs and upheld the rights of others persisted in secular political theory; and the idea of mixed government as reshaped by medieval theologians formed a major strand in later constitutional thought." Tierney, "Church Law and Alternative Structures," 60–61.

creatures. It does not choose its cultural location, and its way of life is not self-contained. The life that God creates and sustains, including the life of the church, is relational, dynamic, and vulnerable. To view the church as having a special role in God's purposes neither diminishes the church's creatureliness, nor withdraws it from the realm of human processes. God raises up disciples of Jesus Christ and sustains communities of praise and witness within an ongoing flow of overlapping and shifting human cultures. This dynamic, interdependent cultural world is not a barrier to the church's faithfulness, but the context for its discernment of what continuing faithfulness looks like. It is indeed the task of theologians to speak of the order and ministries of the church with reference to the work of God; but that reference must include the work of God the Creator.

This essay explores what North American denominationalism, a relatively new arrival on the scene of church governance, can contribute to church unity. Denomination is a Protestant way of being church, not embraced by Catholic and Orthodox Christian communions, though these churches have sometimes *functioned* as denominations in particular religious ecologies. Roman Catholics are my main ecumenical conversation partners in these reflections, and my approach will reflect my own Presbyterian sensibilities while attempting to reflect on North American denominationalism more broadly.[3]

Protestant denominationalism has taken several historical forms since its origins in late eighteenth-century North America, including ethnic enclave, purposive missionary organization, and corporation.[4] However, the denominational form of church has fallen on hard times in recent decades, and many think its glory days are over. Protestant denominations are facing financial crises and sharply declining membership, alienation of ordinary members from denominational leadership, growing parochialism in congregational spending, and unrelenting conflict over hot-button issues. Nondenominational churches now represent the second largest group of Protestant churches in North America.[5] Some nondenominational Protes-

3. See my essay "Presbyterianism and Denomination," 133–46. Because Protestant denominationalism has functioned quite differently in other global contexts, I will confine my reflections to North America.

4. These terms are from Russell Richey, who charts various overlapping forms that North American denominations have taken over their history; see "Denominations and Denominationalism," 74–98.

5. "American Piety in the 21st Century" (selected findings from the Baylor Religion Survey, September 2006).

tant churches have seen enormous growth, to the point of becoming mini-denominations in themselves, duplicating many denominational functions such as training clergy, sponsoring mission, and producing worship and educational resources. Transdenominational affinities based on shared theological perspectives or commitments to particular social causes often seem to trump denominational loyalties. For millions of Protestant Christians around the world, the European and North American struggles and divisions that gave rise to different denominational traditions seem irrelevant to their lives of faith. Many Christians in Africa and Asia wonder why they should perpetuate these Western patterns of denominational loyalty. Many Christians in North America wonder the same thing.

Given this dire state of affairs, it is worth asking why denominationalism deserves theological attention. The Baker *Evangelical Dictionary of Theology* says that "there is no indication that denominations will soon disappear; but neither does it appear that anyone is eager to justify them theologically."[6] I take that statement as a challenge. My aim is not to propose strategies for turning denominational fortunes around, but rather to suggest theological reasons why North American Protestants should not give up on denominationalism just yet. My attempts to provide some modest theological justification for North American denominationalism are accompanied by theological reflections on its sins. Honest ecclesiology cannot escape lament and penitence. In this essay I point out what I see as the strengths of Protestant denominationalism, but I also attempt to be candid about its terrible failings and its uncertain future. I do so as a contribution to ecumenical progress. It is only in mutual acknowledgment of our failures and shortcomings that different Christian communities can find true reconciliation and communion.

Paradoxically, much of my encouragement for not giving up on Protestant denominationalism has come from Roman Catholics. My reflections on denominationalism have been enriched and stimulated by the work of a range of progressive Catholic theologians and historians. Their understanding of the church's historical dynamism and their willingness to criticize the failings of their own church resonate with my Reformed sensibilities about ecclesial change and peccability. I will argue that some recent Catholic explorations in ecclesiology reflect theological views of the church that are consonant with denominational self-understandings and encourage a

---

6. Elwell, *Evangelical Dictionary of Theology*, 336–37.

more appreciative perspective on North American denominationalism and its contribution to church unity.[7]

Comparative ecclesiology, exemplified in Roger Haight's three-volume *Christian Community in History*, takes as its starting point the reality of religious pluralism. According to this approach, a community of faith has no responsible choice except to live in open dialogue with other communities of faith. As Christians we are called to cordial and constructive interfaith relationships; likewise we are to approach other *Christian* communities with a hermeneutic of generosity, trying to understand them as they understand themselves. Expanding the teachings of Vatican II, comparative ecclesiology insists that the whole church "subsists" in every church, but that no church can by itself be considered the whole church.[8] The church universal is a communion of churches. The plurality of ways of being church is both a historical reality and a resource for the church's ongoing renewal. In Roger Haight's image, the church is like "a multi-colored tapestry, or a large river that has branched out . . . to carry the full flow of Christian life."[9]

The notion of the church as a communion of churches resonates with denominational Protestants. There is a non-exclusive impulse at the heart of denomination: to claim a denominational identity is to see one's own body as a part of the universal church, but not as the whole church. To be *denominated* a Methodist or a Lutheran or a Mennonite in the North American context is to recognize the legitimacy of other Christian communities. Humility doesn't come easily for most Christians, but a degree of humility is built into a denominational self-understanding.

Denominational Protestants in North America have lived into this humble, self-relativizing form of church gradually and unevenly across their history, and mostly not by choice. There were Protestants before there were denominations. Denominationalism assumes the legitimacy of at least some degree of ecclesial pluralism in polity and theology, and the earliest Protestants by and large neither desired nor anticipated that within a given civil government there would be a plurality of religious adherence. In that sense, Protestants have accepted denominationalism as a kind of consolation prize. It is not that they were instinctively generous

---

7. See for example, Haight, *Christian Community in History*; Lakeland, *The Church*; Mannion, *Comparative Ecclesiology*; Mannion, *Ecclesiology and Postmodernity*; Oakley and Russett, *Governance, Accountability*; and Murray, *Receptive Ecumenism*.

8. Haight, "Preface," xx.

9. Ibid., 6–7.

and deferential towards other Christians; rather they saw clearly that in a society in which they were not the sole established church, they would have to find ways of coexisting with other Christian churches. As Russell Richey points out, to be a denominational church is to concede the authenticity of other churches even as you claim your own.[10] Ecumenical sensibilities about who else was included in the term *church* expanded only gradually for North American Protestants; in the mid-nineteenth century, for example, Charles Hodge was still unsuccessful in persuading his fellow Old School Presbyterians to accept the validity of Catholic baptism. But at its best, denominationalism has cultivated respectful and cooperative relations among all who claim the name *Christian*.

Denominational churches have generally understood that no single Christian community or tradition ever instantiates a full and non-defective form of church. All expressions of church are partial and problematic. As George Hunsinger has put it, "The divided churches as we know them are not mutually self-sufficient but mutually (though differently) defective."[11] As a result, denominationalism emphasizes what we can receive and learn from other Christians. It acknowledges the provisional, unfinished character of every form of Christian life, and the consequent need of every church community to receive enrichment from fellow Christians. As the Apostle Paul puts it in 1 Corinthians 12:21, no member of Christ's body can say to another, "I have no need of you." All churches are pilgrims, on their way to God's promised future. The members of the Christ's body mutually constitute each other: each member brings gifts needed for the well-being of the whole.

This basic Pauline insight has never lost its urgency, because the Christian tradition has always been internally diverse. The historian Dale Irvin borrows a term from botany to insist that Christianity has had a rhizomatic development, "agglomerating and stabilizing at times," he says, "around common experiences or locations, but then branching off and spreading rapidly at other times, in several directions at once. It is a decentered, or multicentered, system flowing across multiple material and subjective fields."[12] The natural result of this development has been a plethora of strong, distinctive theological and liturgical traditions. In any given ecclesial context, some traditions are given official expression and others

10. Richey, "Denominations and Denominationalism," 76.

11. Hunsinger, *Eucharist and Ecumenism*, 231.

12. Irvin, *Christian Histories*, 47.

are neglected or submerged, ready to be drawn on as new circumstances demand. The Christian faith has always been complex and multicentered, and this fact should inform theological reflections on the kind of structural unity for which we aim. Church unity, as Hunsinger insists, can only result from the joint recognition of the need for "mutual learning, reciprocity, and conversion"[13] among the world's churches. Denominational churches may have a head start in recognizing both the fact of ecclesial pluralism and the need for interdependence.

Differences in polity generally prove more intransigent than doctrinal differences in ecumenical relations. Yet it is arguably a prerequisite for denominational self-understanding to recognize the need for flexibility in ways of ordering Christian communal life. Though they have stubbornly championed their own forms of church order on both scriptural and pragmatic grounds, denominational Protestants have generally recognized that God has given the church no single mandate regarding polity. No one form of church order is a good in itself, but derives its authority and legitimacy from its faithfulness to scriptural teaching and from how it serves the worship, edification, and mission of the church. This pragmatic, self-relativizing view of church polity is hard to find outside of denominational churches, but it is arguably a prerequisite for generous ecumenism.

Disagreements about the status of ecclesial polity introduce an awkward asymmetry in ecumenical relationships. The refusal to regard any church order as normative and immutable, including their own, puts Protestants at odds with their Catholic and Orthodox ecumenical partners. Protestants who lack episcopal structures can appreciate the contribution of the historic episcopate to the unity and stability of the church both across the centuries and in the present. But many of them concur with the assertion of the ecumenical document *Baptism, Eucharist and Ministry*:

> [I]t is increasingly recognized that a continuity in apostolic faith, worship, and mission has been preserved in churches which have not retained the form of historic episcopate. This recognition finds additional support in the fact that the reality and function of Episcopal ministry have been preserved in many of these churches, with or without the title "bishop."[14]

Denominational Protestants are convinced that the church in its many forms continues to be guided and nourished by God, indeed, as Roger

13. Hunsinger, *Eucharist and Ecumenism*, 197.

14. *Baptism, Eucharist, and Ministry*, "Ministry," para. 37.

Haight avers, that "the Spirit of God impels particular organizational structures as a way of ensuring the church's well-being" in a given time.[15]

The ecumenical goal of visible unity has often been defined in rather clerical terms, with unity in structures of ministry being a prerequisite for sacramental unity. By contrast, denominational churches, with their tradition of an open table, provide a glimpse of the visible unity of the church as a gathering of the baptized from all Christian traditions sharing the food Christ has provided. Visible church unity is about the new life in Christ through the Spirit being communicated around the whole body, and the flow of this life does not always go from clergy to laity. From a denominational perspective, the role of a visible head or heads of the church, on both local and global levels, is above all to mirror and nurture this local unity.

Could the Spirit of God now be impelling Protestant churches that lack episcopal structures toward the episcopate? George Hunsinger has recently argued that any church rejecting the historic episcopate cannot be regarded as ecumenically serious.[16] Without the alignment of Protestant churches into the historic episcopate, he sees little hope of an ecumenical future.[17] Hunsinger urges the acceptance of bishops in Reformed churches in particular "for the sake of ecumenical unity and rectification."[18] Though their unhappy historical experiences have sometimes led to vehement denunciations of the episcopate, especially in its Roman Catholic form,[19] Reformed Christians, it seems to me, should not be opposed to the episcopate in principle. There is no distinctively Reformed polity: within the Reformed family of churches congregationalist, Presbyterian, and episcopal structures have all been embraced in different contexts.[20] According to Eberhard Busch, this form of denominational weakness has paradoxically been a Reformed strength.[21] As the Presbyterian *Confession of 1967* insists, "The institutions of the people of God change and vary as their mission requires in different times and places. The unity of the church is compatible

15. Haight, *Christian Community*, 194.

16. Hunsinger, *Eucharist and Ecumenism*, 209.

17. Ibid., 211.

18. Ibid., 207.

19. See, for example, the Reformed critique of the papacy in the Second Helvetic Confession, in *Book of Confessions*, 5.131–32.

20. See in particular Todd, "Bishops in the Kirk," 300–312, for an account of the acceptance of bishops in early Scottish Presbyterianism.

21. Busch, "Reformed Strength," 21.

with a wide variety of forms."[22] In my view, the ultimate aim of ecumenism is a vibrant connectionalism that preserves "the reality and function of Episcopal ministry,"[23] rather than the historic episcopate in particular. However, the Reformed acceptance of the episcopate could be a helpful intermediate step toward that visible unity.

Few could argue that the mission of Reformed churches would not benefit from governance structures that would tamp down the Reformed propensity towards divisiveness. My own denomination, the Presbyterian Church (USA), seems to be heading towards yet another fracture at present. Reformed churches have been like the child who plays beautifully with others at school and then is a real monster at home with her siblings. The Reformed has been both one of the most ecumenical of denominational traditions *and* among those the most likely to divide the church by the inability of its members to live with those theologically and culturally closest to them. Any argument for introducing bishops into the Reformed churches would need to reckon with the rather well-developed Reformed sense of the dangers of ecclesial tyranny. This argument would have to be made on scriptural and functionalist grounds and in a way that did not exclude a central role for conciliar forms of Christian discernment.[24] A Reformed willingness to adopt a pragmatic, self-relativizing attitude towards their own polity and consider changes for their own good and for the good of the larger church would in my judgment be a demonstration of the strength of denominationalism, though it is a difficult step to imagine Reformed churches taking.

If comparative ecclesiology affirms the reality of religious pluralism, inductive forms of ecclesiology maintain the importance of reflecting theologically on the church as it is, rather than on an idealized image of it. Systematic theologians have been tempted to let historians deal with the church in its concrete imperfections and instead focus their attention on some transcendent ideal of the church: the church as "perfect society," the temple of the Holy Spirit, the bride of Christ. Theologian Nicholas Healy warns against a "blueprint" form of ecclesiology that describes the church "in terms of its final perfection rather than its concrete and sinful existence,"

---

22. Presbyterian Church (USA), *Book of Confessions*, 9.34.

23. *Baptism, Eucharist, and Ministry*, "Ministry," para. 37.

24. See Hunsinger, *The Eucharist and Ecumenism*, where he urges the acceptance of bishops in the Reformed tradition "for the sake of ecumenical unity and rectification" (207).

and treats the church's ideal being as theologically normative, "rather than presenting careful and critical descriptions of its activity within the confusions and complexities of a particular ecclesiological context."[25] Paul Lakeland's inductive approach to ecclesiology also insists on the importance of theologizing about the church as we find it. He notes that the church is not a static, unchanging, "perfect" reality, but more like a "collective incarnate subject," moved and changed by the forces around it.[26] To think about the church as we find it includes thinking about the church's imperfections and divisions. As the former archbishop of Canterbury, Rowan Williams, insists, we have to theologize about the church's misconstruals, its premature totalizations, the victims of the historical church.[27] As the body of Christ in the world, the church is a broken and diseased body, mirroring the ills and fractures of the larger society. The church can point neither to its present instantiation nor to some past golden age as the perfect realization of God's intentions for it.

When it comes to imperfections and divisions, it is tempting to say that denominational churches are experts! One of the cardinal sins of denominational churches is divisiveness. The fissiparous character of Protestantism manifested itself long before the advent of denomination. The hope among sixteenth-century reformers, that a wholly biblical theology purged of dangerous speculative and devotional accretions would unite the church, was dashed early on by divisions over the practice of baptism, and Protestants have gone on to fulfill the gloomiest Roman Catholic predictions about the tendency of their movement to divide the church. The incentives provided by the structures of denomination in Protestantism have only exacerbated this propensity to choose division more often than reconciliation. In addition to dividing along national boundaries, denominations have readily divided to accommodate members' convictions and affinities of every sort. Denominationalism has both reflected and perpetuated the racial and socioeconomic divisions of North American society. In the contemporary period, the almost inexhaustible accommodations of religious preference within denominational Christianity mirror the consumerist patterns of the larger capitalist culture. Faced with conflicts about theology, polity, and cultural engagement, Protestants have repeatedly opted to form small, homogeneous groups of the like-minded, preferring to settle the

25. Healy, *Church, World and the Christian Life*, 54.
26. Lakeland, *Church*, 123.
27. Williams, "Saving Time," 323.

truth about a controverted issue in the church by breaking fellowship with all who disagree. In this way they have profoundly betrayed their calling as a witness to the reconciliation Christ has accomplished.

Should denominational churches then be written off as contributors to church unity? No. Despite its manifest failings, denominationalism has been a durable medium for preserving particular traditions of Christian theology, worship, and mission. Authentic Christianity always takes a local form; it is always spoken with a distinctive accent. From this perspective, denominations have in fact been a unifying and conserving force in Christianity, nurturing and carrying forward distinctive theological traditions. According to James Nieman, denominations create multistranded identity narratives that are strong and flexible enough to recall denominational mistakes and failures, preserve marginalized or forgotten voices, and situate themselves within a larger ecumenical ecology.[28] This role is especially significant against the backdrop of the contemporary Protestant trajectory towards non-denominational expressions of church that often seem to lack any acknowledgment of their debts and ties to larger church traditions. For now, these non-denominational churches are living off the theological capital of more established Christian communities, including those of denominational Protestantism. However, it is not clear how the distinctive resources of Wesleyanism, for example, will remain available without the efforts of Methodist denominations. The earthen vessels of denomination have been used to conserve precious theological ointment. We can deplore divisiveness while affirming a legitimate cultural, theological, and liturgical diversity in the global church, and the role denominations can play in that. However, denominational churches clearly have much to learn about unity from other members of Christ's body.

No one is going to confuse denominationalism with God's good and perfect will for the church. The denomination is a provisional structure of Christian existence that has taken diverse forms across space and time. In the North American context, it is currently experiencing many strains and fissures, and may evolve in new ways or even disappear altogether. For denominational churches, this radical contingency is part of their identity. If denominational churches had a slogan, it would be "We're not the only one, we're not perfect, and we need help from others!" These modest convictions have always been part of denominational self-understanding to some extent, though they were easier to downplay when North American mainline

28. Nieman, "Theological Work of Denominations," 625–53.

churches enjoyed greater membership, wealth, and social prominence. Now that these church structures have fallen on harder times, denominational Protestants have the opportunity really to live into their self-relativizing understanding of church, their realism about their own imperfections, and their acknowledgement of the need to receive wisdom from others, both inside and outside the church. They can reclaim the Protestant insistence on what John Webster has called "the sheer gratuity" of the church's existence, and "the permanently derivative character" of the church's work.[29] They can be a living example of Christ's power made perfect in weakness (2 Cor 12:9), a model of what it means for the followers of Jesus Christ to be a humble sign of God's saving love for the whole world.

29. Webster, "Visible Attests the Invisible," 104–5.

7

Karl Rahner's Ecumenism and Its Challenge for Today

–David H. Jensen

RAHNER'S VOICE AMID THE EBB
AND FLOW OF THE ECUMENICAL MOVEMENT

The past century (and particularly the past half-century) has witnessed enormous changes in what is commonly referred to as "the ecumenical movement." These changes have been felt at both the local level of the congregation and the national (or international) level of the various Christian denominations. Though the shifts are too vast to summarize briefly, a few highlights capture the scope of the changes. Most historians chart the beginnings of the modern ecumenical movement starting with the Edinburgh Missionary Conference of 1910, a conference devoted to world mission that was overwhelmingly North Atlantic and exclusively Protestant in its makeup. The conference emphasized the need for denominational collaboration in mission work and training, as well as the tangible goal of evangelizing the world in this generation. Within a few years, however, this spirit of missionary zeal and denominational cooperation was chastened by the outbreak of the First World War. Yet, much of its spirit continued in the aftermath of that war, in a 1937 Edinburgh conference on Faith and Order, which was broader in its denominational and geographic representation, and in the eventual founding of the World Council of Churches in 1948. In some respects, the high point of the ecumenical movement—at least in its official pronouncements and efforts at denominational reconciliation—occurred within the first few decades of the WCC's inception. Church bodies such as the United Church of Christ (USA), the United Church of Canada, and the Evangelical Church in Germany emerged out of a spirit of reconciliation and Christian unity characteristic of these decades. By the time the most significant ecumenical statement of the twentieth century, *Baptism, Eucharist, and Ministry* (1982), was published, however, the evangelistic goal of 1910 had mostly evaporated. And though the denominational makeup of the World Council of Churches was as broad as it had ever been (including Roman Catholic representation in an observer capacity), the denominations present at most ecumenical gatherings were perhaps even less representative of the diversity of Christianity worldwide than they were at the dawn of the century (given the relative lack of charismatic, evangelical, and Pentecostal participation). Meanwhile, as many Protestant denominations began to shrink, fewer resources and attention were devoted to ecumenical discussions. In other words, by the time *BEM* was heralded as a major ecumenical achievement and a decade later when Roman Catholics and Lutherans signed the Joint Declaration on the Doctrine of Justification, many of the founding traditions of modern ecumenism were becoming increasingly concerned with denominational survival. The heady missionary and ecumenical optimism of 1910 was replaced by the need to focus attentions inward as the century closed.

As the ecumenical movement both gained momentum and sputtered over the twentieth century, the voice of Karl Rahner often appeared in the theological mix. Though much of his writing was occupied with theological questions posed primarily to Roman Catholic audiences, the closing years of his life were increasingly occupied with ecumenical concerns, as evidenced by several essays in the concluding volumes of his *Theological Investigations* and one of his last monographs, co-published with Heinrich Fries, *Unity of the Churches: An Actual Possibility* (1983). Though these works generated numerous responses after their publication, they have elicited less commentary in subsequent years, paralleling the waning of many ecumenical efforts and the movement of Rahner's theology from vogue to passé, especially among Protestants. Indeed, when a recent essay makes the assertion, "Rahner has not been directly influential on Protestant theology, either dogmatic or philosophical, and in my judgment is unlikely to be in the future,"[1] it is perhaps not surprising that a specifically Protestant engagement of Rahner's reflections on ecumenism has been largely absent. Nevertheless, there are strands of Rahner's ecumenism, particularly in *Unity of the Churches*, which are resonant today, even if the ecumenical context has shifted. My intent in this essay is to probe some of Rahner's contributions to furthering ecumenical understanding and broader union among Christians, while also exploring some difficulties in his concrete proposals for unity. I will conclude by offering a complementary approach to efforts at achieving greater unity among Christians, one that is resonant with some themes in Rahner's ecclesiology and Reformed Christianity.

A HERMENEUTIC OF GENEROSITY: RECOGNITION OF PLURALISM

Rahner and Fries published *Unity of the Churches* at a time when progress in North American and European ecumenism was beginning to ebb and new problems obstructing further ecumenical collaboration were beginning to arise. Both authors had been engaged in ecumenical issues for some time and had witnessed the tides prior and subsequent to Vatican II in the Roman Catholic Church. Their book, as the subtitle indicates, claims that the conditions for Christian unity are already present among the churches, but are yet to be realized by the diverse Christian bodies. They propose eight theses that the various churches might embrace as common points of agreement, which will result in structural changes. Under these theses, agreement on common theology and adaptation of the presently existing ecclesial polities can result in visible forms of Christian unity beyond what is present today. Though this "actual possibility" of church unity might be readily dismissed as a late-twentieth century version of heady optimism, it becomes clear that Rahner and Fries's proposals involve thorough critiques of existing models of ecumenism. They seek not a furthering of the World Council of Churches, but a greater unity borne out of a spirit of hermeneutical generosity in theology, agreement on core confessions, and a shift in existing church polities.

1. Adams, "Rahner's Reception," 211.

The opening paragraph of the book is indicative of its context and the urgency of the task at hand: "Unity is a matter of life or death for Christendom at a time when faith in God and His Christ are most seriously threatened by a worldwide militant atheism, and by a relativistic skepticism even in those countries where atheism is not yet a state religion."[2] The present context, the authors claim, is in many ways inimical to Christian faith. The more fragmented Christianity remains, the less it is able to address the threats to its message. But the task of ecumenism is not merely a strategic one of the survival of Christian religion; it is primarily a theological responsibility, borne out of Christ's command to exhibit unity: "To abandon the goal of ecumenism and to end one's ecumenical commitment is a violation of the mandate and mission of the Church as expressed in the testament of Jesus, 'That they may become perfectly one . . . so that the world may know that thou has sent me (John 17:23).'"[3] A few things are worth noting in these opening salvos: First, the primary threats to the gospel are atheism and skepticism. Without naming them as such, the authors discern threats in Eastern European Marxism and Western European skepticism, both of which prove intolerant of faith. Soon after these theses were posted, however, communism in Eastern Europe fell. In the intervening decades, moreover, religious fundamentalism has emerged as a more potent force across the globe. Perhaps relativistic skepticism holds sway in some isolated corners of the North Atlantic nations; but, viewed globally—and increasingly even in so-called "secularized" nations—militant fundamentalisms in all kinds of religious traditions have been escalating. This is a threat that hardly seems foreseeable in Rahner and Fries's introduction.

A second item worth noting is that the authors view the goal of ecumenism as visible unity that is evident in church polity. Ecumenical efforts sell themselves short (or sell out entirely) unless there is some greater unity in mind. Ecumenism, as the authors see it, is not merely an effort at greater understanding among Christian bodies; it ought in some way to result in structural unity. This goal of ecumenism is discernible as the pages progress. Otherwise, the authors claim, ecumenism becomes a furthering of the *raison d'etre* of the World Council of Churches rather than following of Christ's command that all may be one. The model of ecumenism that Rahner and Fries offer is ambitious and challenging. Indeed, it is as far-reaching

---

2. Fries and Rahner, *Unity of the Churches*, 1.

3. Ibid., 3–4.

as any ecumenical proposal on the contemporary scene in that it envisions the full communion of Catholic, Orthodox, and Protestant churches.

The authors claim that such communion is possible in the near future. The theses they offer appear—with one possible exception[4]—to be within reach of most ecclesial communities. Three aspects of these theses, indeed, mark significant ecumenical progress: 1) their focus on the Apostles' Creed and the Creed of Nicaea-Constantinople, 2) their hermeneutical generosity, and 3) their welcoming of plurality in ecclesial structure.

The proposal begins with a straightforward affirmation of the basic creeds that are shared broadly throughout the churches. By focusing on the confessional texts that are shared most in common, Rahner and Fries emphasize the nature of the church *as* confessional. The creeds do not simply summarize the basics of Christian faith, they signify that faith is *responsive*. Faith, as the authors see it, is a response of the people of God. The language of the creeds signifies the church's response to the response of faith: "The Creed is response to response. . . . The Creed is linked to the content of faith, but does not articulate all its details; rather, it articulates the contents in their concentrated center."[5] The ancient creeds are witnesses to a responsive faith not only because of their longevity, but because they draw "attention to the fact that faith is not a private matter; rather, it turns toward the public, toward the public community of faith itself . . . [and] also turns toward the public world."[6] The creeds turn believers and the community outward; they are exercises of accountability, toward the faith, toward the world. They are not uttered alone, but with others and, therefore, in some way bind us to others.

The authors are clear about the normativity of the ancient creeds; they indicate that all subsequent traditions are to be judged in light of the Creed and subject to it.[7] They provide a theological foundation to build on, but also to fall back upon. Yet their normativity does not suggest that their interpretation is fixed for all time. Indeed, the authors emphasize the continual reappropriation and assessment of these ancient pillars: "Although the fundamental truths of Christian faith have been formulated in the Confession of Nicaea and Constantinople, this does not exclude but instead

---

4. The exception regards their theses regarding the papacy, which I will explore in the following section.

5. Fries and Rahner, *Unity of the Churches*, 15. This section was written by Fries.

6. Ibid., 16.

7. Ibid., 19.

includes their further interpretation and development, through all those motivations and challenges that determine the history of faith and of theology, and also of dogmas."[8] The responsiveness of faith, in other words, demands the continual recitation of creeds and their creative re-engagement and theological development as the church lives in response. Greater clarity of both the content and implication of the Creed may well occur as time goes by.

This focus on the content and theological implication of the Creed impels one to ask about the teaching authority of the church. If the Creed provides the bedrock of the church's responsiveness, then who delineates the boundaries of the Creed's theology? The individual? The teaching authority of the church? The community of faith? The authors' commentary (written by Rahner) on Thesis II addresses some of these questions with a clarification: "Nothing may be rejected decisively and confessionally in one partner church which is binding dogma in another partner church. Furthermore, beyond Thesis I [concerning the ancient creeds] no explicit and positive confession in one partner church is imposed as dogma obligatory for another partner church."[9] In this section, Rahner emphasizes the astonishing amount of information and knowledge that is present in the modern world. It is not possible for one person to master any one discipline, or to amass all knowledge in one field, let alone multiple fields. The intellectual pluralism of the modern age means that there will be manifest modes (sociological, psychological, philosophical, etc.) of interpreting creeds, drawing out theological implications of the church's confession. "Theologians too know more and more, and for that very reason can understand each other less and less."[10] Once the churches move beyond the content of the ancient creeds, they recognize different ways of knowing and accessing truth. The present situation of intellectual pluralism, moreover, may render it difficult for many to respond affirmatively to truth. This, too, is to be recognized not as a deficiency. "If a person withholds an affirmative verdict regarding a true (certainly or possibly) proposition, he does not err."[11] The posture of the churches, in light of these realities, ought to have a common recognition of the "basics" of faith and a tolerance of those things that fall outside the realm of

8. Ibid., 20.
9. Ibid., 25.
10. Ibid., 29.
11. Ibid., 32.

the basics. Indeed, the theological treasures of the churches as a whole are greater than any one of them has on their own. The portrait of church theology that emerges from commentary on this thesis is one of mutual informing, of bodies needing one another in order to be more accountable to the mystery of faith. A tolerance, bounded by the requirements outlined in the thesis, yields to generosity in the church's interpretive life.

This generosity toward the partner churches, for Roman Catholics, extends in some way to the teaching authority of the church: "The doctrine regarding the binding teaching authority of the church is not the first or most fundamental truth of the Christian faith in either the objective or subjective hierarchy of truths."[12] It occurs, Rahner claims, after the fundamental themes of Christ, revelation, God, and the founding of the church. This recognition does not relativize the church's teaching authority, as much as it situates the partner churches' potential relationship to that authority. The proposal for unity does not demand Protestant (or Orthodox) acceptance of all matters of Catholic doctrine (or vice versa), as much as it advocates a suspension of judgment in regards to some matters that partners view as "binding." For Protestants, this means that "the Protestant Christian would not need to make a doctrinal and definite agreement right now to many of the propositions that the Catholic regards as binding on the faith. But he does not need to reject them definitely either."[13] The posture of the churches, then, might be conceived as mutual listening and learning in the name of a greater call to unity.

This generosity in theology and epistemology also extends, in some regard, to church polity. Efforts toward greater church unity—full communion—need not result in a uniform polity. Here, the burden lies squarely with Rome not to envision itself as the form of unity that dissolves other legitimate church polities: "The demand that these churches [of the Reformation] surrender themselves is an illegitimate and unjust demand."[14] Commentary on Thesis III (also written by Rahner) emphasizes that partner churches maintain their existing structure; regions of the globe will have several overlapping polities and structures. The partner churches have a degree of independence, but are also bound to one another. Homogeneity in polity is no more desirable than uniformity of theology. "Unification results in a more encompassing catholicity if it retains independent part-

---

12. Ibid., 33.

13. Ibid., 37.

14. Ibid., 43.

ner churches."[15] What this kind of pluralism in polity looks like, however, may be difficult to predict: whether like Rome's relationship to Eastern rite churches, or more like its ongoing engagement with the Orthodox churches, or something that fosters an even greater sense of the independence-yet-connectedness between traditions.

The hope of the theses, however, is clear. In some way, the exchange of theology, polity, and response to the church's response in creed ought to evoke a greater openness to others, whereby openness to the other is also "openness to something greater. Indeed, it may even mean a greater loyalty to one's own."[16] This model of ecumenism does not result in a watered down theology or a more organized assembly of church representatives, but a relationship that involves greater faithfulness to one's own tradition and that sees union as a result of that faithfulness. The task of union, for Rahner and Fries, belongs to us: "People . . . have caused the separation of the Church into confessions. People can alter history and renew it; and they must do so if what happened was not good and if it brought harm and scandal."[17]

THE PAPACY: A CHALLENGE
IN THE PROPOSALS FOR UNITY

Rahner and Fries's plea is clear: people have caused division. The means for overcoming this division is strikingly generous toward a variety of theologies and polities. Nonetheless, their proposals also present significant issues for Protestants, primarily regarding the papacy. Rahner poses this challenge directly: "Of course, a unification of the churches is possible only if the Petrine office and its powers and functions are recognized sufficiently by all partner churches."[18] What is meant by the "powers and functions" of the Petrine office? The authors' explanation of them is surprising in its yielding yet insistent stance that the Petrine office stands as one of *the* marks of church unity. The role of the pope, in their proposals, is as "the concrete guarantor of the unity of the Church in truth and love."[19] The pope is more than a symbol of unity, more than a token that the partner churches

15. Ibid., 44.

16. Ibid., 114.

17. Ibid., 140.

18. Ibid., 47.

19. Ibid., 59.

acknowledge as valid for Roman Catholics and their polity. He is in some way to be regarded as valid for the partner churches as well.

Rahner and Fries are careful to note the evolving nature of the pope's primacy; how the role of the bishop of Rome in 1054 differed from his role in the fourth century. They are also careful to trace the emergence of the *ex cathedra* dogma in the nineteenth century, alongside many of the other statements regarding the papacy at Vatican I. They also describe the problems inherent in some of these historical developments: "The nineteenth century, which saw the end of the imperial church and which imposed a heavy and humiliating fate on the popes, gave rise to a pronounced papalism under the sign of the Restoration. Indeed, a veritable papal cult started to bloom, which frequently approached tastelessness and blasphemy."[20] Readers of the commentaries on Thesis IV a (written by Fries) and b (written by Rahner) will no doubt be quickly dispelled of the impression that the papacy is the ax that will fell any earlier nods to pluralism in polity or tolerance in theology. The papacy, in their vision, is part of the broader scope of tolerance and generosity. Indeed, papal primacy as a dogma is rejected, at least for the partner churches: "No explicit confession of dogmatic necessity of the primacy of the pope should be required of the Protestant partner churches of the one Church."[21] What is instead envisioned is a form of subsidiarity, where the papacy abandons "a centralized and isolated form . . . subsidiarity is the result of legitimate diversity and collegiality."[22] Nonetheless, the papacy exhibits a *function* among the partner churches that is recognized as valid: for "the preservation and the clarification, appropriate to the situation, of *the* substance of faith already expressed in the ancient creeds."[23] The pope both provides a sign of the unity of the churches and exhibits a teaching function. In the common life of the churches, clarity—even within the bounds of theological diversity—is needed. Such clarity is provided, at least in part, by the pope in his teaching role. For the Orthodox churches, recognition of the pope's role would involve no more than acceptance of the pope's role prior to the Great Schism (and not subsequent developments in papal primacy after the Schism). For the Protestant churches, recognition would seemingly involve acknowledgement of the pope's teaching role within the structures of their already existing polities.

20. Ibid., 60 (Fries).
21. Ibid., 71 (Fries).
22. Ibid., 71–72 (Fries).
23. Ibid., 89 (Rahner).

In this reconfiguration, Rahner and Fries also hint at new (and somewhat radical) forms of papal election. The presence of partner churches' bishops in the College of Cardinals is suggested as a viable possibility. Partner churches, thus conceived, would have a voice in the selection of subsequent popes, and "a completely different election board" could legitimately be thought of, where "members do not have to be appointed specifically by the pope."[24] If the pope is conceived as the guarantor of church unity, there may be other forms of papal election that better voice that unity.

By situating the pope within the pedagogical realm, Rahner and Fries also recognize an ongoing need for the Congregation for the Doctrine of the Faith. The configuration of this body, however, would also be less centralized, able to recognize "the theological peculiarities of the individual partner churches." The Congregation would likely "exert its influence on the individual partner churches, and on their individual teachers and doctrines, only by way of the bishops of these partner churches."[25] Fries concludes his observation on Petrine service and teaching by posing an intriguing question:

> Do these churches consider the Roman Catholic doctrine regarding the function of the pope—as we understand it today and as Rome already practices it (even though it is in need of correction)—a doctrine and practice so radically contradictory to the essence of the Protestant message that they must reject this doctrine and practice as a deadly contradiction to their faith and as an extreme threat to their eternal salvation? If they do not dare say that, the plain question is why they do not want to live together with us Catholics in the one Church, since this Church . . . in practice demands no more than what is already being lived out in the relationship of its members to its officials.[26]

This is, to be sure, a pressing and provocative question. Very few mainline Protestants would consider the papacy an "extreme threat" to salvation. But does a "no" to the question Rahner and Fries pose lead necessarily to the reconfigured practices surrounding the papacy? And, if not, what would be the theological grounds for questioning the far-reaching proposals for church unity that they outline?

24. Ibid., 92 (Rahner).
25. Ibid., 86 (Rahner).
26. Ibid., 82.

Protestant readers are likely struck by how much is retained and how much is reconfigured in such proposals. Papacy and Congregation of the Faith remain, albeit in somewhat different modes, at least for partner churches. Yet the authors are clear that what they propose is not simply a "give and take" scenario, where Catholic concessions to Protestant theology are made in exchange for recognition of the papacy and its teaching office. Indeed, from their perspective, the grounds for theological tolerance are the same ones for recognition of the teaching role of the pope. The unity of the churches is evidenced in its rich theology that transcends any one tradition and gains symbolic expression in both the mutual recognition of ministries (and sharing of word and sacrament) among the partner churches and acknowledgement of the pope as the guarantor of unity. Most Protestants will find little to quibble with in the theses' theological generosity; but on the question of the pope's role, many will encounter difficulties. I now turn to one reaction that raises important questions in these remarkable proposals for unity.

ONE PROTESTANT RESPONSE: HAROLD DITMANSON

Rahner and Fries's theses did not generate a flurry of Protestant responses in the aftermath of their book's publication. Most of the responses, moreover, came from traditions that had polities most similar to Rome's, namely Lutheran and Anglican. Harold Ditmanson, a former professor of theology at St. Olaf College, offered a response in *Lutheran Quarterly* that stands as one representative, both in its appreciation and critique. Like his Catholic counterparts, Ditmanson sees the goal of ecumenical discussion not to be bargaining and compromise "to reduce the two to one. It is rather that together they should be able to achieve a more authentic reformation than either of them could achieve in isolation."[27] Ecumenical proposals for greater unity become cheapened if they are viewed as tit-for-tat exchanges. Yet Ditmanson claims that *Unity* invariably conveys some degree of exchange, whereby something is given and something received. He admits that this perception is doubtless colored by his own American context, "unduly influenced by commercial and political transactions in a strongly pluralistic society."[28] And when confronted with the items for exchange, he is less than convinced.

27. Ditmanson, "Response to the Fries-Rahner Proposal," 375.
28. Ibid., 376.

On the one hand, Ditmanson is enormously appreciative of the proposals themselves. They represent, in his estimation, a step forward in efforts to achieve more authentic reformation. He finds the willingness to "find room for Protestant concerns" earnest and ingenious.[29] He appreciates the tone of the document, with its "absence of polemics."[30] And he shares and stresses the deep unity of Spirit in the church that is "God's doing," and the solidarity among Christians that render the divisions between the churches "almost trivial."[31]

Despite this sympathy, however, Ditmanson (perhaps unsurprisingly) is convinced that the movement of Rahner and Fries's theses is "toward Rome."[32] On the one hand is a single entity, the Roman Catholic Church, and on the other a plural, the partner churches.[33] Even if the Roman Catholic Church is "transformed," the trajectory—at least through Ditmanson's eyes—seems more a Catholic welcoming home of erstwhile separated siblings than a forging of a common home. His chief objection to the proposals concerns the role and nature of the papacy. Ditmanson responds to the provocative question posed on whether current Catholic doctrine on the papacy constitutes an "extreme threat" to Protestant understandings of salvation with an emphatic "no." "There is nothing in Catholic polity that contradicts the essential Christian 'tradition,' namely, God's redemptive act in 'handling [*sic*] over' and 'handing down' (*paradidonai, tradere*) Jesus Christ to share our human lot and to reconcile the world to himself."[34] Ditmanson admits that Roman Catholic polity is not only theologically acceptable; it also represents a valid interpretation of many of the varied texts in the New Testament devoted to church order. Yet he objects to the stark alternative that Rahner and Fries's question poses: either accept the pope and find oneself in relation to his authority or reject the papacy altogether. His reason for rejecting this stark alternative is that he finds little support for any one model of polity within the New Testament: "It is very doubtful whether the Spirit's guidance was so detailed or so faithfully implemented that any one order could be regarded as absolute or indispensable. In fact, the variety and changeability

29. Ibid., 381.

30. Ibid., 375.

31. Ibid., 383–84.

32. Ibid., 378.

33. Ibid., 376.

34. Ibid., 382.

of church orders points to the continual need to express in updated form the relation between what is normative and what is situational in the life of the church."[35] Just as the New Testament suggests some degree of openness and plurality in church structure, we should expect differences in Christian polities today. The drive to adhere to any one polity, seemingly, may suppress some of the witness of the worldwide church.

This leads Ditmanson to view the existing divisions among Christians, at least in part, as gift. What Rahner and Fries deem a scandal seems, in Ditmanson's eyes, to be a legitimate response to "the reality of God" that "overflows our theological categories."[36] The difference between his observations and the proposals evident in *Unity* is less a matter of theological conviction and more a matter of how one situates church polity within the broader field of theology. Rahner and Fries tend to view separate polities as a theological scandal; Ditmanson sees polity as a necessary outgrowth of differing theological intonations. At their best, these varied polities express a greater unity than is found in any one tradition.

Rahner and Fries's proposals on the papacy, moreover, run head on into a touchstone of Protestant theology: "Protestants do not easily find a place for any human being who would serve as 'the concrete guarantor of the unity of the church in truth and love.'"[37] Ditmanson voices reservations about attributing to any one person the kind of authority present in current Catholic doctrine, not because he deems it threatening to faith or even to unity, but because—given the conflicted history of the church and its interpretation of its scriptural and apostolic heritage—"God evidently wants us to live without external guarantees."[38] Protestants tend to locate teaching authority, moreover, "not in the pope or any other bishop, but in the community itself."[39] At this point, one wonders whether Ditmanson is reading the proposals of *Unity* clearly or not. Rahner and Fries make it clear that the teaching authority of the papacy is connected intimately to the church as a whole. As *Lumen Gentium* makes clear, "the assent [*assensus*] of the church must accompany papal definitions."[40] Ditmanson may be making the gulf between his own and *Unity's* understandings of church polity and teaching

35. Ibid., 382–83.

36. Ibid., 387.

37. Ibid., 389.

38. Ibid., 390.

39. Ibid.

40. Fries and Rahner, *Unity of the Churches*, 80.

wider than it actually is. Nonetheless, his reservations are significant and do point to a key question: Must the cause of unity result in greater sharing of polity? Or, might the aim of unity be served precisely by the diversity of polities represented in the already existing Christian bodies?

On this question, Ditmanson proposes a slight change in terminology. Whereas Rahner and Fries use the term *unity* to speak both to the presence of Christ in the churches that already unites Christians *and* the aim of bringing the churches closer to one another in fellowship, ministry, and sacramental life, Ditmanson proposes distinguishing these two meanings. The former should be dubbed "unity," while the latter "unification or union." Indeed, in his eyes, "the *one* church already exist[s]" and "it already has all the *unity* it needs."[41] This unity is nothing less than a gift of Christ bestowed to all. Union or unification is something that human beings accomplish at the level of organizational behavior, as an expression of our already existing unity in Christ.

That leaves the reader with a question: Is union or unification desirable? Ditmanson answers affirmatively, and suggests an alternative route. Instead of reconfiguring the role of the papacy, he suggests a more direct (and in his eyes, simple) route: "a general declaration of unrestricted fellowship between churches, the full mutual recognition of ministry and sacraments based on common faith."[42] Rahner and Fries also emphasize this aim; but for them, the aim grows from the various churches' relation to the Petrine office. Ditmanson disentangles the polity question from the theology of Eucharist and ministry. More can be advanced in the cause of union by full recognition of ministry, sacrament and fellowship at Table than can be secured by any reconfiguration of the Protestant churches relationship to the *magisterium*. With the same aim in sight, Ditmanson proposes an alternative route.

A MORE MODEST ECUMENICAL WAY?

The proposals outlined by each author are convincing, substantive, and potentially far-reaching. The three authors suggests changes both within their respective traditions and within traditions that are not their own. *Unity* envisions changes in partner churches' understanding of the papacy while it also stresses the transformation of Rome's relationship to partner churches

41. Ditmanson, "Response to the Fries-Rahner Proposal, 387.

42. Ibid., 389.

and recognition of their independent-yet-related polities. Ditmanson emphasizes a mutual recognition of ministries that is not yet present in any tradition, while calling upon Rome to practice open table at the Eucharist. There is not a "one-sidedness" to either proposal for greater union. Yet a close reading reveals two commonalities in the competing proposals: 1) Both envision a way forward in ecumenical relations that begins with official pronouncements made by ecclesial bodies. For Rahner and Fries, this involves official Roman Catholic recognition of the polities and structures of the partner churches and the partner churches' official recognition of the role of the pope as the concrete guarantor of the church's unity, primarily in a teaching role. For Ditmanson, this involves official pronouncements of fellowship, recognition of ministry, and Eucharistic fellowship made by the various bodies. Despite their differences in proposals, both seem to agree that for ecumenical efforts to succeed, they need to be reflected in denominational documents. 2) Both proposals also envision the way forward to begin with the "other" party adopting practices that more closely resemble its own. In Rahner and Fries's case, the way forward will begin to be clear if the Protestant churches (primarily) find room for themselves under the umbrella of the Petrine office. In other words, much ground can be gained by even a limited Protestant endorsement of the pope's teaching role. In Ditmanson's case, the way forward will gain much momentum once the Roman Catholic Church is willing to practice open communion and fully recognize Protestant clergy in ministry. In other words, once the Catholics are ready to understand who is gathered at table more similarly to Protestants, some of the way will be clear. Perhaps it is not surprising that each proposal senses much to be gained when the partner more closely resembles themselves. But such proposals are also somewhat disappointing, if only because they stress that the most transformation needs to happen in places other than one's home church.

As much as I appreciate both of the proposals outlined, I want to suggest something different—perhaps more modest, perhaps more radical—as a possible way forward in the new century when ecumenism seems sputtering at best. My suggestions avoid the official pronouncements that seem part and parcel to the corresponding Catholic and Lutheran suggestions I have considered. Such pronouncements seem unlikely as auspicious places to mark forward progress in the ecumenical movement. On purely pragmatic grounds, such pronouncements rarely garner the attention of local congregations. My own tradition, the Presbyterian Church (USA),

routinely adopts statements, policies, and makes ecumenical pronouncements at its General Assembly, and unless these statements have something
to do with human sexuality, they are barely noticed (or are even unheard
of) at the congregational level. Sometimes, moreover, official pronouncements may run in tension with some of the root metaphors of church in the
broad catholic tradition—people of God, body of Christ, a pilgrim people,
a priesthood of believers—that stress the nature of church as communion.
At their worst, such statements become examples of laity receiving proclamations from leaders in distant places, unconnected to the rhythms of
congregational life.

Official pronouncements, of course, are necessary. Without them, it
is hard to conceive of any progress in ecumenical discussions and efforts
toward greater unity. The proposal that I am offering is not meant as a
counter to denominational agreements, but as a complement to them.
It is at once simple but also difficult to embody in practice: ecumenical engagement, discussion, and progress toward union (which I see as
desirable and grounded in our understanding of the unity of God) is best
begun at the congregational level. Ecumenism, at its most basic level, concerns our relationships with one another in Christ. And it best begins as
congregations build relationships with church communities whom they
grow to understand as partners in common ministry. This way forward is
resonant with the ecclesiology of Rahner and Vatican II as well as some
of the foundational tenets of Reformed understandings of what it means
to live as church. At the risk of oversimplifying, relationships rather than
pronouncements are what make ecumenical engagement move toward
possible union and reconciliation.

In one of Rahner's most cited works, composed shortly before *Unity*,
he writes, "The historical continuation of Christ in and through the community of those who believe in him and who recognize him explicitly as
the mediator of salvation in a profession of faith, is what we call church."[43]
The church is the ongoing presence of Christ given for the world, present
in the community that gathers in his name and professes him as Savior. The
offer of salvation is continually present for the world in this church, me-
diated through its sacraments, present as the community gathers around
the table that he sets. This church, for Rahner, always exhibits both visible
and invisible dimensions. It is visible because salvation is offered in history
to a people, not apart from history or community. But the church is also

43. Rahner, *Foundations of Christian Faith*, 322.

invisible in that the grace of God and the offer of salvation extend beyond those who gather in Christ's name or explicitly confess Christ as Savior. In all cases, however, the church comprises relationships: to Christ, in Christ, in the community of faith. Rahner emphasizes the church's hierarchical nature, its apostolicity, and its sacramental life, but what is common to each of these aspects of church is that the church is *connected, related* to those who have gone before. The church is bound to others as it confesses Christ as Savior and Mediator of God's revelation and salvation. We understand the church as it is a community of continuous relationship to those whom Jesus gathered, and through them to Christ himself. Relations form the fabric of the church. There is no isolated individual in Christian faith: "Faith may not be regarded as something which happens in the private interiority of the individual. . . . It must be public, it must be a profession, it must be the faith of a community."[44] Our experience of Christian faith both comes from and is grounded in the faith of the community. Without those relations, there is no Christian faith.

This expression of the communal nature of Christian faith occasions some of his remarks on church unity: "We are united in the hierarchy of truths in a unity which is deeper than the unity which is hindered by the controversial theological questions which divide the churches . . . Christians are united in a more radical sense than they are divided."[45] The source of this unity, however, is found not in the efforts of the people (though they may contribute to unity). It is grounded in the triune life and God's initiative. This echoes *Lumen Gentium*: "The universal Church is seen to be 'a people brought into unity from the unity of the Father, the Son and the Holy Spirit.'"[46] For Rahner, the church's unity in Christ is already given, but it is also an aim toward which God's people work in efforts to reconcile separated people.

Some of Rahner's reflections on the nature of church also echo with Reformed concerns, especially in one of the classic, and less familiar, statements of the Reformation, the Second Helvetic Confession. Second Helvetic also stresses the church as communion: "The Church is an assembly of the faithful called or gathered out of the world; a communion, I say, of all saints, namely, of those who truly know and rightly worship and serve the true God in Christ the Savior, by the Word and the Holy Spirit,

---

44. Ibid., 330.
45. Ibid., 367–68.
46. Flannery, *Vatican II*, 352.

and who by faith are partakers of all benefits which are freely offered through Christ."[47] Church is marked by a gathered people, assembled in Christ's name, united in worship, knowledge, and faith. Second Helvetic also makes clear that the fundamental unity of the church is not tied to its external actions: "Unity consists not in outward rites and ceremonies, but rather in the truth and unity of the catholic faith." This confession emphasizes an ecclesial harmony and unity in matters of doctrine, preaching, and "in rites that have been expressly delivered by the Lord."[48] Right worship, in this light, is an outgrowth of right belief. Though this confession seems to stress the priority of orthodoxy in church unity a bit more than Rahner (or *Unity*), both stress the nature of church as *communion*. Where we see the church exhibiting unity, there we can also see a people reconciled in Christ's name. The unity of Christians is manifest in their relationships with others in the faith.

I do not think it stretches the sense of either theological perspective on the church to note that efforts toward greater union (as responses to the unity already given the church in Christ) might be most immediately evident as different congregations build relationships with one another. This kind of "grassroots" ecumenism is not a substitute for the conversations going on at denominational levels, but can inform and enrich those conversations. It is, after all, at the congregational level that pronouncements on the church's life take root and grow. This suggestion is not meant to further the individualization and compartmentalization of faith that is often evident in American society. Severing ties with national church bodies or ignoring church policies regarding ecumenism is hardly what I have in mind. Rather, it is as a communion that the local congregation—in relationship with others—lives into the promise of Christ that all may be one. As congregations form relationships with one another, they witness the pain of division, the disagreements that often seem insurmountable, but also the deep sense of how much is shared, and the promise of something new. Such relationships, of course, transpire over the long haul of time. They are not accomplished by annual gatherings between two congregations for a choir concert or a mission project. They are, rather, lived into as possibilities in rather mundane affairs and acts of sharing over the years.

What might this kind of grassroots ecumenism look like? It can take multiple, perhaps endless, forms. But at minimum, it can include

47. "The Second Helvetic Confession," 5.125.

48. Ibid., 5.141.

practices of shared worship, educational opportunities, and meals. Regular pulpit exchanges and combined worship services between congregations are fruitful places of ecumenical interchange. Congregations might also have a common educational hour, where adult and children's Sunday school is shared by partner churches. In an age of the much-discussed decline of mainline Protestantism and shrinking educational resources, this may have a practical import, too. Imagine a class on the Protestant and Catholic Reformation where persons of both traditions are gathered over weeks in common space. Imagine a class on the Eucharist for children and youth of both traditions. In settings such as this the promise and pain of ecumenism might be lived out more fully. Here efforts toward ecumenical understanding can become animated in ways that denominational statements and policies can only anticipate.

Christian faith, in the end, is about basic things: worship, teaching, meals, baths, bodies, and space claimed as holy. When Christians who are separated from one another take steps toward sharing those basic things together, we see some of the promise of a possible next stage in ecumenism, especially in an age that often seems to focus on denominational survival. The concrete practices of congregations may in some way eventually lead to pronouncements and policies that are stated at the denominational level, but they also may not. When Christians gather together, however, they anticipate deeper expressions of unity than are often currently visible. The gathering makes all the difference. The challenges that Rahner and Fries's theses present are very much alive today. So, too, are the reservations and alternative proposal that Ditmanson voices. But no concrete proposal for deeper unity will be able to gain much momentum unless it is accompanied and even preceded by the small and often mundane things that congregations undertake to gather together with their neighbors. As international discussions seem to flounder, other conversations and practices may be becoming more vital.

8

Knowing Our Limits and Laughing with Joy

Theology in Service to the Church Invisible

–Cynthia L. Rigby

Humor is the opposite of all self-admiration and self-praise.

—KARL BARTH[1]

INTRODUCTION

This paper explores what theology has to offer in the face of the growth of the numbers of "unaffiliated"—that is, people who do not identify with any religious tradition. This phenomenon has been touted and/or fretted upon, of late, in the United States. It has long been a trend in many European countries. And it is beginning to be noticed in some Asian, African, South American, and Latin American countries, as well.[2]

---

1. Barth, *Church Dogmatics*, III/4, 665.

2. Some statistical evidence for these trends will be noted below. Also, important global questions include these: How will the visible church in countries in which the unaffiliated are the single fastest-growing group relate to the visible church in countries (e.g., in Africa and Latin America) in which Pentecostalism is the single fastest-growing religious group? How will we find ways to be united with one another in these very different ministerial/missional contexts?

How might theology better serve the church in the face of our changing, global, increasingly "unaffiliated" landscape? Believing that theology in service to the church must be engaged with actual persons (even as it keeps an eye on cultural trends),[3] I frame the problematic I am addressing from the vantage point of a single, perceptive, person—a man named Eric Weiner—who identifies himself as someone unaffiliated with any religion. I then remember and review theology's commitment to the church *invisible* as well as *visible*, suggesting that we are called to serve the unaffiliated as those who very well might be seeking to believe. In the remainder of the paper, I explore what it might look like to serve those who are claimed by God but do not (yet) perceive this. Specifically, I argue that if we are committed to serving those like Weiner, then the time is ripe for us actively to reclaim, reshape, re-present, and be reformed by the elemental truth that even the very best words we speak about God are limited and provisional. When our service to the church invisible is first and always service to the sovereign God before whom we believe "not one is missing,"[4] we are free to engage "religion" with openness and creativity. We listen as well as speak, doubt as well as defend, and laugh at ourselves even as we testify with great seriousness out of "all the riches of assured understanding" and "knowledge of the mystery of God" that is "Christ himself."[5]

Finally, I offer a challenge both to theologians of the church and a challenge to "Nones." Each of these challenges is meant to put a crack in whatever barriers[6] are keeping us from enjoying an approach to religion founded in the idea that the highly interactive (Creator, incarnate, triune) God is with us and for us. I end by suggesting some implications of all this for the global, ecumenical church.

---

3. This is consistent both with the central Christian conviction that "the Word became flesh" (John 1:14) and with the example of Jesus himself. Jesus, in his ministry, always reached out to particular people in their particular contexts.

4. See Isa 40:26b.

5. See Col 2:2, Basic English Version.

6. These barriers include, but are not limited to, sin and more general "dullness" (as Calvin put it).

THE GLOBAL INFLUENCE OF THE "NONES"

On Sunday, December 11, 2011, Eric Weiner published an op-ed piece in the *New York Times* titled "Americans: Undecided about God?"[7] He expresses his frustration that current U.S. discourse about God "has been co-opted by the True Believers, on the one hand, and Angry Atheists, on the other." "What about the rest of us?" he asks. He himself makes up the 12 percent of those who say they have no religious affiliation, or at least none yet. "We 'Nones' may not believe in God, but we hope to one day. We have a dog in this hunt." Weiner goes on to note that there is "not a lot of good religion out there." He characterizes the religions he rejects as asking him to "return to an age of raw superstition" (he says he can't do this, because he is a "rationalist" who thinks the Enlightenment "was a very good thing"). The only God he sees religion offering is "an angry God" who is talked about by people who (like this God) "judge," "smite," and "shout." In contrast to this, Weiner wishes for a God who is "fun" and for religious leaders who "laugh." "God is not an exclamation point," Weiner insists. God is, at best, "a semicolon, connecting people." Finally, Weiner suggests that what we need is a "Steve Jobs of religion . . . someone (or ones) who can invent not a new religion but, rather, a new way of being religious . . . that celebrates doubt, encourages experimentation and allows one to utter the word God without embarrassment."

I have been thinking about this editorial ever since reading it. Allow me, briefly, to disclose the content of my reflections, since they have no doubt driven the framing of this paper. I think they can be broken down into two main categories: (1) the things I appreciate about Weiner's way of understanding, and (2) the things I want to change, as a theologian of the church and Christian believer, in response to Weiner's appeal.

I appreciate that Weiner understands that the so-called "True Believers" do not necessarily speak for all of us "religious" folks, even if he is having trouble hearing religious voices *other than* these folks (presumably because they are always shouting). Weiner respectfully presumes there is something worth hearing from some religious people he has not heard from, yet. This in contrast to others, including Richard Dawkins, who are not willing to listen for religious voices that more quietly and less judgmentally testify to a God whose work is a semicolon. Dawkins, like Weiner, self-identifies as

---

7. Weiner, "Americans: Undecided." Weiner is also the author of *Man Seeks God: My Flirtations with the Divine*, which came out in December 2011.

a "None." While Weiner is a "None" who still seeks to know God, however, Dawkins is an atheist. Dawkins argues that anyone who believes in God is necessarily "delusional."[8]

I also appreciate the fact that Weiner respects and hopes for *religion*, refusing (for example) to accept "spiritual but not religious" philosophies as antidotes to the rhetoric of both the "True Believers" and the "Atheists."[9] Related to this, he states a need for and seems to expect theological leadership and guidance: he specifically asks for a "Steve Jobs of religion," that is, *someone who knows better than him*, when it comes to God. While it is clear he wants this person or persons to develop an approach to religion that is "straightforward, unencumbered . . . and highly interactive," he wants help with what such a religion would look like. Beginning to think with him about this, I don't believe, by "straightforward," that he is asking for something simplistic. He seems to know that, if interactive religion could be obtained simply by culture ordering it up from theologians who could serve it, he would already be eating it by now. Weiner seems to expect and desire that the "Steve Jobs of religion" who will help us will not react to cultural demands as much as perceive cultural needs. Maybe I'm giving Weiner too much credit, but my suspicion is that, in an age where theologians, pastors, and other church leaders feel incredible pressure to cater to what people *say* they "want" in religion, Weiner is exceptional in that I think he would appreciate Barth's comment—directed to theological scholars—that

> Those who urge us to shake ourselves free from theology and to think—and more particularly to speak and write—only what is immediately intelligible to the general public seem to me to be suffering from a kind of hysteria and to be entirely without discernment.[10]

That said, it is clear Weiner wants theologians to work very hard at making their deepest insights accessible (even as Steve Jobs did this, in a different

8. See Dawkins, *The God Delusion*. Dawkins' influence is global. His book has sold two million English copies and has been translated into thirty-one languages, according to wiki sites. In June 2011 he keynoted, in Dublin, at the "World Atheist Convention." The convention was sold out.

9. This is an important point because "Nones" and "SBNR" ("spiritual but not religious") folks are often identified in blog posts and other publications. They are not one and the same. Weiner is not, for example, the caricaturized SBNR person Lillian Daniel mercilessly mocks in her controversial *Huffington Post* piece "Spiritual but Not Religious? Please Stop Boring Me."

10. Barth, *Epistle to the Romans*, 4.

realm). This is what theologians should offer in service to the "Nones": deep thinking about God, made accessible enough that the world can benefit. It is hard to appreciate the value of this request, and difficult (for those of us called to serve the world in this way as our day job) not to ponder a way to respond.[11]

Reflecting on Weiner's clear admittance that he doesn't know exactly what he wants, but hopes there will be a God-expert-creative-genius who emerges to help him figure that out, I remember one of Steve Jobs's insights, circulating especially around the time of his death. As one business website reports, Jobs taught us that "customers today don't always know what they want, especially if it's something they've never seen, heard, or touched before."[12] Considering this, I wonder if Weiner's "Steve Jobs of religion" might need to spend *less* time trying to respond to what the Nones *say* they want, and more time *testifying to* what he or she *has* "seen, heard, or touched" and *inviting* them to interact with it.

This, of course, would not exactly be a new approach to religion. The writer of 1 John, for example, bears witness to "what we have heard, what we have seen with our eyes, what we have looked at and touched with our hands"—that is, the "word of life" that invites all who have not yet seen, heard, or touched to join in fellowship, to share together in joy.[13]

I have moved, in these last few sentences, from discussing *what I appreciate* about Weiner's comments to *what I want to change.* I want to change the perception that Christianity, as a religion, endorses a static, distant, non-interactive God. I want to proclaim the Good News that—in Jesus Christ—God is heard, and seen, and touched with our hands. This is

---

11. We are suckers for people who want us to save them, both for good reasons and bad!

12. See Jackson, "Top Ten Lessons Steve Jobs Can Teach Us." Here is a longer excerpt: "*To create the future, you can't do it through focus groups.* There is a school of thought in management theory that—if you're in the consumer-facing space building products and services—you've got to listen to your customer. Steve Jobs was one of the first businessmen to say that was a waste of time. The customers today don't always know what they want, especially if it's something they've never seen, heard, or touched before. When it became clear that Apple would come out with a tablet, many were skeptical. When people heard the name (iPad), it was a joke in the Twitter-sphere for a day. But when people held one, and used it, it became a 'must have.' They didn't know how they'd previously lived without one. It became the fastest growing Apple product in its history. Jobs (and the Apple team) trusted himself more than others. Picasso and great artists have done that for centuries. Jobs was the first in business."

13. See 1 John 1:1–4.

the old, old, story, of course.[14] But it is a story we need to tell in new, new ways if it is going to get out. What does it mean, I ask myself, that a person who, like Weiner—a person who seems actively to be pursuing relationship with a God-made-flesh—has not "gotten there" from where he is? Where have we failed?[15] And how can we—theologians from the visible church who are also for the church invisible—respond to his request for help?

In a moment I will move on to considering what it would mean to serve Weiner as an assumed member of the invisible church. But first I want to note that the trend toward being a "None" out of which he speaks is an issue not only in the United States of America and for the U.S. churches. It is a phenomenon that is widespread in the Western world, and one that has implications for the unity and work of the global church, now and into our future. According to a well-publicized study published in March of 2011, organized religion "may become extinct in nine nations": "Australia, Austria, Canada, the Czech Republic, Finland, Ireland, the Netherlands, New Zealand, and Switzerland."[16] While such a threat does not yet loom large in all African, Asian, or Latin American countries, the growth in the number of self-identified "irreligious" in the Western world will certainly impact the character of our ecumenical partnerships and the way we think about evangelism and mission.[17]

Some studies have suggested that at least a third of the self-identified "Nones," like Weiner, "still have a dog in the hunt" for God.[18] How, again, might our theology serve them? I turn now to offering a brief review of what it might mean to serve the church "invisible," moving then to my constructive proposal that we should undertake the re-creation of a highly interactive/incarnational "religion" by being more humble, and laughing more, before the sovereign God we have indeed seen, heard, and touched.

14. Referencing, here, the lyrics to the old hymn, "I Love to Tell the Story," by Hankey and Fischer.

15. I think it is important to ask ourselves this question rather than merely divorcing ourselves from the caricatures of (a judgmental) God and "True Believers" that do not resonate with us.

16. See Palmer, "Religion May Become Extinct in Nine Nations."

17. For a more complete list of countries with respective percentages of the self-identified "irreligious," see http://en.wikipedia.org/wiki/Irreligion.

18. These would be those who identify as "agnostics" or "non-affiliated theists" as opposed to "atheists."

WALKING MORE HUMBLY: THE SOVEREIGNTY OF GOD, THE INVISIBLE CHURCH, AND THE PROVISIONAL CHARACTER OF OUR EFFORTS

A new approach to religion, if it is to welcome—and perhaps even share in—the "doubts and experimentations"[19] of the "Nones," needs to be intentionally committed to humility.[20] Frankly, it is hard to imagine any person in the United States who is disillusioned with religion disagreeing that a good dose of humility is way past due, for us religious folk. What they might balk at, however, is my following suggestion: that a way "to" that humility that allows for interaction and even doubt is the reclamation of the idea that God is sovereign. They would balk because they associate the idea that God is sovereign—for many understandable, historical reasons—with the angry God of exclamation points. The idea that God governs us has been used, consistently, to justify the domination of some over others. Why not lay it to the side in favor of an understanding of a less-than-sovereign God that would immediately disassociate our new approach to religion with religion of the past?[21]

The bottom-line answer to this, for those of us who believe it, is of course because God *is* sovereign. But the question I want to address here is, how might our conviction about God's sovereignty impact the tone of our engagement with the "Nones"? Here I would like to offer two suggestions, both of which draw further and in particular from the depth of the Reformed theological tradition. First, I think our confession that God is sovereign should lead us to reclaim in new ways the distinction between the visible and invisible church, engaging "Nones" such as Weiner with the presumption that they participate in the church invisible, rather than approaching them as though they are mere "outsiders" to the community of faith. Second, I hold that our confession that God is sovereign should lead us to remember what Barth identified as "the eschatological reservation"—that is, the idea that all of our words and efforts as the church are provisional. We are, even still, awaiting consummation with the Christ who will come again and take us to himself.[22] I realize this language is not the

19. Weiner's words.

20. This, after all, is not only what Eric Weiner asks of us, but also what God requires. We "religious" folks have not been showing the world what it looks like to "walk humbly with our God" (Mic 6:8).

21. This, of course, is an approach consistently taken by process theologians.

22. See John 14.

"intuitive and unencumbered" language Weiner calls for, but is, rather, the highly encumbered language of confessional Christian faith. But I believe what this confession is about, when it comes to our engagement with the "Nones," is speaking with conviction about God's certain reign while at the same time having plenty of space for including doubt, and experimentation, in our reflections on God and in our work in this world.

RESPECTING THE INVISIBLE CHURCH: SEEKING BETTER TO PERCEIVE GOD ALONGSIDE THE "NONES"

There is some evidence that a theological distinction had been made, by the time of the fourth-century Donatist controversy, between the church visible and the church invisible. While there is disagreement over whether Augustine used this actual terminology, there is no question that, by the time of the Reformation, Protestant theologians were holding these terms in tension both as a way of accounting for the corruption in the institutional Roman Church and as a corollary to their uncompromising teaching that God—and only God—is sovereign.[23] John Calvin taught, along these lines, that it is God who elects God's own sons and daughters "before the foundation of the world." Those who profess faith in Christ and are members of a church in which "the Word is proclaimed and the sacraments rightly administered" are generally those on the path to recognizing their identity in Christ and as the children of God. They are, in Calvin's terminology, members of the visible church.

While Calvin did hold there were those who appeared to participate in the visible church that were actually not elect by God, his much stronger emphasis was that *not* being a part of the visible church did not preclude one from actually being a member of the church invisible. Again, God elects whom God wills. It mattered to Calvin whether or not the elect *knew*

---

23. The critique has commonly been made, especially by Orthodox theologians, that to distinguish between the visible and invisible church is to create a Nestorian ecclesiology that denigrates the "fully human" (visible) church in favor of the "fully divine" (invisible) one. (See, for example, Barnes, "The Church Is Visible and One.") On the contrary, the Reformers' intent was not to denigrate the visible church, but to honor it and respect it as an authority because it is acting in obedience to the sovereign God (e.g., preaching the Word and rightly administering the sacraments). What we bind on earth will be bound in heaven; what we loose on earth will be loosed in heaven; because the church visible participates always in the church invisible, we can take heart our efforts, in the context of the visible church, will not be done in vain—appearances to the contrary!

their election, but there was no causal relationship between recognizing oneself as a child of God and being elect. Calvin preached and taught and engaged in the work of pastoral care in obedience to the sovereign God who had planted "seeds of faith" in the hearts of the elect. The work of "making disciples of all nations," he thought, was to water these seeds so that the elect could live their lives with the cognizance of God's claim on them.[24] For Calvin, election is the job of God alone. But Calvin thought Christian believers were called to the disciplined work of perceiving their election, and helping others to see it. His entire theological corpus as well as his pastoral ministry was, in fact, devoted to nurturing "firm and certain knowledge of God's benevolence toward us."[25] As Marilynne Robinson has put it, "Nothing in Calvin's thought is more striking than his evocation of perception, which has the potency and the splendor of a true apprehension of God."[26] So to say Weiner might be a member of the invisible church would not be to cease testifying to him, but to work all the harder to help him see the truth of who he actually is, as a child of God.[27]

Some Latin American liberation theologians, including Gustavo Gutiérrez, have developed the idea of the distinction between the visible and the invisible church in a different and important way. To Gutiérrez (fighting the corruption of the Peruvian church of the twentieth century), as for Calvin (fighting the corruption of the Roman church of the sixteenth century), the true church is not always located in the *ekklesia*—the church that is visible.[28] Gutiérrez thinks that the church is wherever the Spirit is present and at work, with or without the name of Jesus Christ being explicitly confessed. He thinks the church as *koinonia*, the true church, is where the hungry are fed, the naked are clothed, the sick and imprisoned visited, as scripture bears witness (for example) in Matthew 25.

---

24. When Jesus ministers to the Samaritan woman at the well in John 4, for example, Calvin explains that she clearly has "seeds of faith" that grew as a result of Jesus' revelation to her (see Calvin's commentary on the Gospel of John).

25. This is the opening phrase of Calvin's definition of faith, in the *Institutes of the Christian Religion*, III.2.7.

26. Robinson, *Death of Adam*, 188.

27. Even as, in fact, Calvin worked to increase such perception in the context of the visible church.

28. This gets tricky, since Calvin does not think the *ekklesia* is actually visible in the Roman Church, because the Word is not being proclaimed there, and the sacraments are not being rightly administered.

Both the idea that the visible church should never be so sure of itself and its own actions that it fails to look beyond itself to learn about God, and the idea that God's claim extends beyond those who are currently cognizant of it might have something to say to the development of an approach to religion that is more interactive and that promotes more laughter. God is not the exclamation point judge who shouts instead of laughs and expects religious people to do likewise. God is not scrapping for power by means of "rightness" and piety. Rather, God is the sovereign, ubiquitous, living and dynamic semicolon who joins together those who perceive that God loves them with those who are still seeking; with those visible and invisible; the *ekklesia* and the *koinonia*.

REMEMBERING THE ESCHATOLOGICAL RESERVATION: MAKING ROOM FOR DOUBT AND EXPERIMENTATION

Recently, I heard a pastor represent the discipline of systematic theology as committed to speaking about God with "certainty." This surprised me, since most of my colleagues in systematic theology are, on most days, so taken by the profound mystery of who God is, and how God relates to us, that they are filled with gratitude for the fact they can say anything true about God at all. I try to remember, however, that faulty stereotypes usually have some basis in reality. Both this pastor and Weiner have the impression people who talk about God are in the habit of thinking of themselves as right. One of my favorite *Peanuts* comic strips, I must admit, concurs with their impression. Snoopy is sitting on his doghouse, typing, when Charlie Brown comes around. Snoopy tells Charlie Brown he is writing a book. "I hope you have a good title," Charlie Brown replies. "I have the perfect title," Snoopy thinks to himself, proudly: *Has It Ever Occurred to You that You Might Be Wrong?*[29]

Theologians who have lost sight of the fact that they might be wrong will be ineffective at serving the church by engaging the "Nones" of this world. More importantly, to work at being "right" rather than on being faithful disciples is to commit the sin of idolatry: if theologians offer their theological systems with the aim of achieving certainty, univocity, or unequivocalness, what they are speaking about is no longer the infinite, mysterious God.[30]

29. This comic may be viewed at http://www.fivecentsplease.org/dpb/bewrong.gif.

30. This is an attempted corollary to Augustine's famous quote: "If you have

Barth reminds us that tight theological systems are not the goal:

> [A] system is . . . above all . . . opposed by the fact that the theological center which comprehends and displays its manifold individual aspects is no blue-print available for the asking. It is, instead, Jesus Christ who, by the potency of the Holy Spirit, is risen, powerful, and speaking. *It is the continuously novel binding and liberating goodness of the living God who comes down to humanity and draws human beings up to Godself in a history that is always freshly in motion.* He reigns, and beside him there is no other ruler. There is no systematic power behind the throne.[31]

Talk about highly interactive! Related to this, Barth advises all of us who speak words about God and understand our efforts in this world to contribute to the coming of the kingdom on earth to keep our sights on the so-called "eschatological reservation"—that is, the idea that all of our words and efforts, though essential to God's work, are at the same time provisional ones. We are the bride awaiting our bridegroom to return; it is at that time that God's kingdom will fully come. As Barth, again, explains it:

> The exaltation of the Head really means for the body a lowering, its demotion to a position of humility and waiting, and a definite limitation of the miracle of Pentecost. The conditional character of the gift of Pentecost must never be forgotten; the gift is never to be taken for granted when one speaks of its power.[32]

The idea that we need remain always open to the possibility that we might be wrong—even when we think we are right!—is, again, consistent with the confession that God is sovereign and we are not.[33] Further, even when we are not "wrong," we can always do better than even what is currently best at bearing witness to, and inviting others to see, what we have perceived. This is because our subject matter is, in fact, an infinite, inexhaustible, endlessly beautiful Subject. The danger of this idea is that it will be misused to stymie creaturely agency and creativity, rather than to free human beings to live and act as creative creatures by removing from them the burden of trying to be little versions of God. With this in mind, I turn in the next section

---

understood, what you have understood is not God."

31. Barth, *Evangelical Theology*, 89, my emphasis. I have taken the liberty of making Barth's language inclusive, but have not included brackets.

32. Barth, "Church and Theology," 294.

33. The Reformed Christian commitment to being "Reformed and always (in the process of) reforming, according to the Word of God" is consistent with this.

to suggesting how it is that both engaging members of the invisible church as partners in the journey toward perception of God, and remembering that the goal is not certainty, since all of our words and actions are provisional, can free us to play, laugh, and be more interactive in our approach to religion.

But before I do this, allow me to risk being experimental. In the list that follows, I begin imagining some of the features of an operating system that might frame a new approach to religion, when the system itself is powered by a commitment to upholding the sovereignty of God.

1. It would actually treat talk about God as analogical, not literal or univocal.

2. It would emphasize knowing what the teachings of the church *are about* more than understanding how *they work*. (For example, it would not attempt to explain how God is at the same time both one and three, nor how Jesus Christ is at once both fully human and fully divine, but it would strive to testify persuasively to why these teachings matter to our lives and the life of the world.)

3. It would not adjust confessed truths that contradict each other with the goal of putting them neatly "in sync," but would work (with mind as well as heart) to hold them in tension.

4. It would treat everyone seeking to perceive God or to perceive God better as co-journeyers, rather than as "insiders" or "outsiders" to the church (i.e., treating apparent "outsiders" as members of the invisible church who simply have not yet recognized God's claim on them).

5. It would be ever cognizant that all our efforts are limited, and in this then would offer creative creatures plenty of free space faithfully to experiment.

6. It would ask questions borne out of the tensions between the real and the actual; between consistency and contingency; between the "one" and the "three" that characterizes life created in the image of the triune God.

With these features taking shape in the background, I turn now to imagining what a new approach to religion might actually look like "in operation."

HAVING MORE FUN: THE SOVEREIGNTY OF GOD AND THE "PLAY" OF THEOLOGY

> The one and only genuine comfort we may offer to others is this reflection of heaven, of Jesus Christ, of God himself, as it appears on a radiant face. Why don't we do it? Why do we withhold from them the one comfort of mutual benefit? Why are the faces we show each other at best superior looking, serious, questioning, sorrowful and reproachful faces, at worst even grimaces or lifeless masks, real Carnival masks? Why don't our faces shine?[34]

A More Interactive Systematic Theology

In the last section I admitted there might be some truth to the stereotypes of systematic theologians. Fortunately, less idolatrous versions of systematic theology abound. Rebecca Chopp, for example, argues that systematic theology is committed to "the creative, productive imaging of Christian faith."[35] Wentzel van Huyssteen similarly understands "the special task of systematic theology" to be "to preserve that tension in creatively designing concepts, models, and finally theological theories, while nonetheless progressing through a problem-solving and thus maximally meaningful appeal to both our insight and our experience."[36] One way to put the question before us in this paper is precisely: How, moving into the future, might systematic theologians "give effort and attention to the *creative, productive imaging* of the Christian faith"?[37] How might we "*creatively* design concepts" that have "*maximal meaningful appeal*"?[38]

My beginning answer to this question, as a Reformed and feminist theologian standing in the tradition of Karl Barth, is that the more creative, maximally appealing theological work that invites interactivity needs to re-commit itself to Chalcedonian patterning[39]—a patterning that insists

---

34. Barth, *Prayer and Preaching*, 123–24.

35. Chopp, *Power to Speak*, 23.

36. Van Huyssteen, *Theology and the Justification of Faith*, 197.

37. Chopp quote, again, with my emphasis.

38. Van Huyssteen quote, again, with my emphasis.

39. The Council of Chalcedon was held in 451. It adopted the Chalcedonian statement, still the measure of christological orthodoxy. It states that Jesus Christ is "fully human, fully divine . . . As to his deity, he was born from the Father before the ages, but

on the fullness of both the "humanity" and the "divinity," the contextuality and the transcendence, of the theological enterprise. On this I agree with Paul Lehmann, who all the way back in 1941 wrote that, "The realization of theological vitality requires a fundamental rediscovery . . . a compelling direction to which all human life may be committed . . . [a return to] the meaning of Christ's coming in the flesh."[40] It is not, from my point of view, that we first and foremost need to make our theological discourse more winsome so that it will appeal to Eric Weiner, the "Nones," or the rest of the public. Rather, we need be renewed in our deepest convictions about who God is, and who we are, in Jesus Christ. We need to show Jesus in our work. And when we do, our work will be engaged in the creative tensions between divinity and humanity, between transcendence of contexts and contextuality, between the sovereignty of God and the essential involvement of the human creature in the coming of the kingdom of God.

Related to this, I don't think we may proceed, in our theological deliberations, as though there is no radical in-breaking of anything beyond the conditions of our historical existence. In the current political climate of our global society, all of us are—or should be—concerned about how theological discourse serves to support the dynamics of Empire, and (in contrast to this) how it serves to promote "counter-movements on behalf of humanity and against its denial in any form."[41] A great contribution of liberation and feminist theologians has been to show how appeal to a transcendent God has been used, historically, to perpetuate Empire by those who try to wash their hands of culpability of any responsibility for human suffering in the name of "God's will." But it seems to me that, absent an understanding of and attentiveness to the radical in-breaking of the transcendent God known to us in Jesus Christ, the danger of perpetuating Empire *via* our theological discourse is just as real. Instead of appealing to the will of God, we appeal to ourselves, our best arguments, and our most powerful arguers. While this is, in a sense, all we can do (as historical, creaturely, beings), without a transcendent, fully divine, even "timeless" dimension to our theological

---

as to his humanity, the very same one was born in the last days from the Virgin Mary, the Mother of God, for our sake and the sake of our salvation . . . one prosopon and one hypostasis . . . existing in two natures . . . without confusion, without change, without division, without separation." See Norris, *Christological Controversy*, 139.

40. Lehmann, *Forgiveness*.

41. Barth, *Church Dogmatics*, III/4, 544. Barth is here talking about the character of the divine command, which we are called to bear witness to in our theology and our preaching.

discourse, there is nothing to pull the rug out from under us—to reorient us, to drive us to confession and restoration, to change our questions, to keep us from the temptation to posture ourselves as gods.

It is my hope that we who are systematic theologians will re-submit ourselves and our work to the transcendent, incarnate God who in every context stands for the marginalized in Jesus Christ; the living God who "binds" us and "liberates" us by speaking in ever new ways, the God who calls us creatively to participate in a history that is "freshly in motion."

Toward an Interactive Theology of Play[42]

Knowing that God is sovereign, we are free to approach our theological deliberations and our religious practices playfully. This, as Barth explains, will mean that we engage them *more*, rather than *less* seriously.[43] But our seriousness, again, will not manifest as the presumption of rightness, punctuated by bouts of shouting. On the contrary, it will be given to the kind of laughter that characterizes children's interactive play. When kids get really engrossed in what they are doing, they laugh out loud at the sheer joy of it. They play hide-and-seek, they concentrate on finding the right place to hide, they anticipate being found and then cry out with glee. They take all the cushions off the living room furniture, they make forts, they assign roles and create rules with great seriousness, adjusting all the way along. They know they are not sovereign: they do not have responsibility for making dinner; they do not have to keep an eye on the clock.

We should be more like them, as we engage the stuff of faith. Immersed in imagining, interacting, laughing, and ever reconceiving those things that matter most. I listen and watch my kids playing, and I hear them processing everything they care about in their lives: the way their parents, teachers, and friends relate to them, the rules they have to follow if they are going to stay safe, the threat of injury, friendlessness, and death, the promise (of all promises): that it will all, somehow, wind up OK. They fight (usually when they can't agree on the rules they are making up). They are not easily distracted because—again—they are very serious about all of this. And they laugh. They laugh a lot.

---

42. For more on a theology of play, see Rigby, "Beautiful Playing."

43. See Barth, *Church Dogmatics* III/4, 553. All further references to this work will be indicated parenthetically.

What if we shaped an approach to religion that drew from the spirit of children playing?

What if this is what the Christian religion has always thought it was doing? What if worship (for example), is all about us "playing" the kingdom of God come to earth, as it is in heaven? What if, when we gather around that table, we are really doing (at least in part) what kids do when they have a tea party (sometimes with real tea, in those little kid cups), imagine themselves getting married, or play school? Are we not, just like the children, both practicing for what is to come and actually, even, bringing what is to come into the present by virtue of our play-acting? And if we are, what could possibly be more intuitive, interactive, straightforward, or unencumbered[44] than this?

A CHALLENGE FOR EACH OF US: SHAPING A "HIGHLY INTERACTIVE" (A.K.A. "INCARNATIONAL") RELIGION

As I near the close of this essay I surmise I am really just beginning the work of imagining what a new approach to religion, grounded in the humility that comes with remembering God is sovereign, might look like. There is not time, nor am I yet prepared, to develop a full description. Having experimented with offering some suggestions that can be fed into the "operating system," and having reflected that our religious expression should be playful, I would like here to pose a challenge first to those of us who are theologians and church leaders in the visible church, and then to those who seek to believe in God, who (I have suggested) we treat as members of the invisible church. My hope is that grappling with these challenges might press us further toward whatever approach to religion is needed next.

First, a challenge for theologians and church leaders in the western world: *How do we resensitize church?* If I am right that the practices of our religious traditions are already meant to be a form of play, a useful question to answer might be: What happened? How did we get from these highly interactive, seeing-hearing-touching religious practices to the sterile, we-have-come-to-church-to-be-talked-*at*, not-to-be-engaged-*in* attitudes so commonly found in, well, those places that have a rise in the number of the non-affiliated?

I know what you're thinking, if you're a leader in the visible church. You're thinking that we've always had a multisensory approach to religion:

44. These are Weiner's words.

an approach committed to chewing bread and drinking wine or grape juice in the Eucharistic feast; an approach that splashes water and makes promises impossible to keep in baptism; an approach that has as its model prayer one that Jesus taught—with senses tingling in expectation for the coming kingdom, with concrete demands for food, and forgiveness, and deliverance from evil. But we have, in some way or another, muddled all this up: we have, somehow, desensitized these gifts that are so very highly interactive; these gifts that are extensions of our God entering interactively in; that Word made flesh.

There are surely plenty of churches where the gospel is known to be experienced through hearing, seeing, and touching. It can, as we have said, be frustrating to defend against stereotypes. But, again, there is usually something to be learned from the way things are stereotyped. Anecdotally, for example, I've lost count of the number of people who tell me they skip church on communion Sundays because it is "just too boring to sit there that long." Pastor friends, frustrated with comments like this, have tried everything to "bring the senses back" to worship: from baking their own communion bread to writing evocative new liturgy to playing extraordinarily beautiful music. What else can be done? Where do we go from here? If perception of God matters, and the senses are the vehicles through which perception takes place, we have to keep trying to do a better job of proclaiming God's majesty by way of all the senses. How do we see, hear, and touch so that we might know?

Second, a challenge for Weiner and all "Nones" wanting, someday, to believe in God: *Would you be willing to interact with and experiment with the not-rational and not-practical?* You say you tried the way of the "True Believers" and that it didn't work for you because you are too rational and practical about religion. I can assure you that I would never want you to check your brain at the door in your pursuit of God. But I do suspect limiting yourself to what is "rational" and "practical" is keeping you from what you really need, and seemingly also from what you seem, really, to want: to believe in God.

Consider what Immanuel Kant gave up, in order to maintain his rational and practical hold on religion. Kant didn't want to "limit reason to make room for faith" and so he instead created "religion within the limits of reason alone." His approach to religion did not include a place for the kind of interaction, doubt, or experimentation you're asking for. These things would be way too inefficient and impractical. Kant advocated, instead, adherence—with no exceptions—to the "universal maxim." "Act in such a way that what you do can be a universal law."[45] That's it. End of story. A purely rational and practical understanding of God. Not what you want, I don't think. But, again I ask: Are you willing to *add to* your reasoning skills other ways of perceiving God? Are you willing to risk faith?

I think the two questions posed here are only the first few that would need to be asked in the process of shaping a new approach to religion. To ask ourselves hard questions like these is not only necessary to coming up with a new approach, but also part and parcel of walking humbly with the mysterious God we are seeking to know better, or even to know at all.

IMPLICATIONS FOR THE GLOBAL CHURCH

A couple of times during the writing of this essay I had to remind myself that what is at stake is not only having more categories to choose from on a religious survey or showing a person like Eric Weiner what we theologians are made of (even if we can't be—or don't want to be—the "Steve Jobs of Religion"). What is at stake is figuring out how the rapid growth of the "unaffiliated" in a significant number of influential countries affects the way we all engage our God-given mandates: to make disciples of all nations[46] and to do the work of justice in the world.[47] How will countries where Christianity is the fastest growing religion respond to the decline of Christianity and the growth of the "unaffiliated" in the Western world? Will they begin sending missionaries to the United States, as South Korea has already been doing for some time? In a global world with shared economic and environmental concerns, it will be necessary for those countries in which the numbers of unaffiliated are not on the rise to learn how to engage in conversation with the unaffiliated, for the sake of the common good.

In relation to the matter of "Nones" like Weiner needing to experience a seeing-hearing-touching, highly interactive approach to religion, there may be an opportunity for the Western world to listen and learn. Multi-sensory religion is being practiced in countries around the world—in countries, for example, where Pentecostalism is the fastest-growing religious affiliation. I am not suggesting that Weiner should become Pentecostal. What I am suggesting is that theologians and churches in the Western world be

45. For more on this, see Kant, *Religion Within the Limits of Reason Alone*.

46. See Matt 28.

47. Mic 6:8 and Amos 5.

intentional about learning, from brothers and sisters in other parts of the world, what interactive religion might look like. Clearly, of late, we seem to be in the market for some new ideas!

CONCLUSION

I have reflected on the possibility of a highly interactive approach to religion that is grounded in the conviction that God is sovereign and we are not. I am responding to what I think is a problem: We have lost sight of the freedom, creativity, and joy that comes with knowing ourselves as beloved creatures in relation to the God who both "measures the waters in the hollow of her hand" and calls each of us by name.[48] We seem to have trouble holding onto the fact that this sovereign God interacts with us in ways we can see, hear, and touch. If we can learn, again, to play before such a God we will, like Woman Wisdom, be drawn to "rejoice in God's inhabited world" and to "delight in the human race."[49] With the honesty of children we will articulate our doubts, and with their fearless creativity we will experiment with new ideas. We will, in short, become ourselves more interactive as we perceive the God of manger and cross interacting with us. We will better bear witness to the invisible church that still hopes, someday, to believe in God. And, perhaps almost as importantly, we may even learn to laugh a lot more![50]

48. Isa 40:12, 26.

49. Prov 8.

50. For more on humor and spirituality, see Martin, *Between Heaven and Mirth*. Also see a video clip of Father Martin talking on the same theme on *The Colbert Report*: http://religion.blogs.cnn.com/2012/01/25/my-take-reclaiming-jesus-sense-of-humor/.

9

Sexual Ethics and the Scandal of the Cross

– David Tombs

INTRODUCTION

THE CATHOLIC AND THE Anglican churches have spent a great deal of time in recent years wrestling with sexual ethics. For the Catholic Church, the revelations of clerical child abuse, and the cover-ups which accompanied it, have damaged the foundations of the Church in ways which may prove impossible to repair fully. Meanwhile, the Anglican Communion is riven by a deep division in attitudes to homosexuality and the LGBT community. On one side of the debate is a more liberal outlook, led especially by many of the bishops in the Episcopal Church of the United States, which argues for a more inclusive and more affirming attitude towards people in loving lesbian and gay relationships. On the other side of the debate is a more conservative outlook, led especially by many of the bishops in Africa and other countries in the Southern Hemisphere, which argues for a stronger assertion of traditional church teaching on the sanctity of marriage between a man and a woman, and opposition to any sexual relations outside marriage.[1]

1. As with any major ethical and theological debate, there is much more complexity

For two global denominations to be so preoccupied with these issues deserves serious theological attention. This will of course include more theological attention to the debates themselves, and the issues that they raise (which is something that has barely begun with the clerical abuse scandal, whereas it seems to be interminable on the sexual orientation debate), but just as importantly, it will involve questions about what these preoccupations indicate about the state of the churches and how theological reflection taking place in the academy might serve them.

On a personal note, I have been wondering how these recent discussions in theological ethics relate to discussions of sexualized violence, and what insights they might gain from it. How does sexual violence relate to the issues which currently so occupy the Catholic and Anglican churches, and how might a better awareness of sexual violence serve the theological and ethical debates taking place in the churches?

The first part of this chapter will review the progress that has been made in recognizing the political significance of sexualized violence in conflicts in recent decades, and situate my own work on crucifixion as a form of sexualized violence in relation to this. The second part will explore how this offers resources for a more theologically engaged reading of two incidents which featured in world news during 2011, the death of Gaddafi and the disrobing of an unknown woman in Tahrir Square, Cairo, on December 17, 2011. The third part will suggest that more focused theological attention to the evils of sexualized violence as a feature in the scandal of the cross might contribute an important dimension to widening the current Catholic and Anglican respective preoccupations with clerical abuse and sexual orientation to a better conversation around sexual ethics.

SEXUALIZED VIOLENCE AND CRUCIFIXION

I have been investigating issues of sexual violence as a feature of war for a number of years. Since the 1990s there has been a growing awareness of rape and other sexualized violence against women as a common occurrence

---

to what is involved than this brief stereotype suggests, and much more variety in either outlook than is allowed for by this simplified dualism. On both sides appeals are made to biblical teaching and to contemporary discernment of divine will, though the emphasis on the conservative side is more likely to be on appeals to biblical teaching and the emphasis on the liberal side is more likely to be on contemporary discernment of divine will.

in wars and political conflicts.[2] At one level, this violence is something that has been well known for centuries. However, despite the awareness of sexualized violence stretching back to ancient times, it is only in the last few decades that it has become a subject of public debate and deeper analysis. Previously it was most likely to be seen as "side effect" or "secondary issue" in war, which involved personal trauma but lacked political significance. The mistaken belief that it was not politically important meant that peace-agreements did not mention it, historians rarely gave it serious attention, courts did not prosecute it, and wider society passed over it in silence. These dynamics were coupled in most societies with strong tendencies for victims and others to self-censor rather than publicize their experiences. Sexualized violence was so readily associated with shame and stigma that most victims did not want to speak of it and in public discussion it was taboo. In this context, sexualized violence was an unspeakable form of violence, and those who suffered it could expect little help or understanding.

Against this background, Susan Brownmiller's book *Against Our Will: Men, Women, and Rape* in 1975 was a landmark study in documenting the extent of rape in twentieth-century wars and analyzing the power issues that shape it.[3] It marks the start of a wave of feminist works breaking the silence on rape and conflict. These have done much to illuminate both why rapes in war are so common, and why they have not been given the attention they should have received.[4] Initially these works did not get the attention they deserved beyond a relatively small circle, but during the 1990s public awareness around the issues started to grow rapidly. In the early 1990s, the experiences of the so-called "comfort women" or "sex slaves" who were forced to work for the Japanese army in World War II became more widely known. After fifty years of silence, Korean, Filipino, Chinese, and other Asian women became more vociferous in calling the Japanese government to account for what had happened. Alongside this, the sexualized violence against women in the ethnic cleansing in Bosnia (1992–95) and the genocide in Rwanda (1994), demonstrated how rape could be a weapon of war. After these conflicts rape could no longer be seen as a mere side effect: its political significance had to be taken into account.

2. For a good collection, see Barstow, *War's Dirty Secret*.

3. Brownmiller's book examines rape more broadly, but it starts with a long chapter on rape in World War I, World War II, Bangladesh, and Vietnam.

4. See Lorentzen and Turpin, *The Women and War Reader*.

The first decade of the twenty-first century has confirmed the importance of this breakthrough. Rape and other sexualized violence remain all too common in contemporary conflicts around the world. In addition, further research continues to uncover the silences around sexualized violence in earlier times. Two books on violence against women published in 2010 show how easy it is to become complicit with this silence. The first is the collection edited by Sonja Hedgepeth and Rochelle G. Saidel, *Sexual Violence against Jewish Women during the Holocaust*.[5] This brings together a collection of essays uncovering the nature and extent of sexualized violence suffered by Jewish women. The other is *At the Dark End of the Street: Black Women, Rape and Resistance—a New History of the Civil Rights Movement from Rosa Parks to Black Power*, by Danielle McGuire.[6] McGuire uncovers the history of the sexual abuse of African American women in the 1940s and 1950s. She shows how the investigation of a racially motivated gang rape in 1944 played a significant role in politicizing women, and how the experience of sexual violence and humiliation strengthened the resolve of African-Americans to struggle for their rights.[7] McGuire also shows how this background to the civil rights movement has been ignored and marginalized despite its importance.

The feminist commentator Gloria Steinem credits these two books as "lighting a match" that prompted her to help create the "Women Under Siege" project through the Women's Media Center.[8] The project explains its purpose as "to figure out what we've missed along the way when it comes to rape in war. From the Holocaust onward, we've documented sexual abuses committed from Bangladesh to Egypt. The idea is to figure out how stigma, shame, and death has prevented us from knowing fully what occurred in these wars." The project's website is http://www.womenundersiegeproject.org. Its purpose is to provide information and analysis of current conflicts with special attention to their impact on women and girls. Steinem's hope for the project is that greater awareness of what is happening can have a preventative role. In addition, it can make a restorative contribution as women in different societies and situations learn from each other's experiences. In

5. Hedgepeth and Saidel, *Sexual Violence*.

6. McGuire, *At the Dark End of the Street*.

7. Rosa Parks was sent by the president of the local NAACP to Abbeville to investigate the rape of twenty-four-year-old Recy Taylor.

8. Wolfe, "Gloria Steinem on Rape in War."

particular, they become more aware of shame as a way of silencing victims and the need to break this silence.[9]

Finding ways to understand and speak about the shame that is so often associated with sexualized violence is critical to this task. Yet it presents many challenges. In particular, how should sexualized violence be discussed so that victims are treated with dignity and the violence is not reinscribed? In some cases, discussion of rape can distort or even eroticize the violence of rape against women.

One practical step Steinem has made in this regard is her attention to language and her use of the terminology "sexualized violence." For Steinem, it is a way of reinforcing the point that rapes and other acts of sexual violence are not about sex but about violence. The website shows just how pervasive such violence against women remains in conflicts around the world.

The fact that most sexualized violence during political conflict (and in times of political peace) is directed against women needs to be central in any discussion of sexualized violence. However, it does not follow from this that sexualized violence is limited to violence against women. Sexualized violence against men in conflict also needs to be recognized. Whilst this is less common than sexualized violence against women, it is much more frequent than many people suppose. It is especially prevalent in torture practices, and can involve male rapes, castrations, beatings on the genitals, and genital mutilations. Yet, like sexual violence against women, it remains largely "unspoken" and in many ways "unspeakable." In many societies it may be even more stigmatized and taboo than sexualized violence against women.

It is important to realize that sexualized violence against men is likely to occur alongside sexualized violence against women in conflicts because normally both are governed by a similar logic and express similar notions of power and conquest. It is rooted in conceptions of male identity, in which male power is expressed through male violence, and sexualized violence is a physical and symbolic expression of domination.

9. Steinem explains her hopes behind the project: "For me, inspiration comes from seeing positive results. For instance, a woman survivor of brutal rape in the Congo is rejected by her family, but learns she's not alone or at fault from the story of a Jewish woman who survived rape and the Holocaust only to be shunned as if she had collaborated. Each example illuminates another. We have to know what's wrong to change what's wrong, but the special problem of sexualized violence is used to silence and shame the victim." See ibid.

For theologians and Christian ethicists a greater awareness of sexualized violence and how it is used to humiliate and degrade can provide insights into the shame and scandal of the act of political violence at the heart of the Christian tradition. It illuminates the Roman crucifixion of Jesus of Nazareth. The central focus of my theological research in this area can be summarized in four brief points.[10]

First, that the crucifixion of Jesus of Nazareth was a form of sexual humiliation, since a key part of crucifixion was to strip the victim and display the victim in public. Second, this enforced nakedness and humiliation needs to be named as "sexual abuse" if its significance is to be understood. Third, this sexual abuse was not accidental or incidental to crucifixion as a form of torture and execution, but rather it was intentional and integral and crucifixion should therefore be recognized as a form of sexual torture. Fourth, it would not have been unusual if Jesus' crucifixion had been preceded by other forms of sexualized violence, such as prisoner rape or other physical forms of sexual assault.

In terms of evidence and support, the first claim, in relation to sexual humiliation, rests on direct evidence from the Gospels as well as from a wider study of Roman practices. The second claim, in relation to sexual abuse, is primarily a claim about terminology and language, and was reinforced by the Abu Ghraib scandal in which humiliating photos of naked Iraqi prisoners were readily, and rightly, recognized as photos of sexual abuses.[11] The third claim, that crucifixion should be recognized as a form of sexual torture also involves a claim about terminology, and a greater awareness of how crucifixions operated in practice, and is significant in linking crucifixion to the many different forms of sexual torture that are documented by human rights observers today. The fourth claim, that Jesus may have suffered prisoner rape or some other form of violent sexual assault preceding crucifixion, is more speculative and open-ended than the first three claims. It is a claim about a possibility to be taken seriously but qualified with the recognition that the Gospels do not provide direct evidence to confirm or to refute what may have happened, and therefore no definitive judgment can be offered. There is substantial evidence that other Roman prisoners suffered sexual violence of many different sorts, and therefore it would not have been unusual if Jesus had suffered in this way, but this is as far as the evidence goes.

10. Tombs, "Crucifixion, State Terror and Sexual Abuse."
11. Tombs, "Prisoner Abuse."

Sometimes I am asked why this research into crucifixion is worthwhile, and what it offers as a service for the church. Part of the answer to this is that my interest in the sexual violence of crucifixion is not just historical; as will already be clear, the historical issues are linked to what is happening today. Sexual humiliation, sexual abuse, sexual torture and sexual assaults remain horrifically common, and an understanding of Jesus' torture and crucifixion may give us greater insight into what is really happening in today's world, just as an understanding of what is happening in the world can give us greater insight into the crucifixion.

For the churches to meaningfully engage with political issues it is important for them to have credible insights to offer on the issues at stake. The pain and shame of sexualized violence is a subject on which the churches could be much more vocal, and could bring important insights to a more sensitive awareness. Two examples related to the Arab Spring of 2011 point to the value of this type of engagement. The first is the death of Muammar Gaddafi in October 2011.

DEATH OF MUAMMAR GADDAFI

The death of Colonel Muammar Gaddafi offers a stark contemporary image of the once mighty now fallen. It has some significant parallels to the death of Saul and his sons told at the conclusion of the first book of Samuel (1 Sam 31).[12]

According to the text, the Philistines defeat Saul and his army at Mount Gilboa. Saul, his three sons and what remains of their force seek to flee. They are overtaken and the three sons, Jonathan, Abinadab, and Malchishua are killed. Saul is spotted by archers and they manage to wound him. With no chance of further escape Saul turns to his armor bearer and commands him (or maybe begs him) to take his sword and kill him before the Philistines can get to him. Saul's language reflects his fears: "Draw your sword and thrust me through with it, so that these uncircumcised may not come and thrust me through, and make sport of me" (1 Sam 31:4).

The armor bearer is too afraid to obey, so Saul has to take his own sword and fall upon it. When the armor bearer sees that Saul is dead he also falls on his sword and dies with him. The next day the Philistines come to strip the slain. They cut off Saul's head, strip him of his armor and put it in the temple at Ashtaroth. Saul's headless body is fastened to

12. 2 Samuel has a slightly different version.

the wall at Beth-shan to be displayed along with the bodies of his sons.[13] Their disgrace and humiliation is made public for all to see.[14] The violation would have been added to as birds (and possibly dogs or other animals) fed off the decaying bodies.[15] According to the text, upon hearing the news of Saul's death and disgrace, the men of Jabesh-Gilead arise and travel all night to retrieve the bodies and bury them with dignity. In the first chapter of 2 Samuel, David grieves the death of Saul and Jonathan, and offers his famous lament "How are the mighty fallen" (2 Sam 1:25). Then, after David is made king in place of Saul, he takes his vengeance on the Philistines (2 Sam 5:17–25).

On October 20, 2011, when Gaddafi's stronghold, his hometown of Sirte, was on the point of falling, he tried to flee. NATO fighter planes tracked the small motor convoy and attacked it before it got too far. Gaddafi survived the attack and took refuge in a large concrete pipe that served as drain underneath the road they were traveling on. When Libyan opposition forces arrived on the scene they celebrated that the one who had insulted them as "rats" was himself now hiding in a drain like a rat.

They pulled him out and initial video footage from mobile phones shows Gaddafi injured, disoriented, pushed, shoved, and surrounded. At one point Gaddafi is heard to say, "What you are doing is forbidden in Islam!" After a gun is pointed at his head, he says, "Do you know right from wrong?"

His killing attracted international criticism and calls for an investigation. Initially the National Transitional Council (NTC) said that he died when the ambulance he was in was caught in crossfire. It subsequently

13. The name Beth-shan means "city of peace" or "city of refuge." It may have taken its name from the practice described in Num 35:6 as a place where the accused or endangered could flee to receive shelter.

14. The Jewish historian Josephus refers to the display of the bodies on the walls using the same Greek word, *anastauron*, that is used for crucifixion (*Jewish Antiquities* 6, 374). Whiston translates this as "hung their bodies on crosses at the walls of the city" (Josephus, *Works*). In the Loeb edition the phrase is translated as "impaled their bodies to the walls of the city" (*Jewish Antiquities*, translated by Thackeray and Marcus).

15. Earlier in 1 Sam 17:44 and 17:46, Goliath and David swap threats that they will leave each other's bodies for the birds and the beasts. In the event, David unexpectedly kills or stuns Goliath with a stone from his sling and then uses Goliath's own sword to behead him (1 Sam 17:51). David is then said to take Goliath's head to Jerusalem (v. 54), presumably for display. In the same way David had his men chop off the hands and feet and display the bodies of Rechab and Baanah when they brought him the head of Saul's son Ishbaal (2 Sam 4:12), though commentators point out that the chronology may be confused here since Jerusalem at that time was still controlled by the Jebusites.

became clearer that he was most likely shot by his captors. His body was taken back to Misruta and displayed in a refrigerated meat container. Visitors were allowed to view his body, which showed bullet wounds to his side and his thorax.

He was buried on October 25 at an unidentified desert site outside Misruta. On the same day, new cell phone footage obtained by the *Global Post* correspondent Tracey Shelton provided disturbing information on a previously unknown part of his treatment before death.[16] As Channel 4 news presenter Krishnan Guru-Murthy put it on British television, "Now it has been revealed that Muammar Gaddafi's final moments were even more gruesome than we first thought. It appears that he was sexually assaulted by one of the men who captured him alive."[17]

Channel 4 did not play the whole video recording. Guru-Murthy explained that it was not appropriate for TV screening, especially for a 7 p.m. program. However, Guru-Murthy assured readers that he has seen the full video and told viewers to watch the man in gray to the left of Gaddafi. Playback was frozen a second or two into the clip and the image cropped to focus on the man in gray and exclude the rest of the scene to his right. Guru-Murthy explained that this man "appears to sexually assault Gaddafi with what looks like a metal pipe." He adds that the assault looks "absolutely deliberate and clearly caused injury." He goes on: "and it may offer an alternative explanation for those last words Gaddafi uttered on the video 'What you are doing is forbidden.'"

Channel 4's decision to leave the assault off-screen is understandable and appropriate. The horrific violence is "obscene" in the classical sense of belonging "off scene" (*ob skene*).[18] However, this does not mean that important questions about the sexual assault and sexual humiliation of Gaddafi should not be taken up elsewhere. Despite the Channel 4 piece, and the availability of the full video on the Internet, there was relatively little mainstream media commentary on this part of the story.[19] A lot remains unclear

16. See "Decoding a Death." *Global Post* is a Boston-based online news agency.

17. Channel 4 News, October 25, 2011. Channel 4 is a well-respected TV channel in the UK, and the *News* (broadcast at 7 p.m. weekdays) is one of its flagship programs. See http://www.channel4.com/news/.

18. This classical sense covered scenes of high emotion as well as sexual scenes.

19. BBC Radio Ulster invited me to discuss it on the Sunday morning show *Sunday Sequence* on October 30, 2011, but this seems to be exceptional. This interview is available at http://www.conflicttransformation.ie/tombs/radio/

and is likely to stay this way unless the calls for a full investigation into the death are heeded.

For example, some British newspaper reports suggested that the instrument of assault was a knife or bayonet rather than a pipe.[20] The possibility that a bayonet is attached to the instrument is very plausible but hard to verify from the jerky, low-resolution and short *Global Post* video. Even a frame-by-frame analysis leaves a lot of the details about what happened unclear. The video starts with Gaddafi already captured and being escorted by a small group of men. After a second or so it skips to a chaotic melee. When the sequence of frames is slowed it looks like a metal pipe (or attachment for the bayonet) has been thrust into Gaddafi's rectum from behind and has caused bleeding in his trousers. It also shows a gun placed to one side on the ground while this is happening. The video does not capture the initial assault or show what the instrument is, but it does very briefly show the instrument in place, and being held and apparently shaken or pushed by the unidentified rebel fighter in gray standing to Gaddafi's left.[21]

Even if there are further investigations into Gaddafi's death these will only shed constructive light on the assault if they make a positive choice to both record and seek to explain this act of violence. In many cases, sexualized violence is left out of the account or only referred to in the briefest terms. Even when it is mentioned, it is often presented without much analysis, as if it is a gratuitous act that lies beyond comprehension. If an inquiry is to be thorough and also serve a wider purpose of promoting a deeper understanding of sexualized violence, it will need to link the assault to the wider phenomenon of sexualized violence against women and men in conflict and the factors that shape and sustain this.

Gaddafi's own use of rape and sexualized violence against those whom he saw as his enemies received coverage earlier in the conflict. The International Criminal Court chief prosecutor, Luis Moreno Ocampo, claimed that Gaddafi was authorizing the distribution of Viagra to his troops with

20. See, for example, Chulov, "Gaddafi Killer Faces Prosecution."

21. It looks like this is the same rebel fighter dressed in gray as the one a little bit farther to the left of Gaddafi in the first frames of the video. The piece by Guru-Murthy explicitly identifies the two together. However, the break in the footage makes it hard to know with certainty whether the figures are a precise match or might be different. Likewise, while Gaddafi is clearly recognizable in other parts of the video record, in the assault frames his face is not visible. While the sequence of events, the clothing he is wearing, and a blood-stained sleeve all strongly suggest that it is him, the video on its own does not guarantee this.

orders to use it for rape.[22] An earlier allegation of gang rape by forces loyal to Gaddafi had made international headlines when a distraught woman, Iman al-Obeidi, burst into an international press conference at a hotel in March 2011. She claimed that she had been selected for rape by fifteen men over two days because she was originally from Benghazi, which was now a rebel stronghold. After a struggle with hotel staff and security minders she was silenced and bundled away into a car.[23]

Likewise, if Saul was a victim of sexual violence by the Philistines he was also a perpetrator. In 1 Samuel 18 he uses the engagement of his daughter Michal to David as a way to exact vengeance on the Philistines. He has his servants tell David that the only wedding present he would like from David is a hundred Philistine foreskins. He seems to have hoped that this would be David's undoing and probably his death. However, David and his men carried out the task successfully and returned to present the hundred foreskins to Saul as a wedding gift. It is therefore little surprise that Saul foresaw and feared sexual violence when he faced capture by the Philistines at Gilboa.

Despite the evocative parallels in the deaths of Saul and Gaddafi, the sexual assault against Gaddafi did not prompt the churches to contribute to a public debate on sexualized violence. This was partly because awareness of the assault and the video remained fairly limited. However, even if there had been more awareness of the video evidence, I suspect that in terms of Christian faith and ethics the assault would be typically seen as irrelevant and probably irreverent. In all likelihood it constitutes too great a scandal to be addressed by theology. Yet here is a theological paradox. The scandal of the cross is central to Christian theology, yet our sanitized conception of the cross does not help us to address the scandal of sexualized violence today. It is more likely to encourage us to avoid it.

22. Bowcott, "Libya Mass Rape Claims." This story was widely reported at the time, though a follow-up investigation did not locate victims who could directly testify to it. The extent of the practice may have been quite limited or part of intentional disinformation; see Kirkpatrick and Nordland, "Waves of Disinformation and Confusion."

23. Iman al-Obeidi (sometimes translated as Eman al-Obeidi) was released after a few days and gave further details of the rape in interviews with CNN (April 7) and NPR (April 11). In May she escaped from Libya to Tunisia and received help for a move to Qatar. However, after an initial welcome in Qatar she was deported back to Libya in June. She applied for asylum in the United States and after a period in a refugee center in Romania moved to Denver, Colorado, at the end of July 2011; see Basu, "A Symbol of Defiance."

With this in mind, I turn to my second example, the Unknown Woman disrobed in Tahrir Square, Cairo.

THE UNKNOWN WOMAN DISROBED
IN TAHRIR SQUARE, CAIRO

One of the tactics used by the security services during the rule of former president Hosni Mubarak in Egypt (1981–2011) was to target women for various forms of sexual humiliation. To intimidate women and discourage them from participating in protests against the regime, or even being present or nearby while such protests took place, security agents would leer at them, grope them, and tear their clothing. For example, on May 25, 2005, during an attack on protesters, bystanders, and journalists, a number of women were attacked and had their clothes torn off. One of the women attacked, Nawal Ali, a journalist with the paper *al-Geel*, became well known for subsequently seeking to press charges against her attackers.

Mubarak was eventually brought down by protests and civil disobedience in the Arab Spring of 2011.[24] Initially there were high hopes for democratic change. One of the first acts of the new military council was to announce that there would be elections after a six-month period of military rule and that the military would not field a candidate. However, as dissatisfaction with the political situation grew, in October the military started to crack down on protesters. In the crackdown similar tactics of intimidation against women started to be reported.[25]

A notorious example occurred on December 17, 2011, as Egyptian soldiers beat, kicked, stamped on, and shot at protesters in Tahrir Square.[26] A Reuters photo shows a group of three soldiers around a woman lying prone on the ground. The woman's black *abaya* (her loose full-length robe) has been pulled open to reveal the jeans and blue bra she is wearing underneath the robe. The soldier on the right (who will be referred here for convenience as soldier A) has his foot raised as if he has

---

24. Encouraged by events in Tunisia, a wave of protests began in Egypt on January 25, 2011, and Mubarak announced his resignation on February 11, 2011.

25. Another aspect of this was the forced virginity tests; see Kirkpatrick, "Rights of Women Were Violated."

26. This was the second day of a new wave of protests that had begun on Friday December 16, 2011.

just stomped on her upper body or is about to stamp on it.[27] The other two soldiers (soldier B on the left, and soldier C in the center) are grasping the sides of her open robe.[28]

A video released on YouTube has nearly a minute of footage showing what happened in a little more context.[29] Initially it shows three men holding the arms of a woman and running with her, desperately trying to drag her away from an advancing rush of soldiers (thirty-one-second mark). As they do so her robe has opened and is showing the blue jeans which she wears underneath. Within a matter of seconds the soldiers catch up with them, two of the men let go of the woman and manage to escape but the other man continues to pull her for a few more strides until he is overtaken by soldiers and knocked to the ground. About a dozen soldiers surround the woman and the man and beat them ferociously with their long batons (forty-second mark). The woman's jeans and bare stomach are now visible but the robe continues to cover her chest and shoulders. She lies unresponsive on the ground as if unconscious, whereas the man can be seen moving his arms and legs as he does his best to protect himself from the blows. During the beating, Soldier A can be seen stamping repeatedly on the woman's head. Soldier C starts to drag her away (fifty-second mark), he seems to be pulling her by her robe, which by now has come apart on her upper body as well to at least partly reveal some of the blue bra she wears underneath. As Solider C drags her, Soldier A kicks hard at the side of her rib cage. Soldier A then stands on the hem of the robe with his left foot and kicks the upper part of the robe with his right foot to uncover the woman's chest and bra more fully (fifty-six-second mark). He then stamps

27. This figure on the right certainly looks like a soldier and is wearing a similar helmet and trousers to all the other soldiers so will be identified as Soldier A for the purposes of this discussion. However, his footwear is different and unlike the other soldiers he does not carry a cane, so it is possible that he has a different status from the other soldiers and may be from a different part of the security services. After a few seconds more stones start to land near the soldiers and the soldiers start to retreat. In a short time (1:24 mark) fellow demonstrators can be seen alongside the woman who has remained on the ground throughout the whole experience and may well have been unconscious the entire time.

28. The *abaya* is often worn by women with a headscarf (*hijab*) and a veil (*niqab*), and it looks like the woman is also wearing a headscarf.

29. http://www.youtube.com/watch?v=4iboFV-yeTE&feature=player_embedded&skipcontrinter=1. The sequence is from the thirty-one-second mark to the 1:25 mark. It seems to be continuous footage but it is possible that some editing has compressed events into a shorter time span.

down straight into her midriff and bra (fifty-seven-second mark). The top part of her robe tears further under the force of the blow and uncovers her shoulders. The Reuters photo captures Soldier A as he lifts his foot up from the stamp, and the woman is at her most exposed with her robe now fully open.[30]

The photo and video were circulated on the Internet and international media and prompted an angry outcry. Whilst the more general images of beating and physical violence against demonstrators made a strong impact, the image of the unknown woman exposed in this way seems to have had an especially powerful effect. However, her name remains unknown. She has not come forward to identify herself, presumably because of anxiety about the shame and stigma that would normally apply to a woman disrobed in public. Instead she is widely referred to as simply "the blue-bra woman."

On December 20, 2011, several thousand women staged a protest demonstration against Field Marshal Mohamed Hussein Tantawi and the military regime. Local historians described the protest as: "the biggest women's demonstration in modern Egyptian history" and "the most significant since a 1919 march against British colonialism inaugurated women's activism here."[31]

Many of the women involved seemed to judge the disrobing of the woman as a greater affront than the physical violence. They reportedly chanted, "Drag me, strip me, my brothers' blood will cover me!"[32]

The incident of an unknown woman is therefore a reminder of the power of honor and shame in societies that take these codes seriously. For a woman to be forcibly disrobed in public is not a trivial incident. It is a momentous symbolic act that can be hard for outsiders to appreciate fully.

For Christians, the stripping of Christ which accompanied crucifixion might provide a resonant narrative that can give some insight into the sense of extreme scandal felt by the demonstrators. The indignity and humiliation

30. The next few seconds reveal something about Soldier C that cannot be known from the Reuters photo. He immediately reaches over to close the woman's robe and prevent her exposure (101-second mark to 104-second mark). He seems to be trying to protect her from indignity and further harm but it is not completely clear what happens after this. The footage then turns to the man who is still being beaten and stamped upon a few meters away. Then the soldiers appear to retreat and leave the woman to demonstrators who come to her aid. Seen in this wider context, Soldier C's earlier actions when dragging the woman away from the beating (at the fifty-second mark) might also have been to protect her rather than to mistreat her.

31. Kirkpatrick, "Mass March by Cairo Women."

32. Ibid.

of stripping a man and displaying him in public was not trivial or incidental compared to the physical symptoms of crucifixion. The shame of public display was almost overwhelming. Yet this aspect of the Passion story is often missed or underplayed. The cross should serve as a reminder that the execution of Jesus was not just a matter of physical suffering, but also an act of extreme shame and symbolic degradation.

As with the death of Gaddafi read alongside the death of Saul, the disrobing of the unknown woman at Tahrir Square read alongside the stripping of Jesus at Golgotha points to the mutual illumination that is possible between scripture and contemporary life.

THEOLOGICAL ATTENTION TO GENDER VIOLENCE

Christian theologians and ethicists, along with Christian believers more widely, need to do more to recognize and understand instances of sexualized violence within their own scriptural tradition. They also need to be aware of the prevalence of sexualized violence in current conflicts and consider what more might be done to understand them, identify the sinful power dynamics behind them, and take meaningful actions to prevent them.

If they do so, they are likely to find insights and applications which might serve them in other areas of theological and ethical debate, especially in relation to sexual ethics. It is striking that so far neither of these two more common discussions within sexual ethics mentioned at the outset (clerical abuse and same-sex relationships) has given serious attention to sexualized violence or the scriptural resources referred to in this paper, or theologically addressed sexualized violence in a sustained way. This is particularly notable in the case of sexual abuse, where the relevance of a deeper understanding of sexualized violence should be very obvious and very direct. Yet little seems to be done to make these links, and sexual abuse is often presented in a naïve way as primarily an inappropriate attraction. This gives insufficient attention to the patterns of power and domination which shape the abuse, and which are played out and reinforced in the abuse.

For sexual orientation, the relevance of sexual violence is more indirect and makes a contribution in a very different way. Because of this difference, there is a danger of being misunderstood when using insights from discussion of sexualized violence for the debate on same-sex relations. The key issue for the Anglican Church to address in the sexual orientation debate should be about whether consensual same-sex relationships should be given a similar respect and status as consensual heterosexual relationships. If the debate is focused only on consensual relationships then the types of sexual violence discussed in this chapter will remain a different and separate issue. However, in practice, at least within my own local context in Northern Ireland, the debate about sexual orientation readily conflates arguments about sexual orientation and sexualized violence, invariably to the detriment of productive discussion, and in ways that are unfair to the LGBT community.

This is especially true in the use that is made of Genesis 19:1–11 (the threats made by the men of Sodom), which is cited as a proof-text against same-sex relations. A greater awareness of sexualized violence issues can help to identify and challenge this. The story of Sodom should be read as a narrative of threatened sexualized violence. It is the threat of rape that is the central and deplorable issue, not the fact that the angels are understood to be male. The story of the Levite and his concubine in Judges 19:10–30, which presents not just the threat of sexualized violence but the actual sexual abuse of the concubine, should preclude any reading of Genesis 19:1–11 as about consensual same sex relations. However, critics of same-sex relations rarely acknowledge that neither Genesis 19 nor Judges 19 can be taken as a guide for consensual sexual ethics. Greater clarity on sexualized violence, what it involves and what it means, may therefore help the debate of consensual same-sex relations by identifying and excluding arguments like this that belong in discussions of sexualized violence not sexual orientation.

CONCLUSION

Sexualized violence in the Bible or in contemporary life is a disturbing and dehumanizing feature of war and conflict. Yet despite the significant resources in scripture that should support a mature and constructive Christian concern for sexualized violence, many Christians prefer to keep it off-scene and leave it unaddressed. Leaving sexualized violence unaddressed is unlikely to help bring it to an end. The temptation to choose a false innocence of ignorance should be resisted. Realities of war and conflict need to be faced, not avoided; only then can action be taken to end them and care for those who have suffered from them. The false innocence of avoidance leads to an unintended complicity for which a level of responsibility must eventually be owned.

The majority of victims of rape and other gender violence in conflict are women. Significant progress has been made on identifying, understanding and dealing with this over the last twenty years. In comparison, gender violence against men is less common but it is much more frequent than many people suppose. It is especially prevalent in torture practices, and can involve male rapes, castrations, beatings on the genitals, and genital mutilations. Like sexual violence against women, it remains largely "unspoken" and in many societies still "unspeakable."

Gender violence against men is likely to occur alongside gender violence against women in conflicts because both are governed by a similar logic and express similar notions of conquest. It is rooted in conceptions of male identity, in which male power is expressed through male violence, and sexual violence is a physical and symbolic expression of domination. The sense of humiliation and shame often make victims prone to despair, withdrawal, and even suicide. Some survivors, both women and men, speak of it as a fate "worse than death."

Taking sexual violence and its consequences seriously in theology and theological ethics is a demanding challenge, and will not always be welcomed, but it will serve the church well if the church wishes to be taken seriously on social issues. It will strengthen the church's contribution in the public square, and will also help the church to discover important insights into its own traditions.

10

Public Theology and the Public Role of Churches in South Africa Today

Insights from the Confession of the Threefold Office of Christ

–Nico Koopman

INTRODUCTION

CHRISTIAN THEOLOGY PLAYS A crucial role in assisting South African churches to fulfill their public calling in South Africa today. The notion of public theology is employed by an increasing number of South African theologians to describe this role of Christian theology. The calling of churches can be described in terms of the threefold office of Christ as a prophetic, priestly, and royal-servant role.

Public theological discourse assists churches to redefine their prophetic role in the context of the quest for truth and justice in a democracy, and to describe it in terms of the notions of prophetic envisioning, prophetic criticism, prophetic storytelling, prophetic technical analysis, and prophetic participation in policymaking processes.

Public theology helps churches to fulfill their priestly calling, namely to witness to and participate in quests for healing and reconciliation.

Public theology thirdly assists churches in their royal-servant task—to be communities of hope and to be moral communities of the formation of faithful disciples and responsible citizens.

This essay discusses this service of theology to churches according to the following structure. First, a description is presented of the prophetic, priestly, and royal-servant offices of Christ. On the basis of this analysis, some suggestions are made regarding the prophetic, priestly, and royal-servant callings of the church.

PUBLIC THEOLOGY AND THE THREEFOLD OFFICE OF CHRIST

This section of this paper investigates the historic-theological development of the threefold office, the Reformed and ecumenical reception thereof, its Trinitarian framework, and some points of criticism thereof that suggest guidelines for a constructive and redemptive use of the threefold office today.

One of the most helpful contemporary works in Christology that focuses extensively upon the threefold office of Christ is the work of United Methodist theologian Geoffrey Wainwright.[1] He describes the threefold office as both a Reformed and ecumenical notion. He discusses the use of the threefold office in the early church, and mentions that one of the first firm and explicit uses of the threefold office was that of Eusebius of Caesarea in the fourth century. Eusebius's aim was to illustrate that Jesus Christ was the fulfillment of the Old Testament and in fact of all religions.[2]

Wainwright helpfully cites the perspectives of theologians of the early church, like John Chrysostom (fourth century), who argued that Abraham embodied the dignities of prophet and priest, and David the dignities of king and prophet. Jesus, the son of both, has all three dignities of King, Prophet and Priest.[3] Wainwright also discusses the perspectives of Peter Chrysologus, a fifth century bishop of Ravenna, who calls Christ the King of kings, Priest of priests and Prophet of prophets.[4]

1. Wainwright, *For Our Salvation*, 97–186.

2. Ibid., 110.

3. Ibid., 110–11.

4. Ibid., 111.

Wainwright cites Erasmus's work on the threefold office as another example of a forerunner and anticipation of the eventual systematic development of the doctrine of the threefold office by Calvin.[5] Erasmus described Christ as the Prophet of prophets, the priest who gave himself as victim to purge all the sins of those who believe in him, and the ruler to whom all power was given. Before this ruler returns as judge, he kindly offers peace, and through his teaching he dispels all darkness.

Wainwright identifies Martin Bucer as the most direct inspiration for Calvin's use of the doctrine of the threefold office.[6] For Bucer Christ is the king (*rex*) who will govern us, provide all good things for us, and protects us against ill and oppression. As prophet or teacher (*doctor*) he teaches us the whole truth. As priest (*sacerdos*) he reconciles us with the Father eternally.

Wainwright affirms that Calvin laid the foundation for the extensive and systematic use of the threefold office in the Reformed tradition,[7] and states that the royal, priestly, and prophetic functions among the people of God for the sake of salvation have been united under a single head, Jesus Christ. Based on Calvin's work, the Reformed confessions and catechetics (amongst others the Heidelberg Catechism and Westminster Confession) and Reformed dogmatics (amongst others Friedrich Schleiermacher, Heinrich Heppe, Charles Hodge, Emil Brunner, and Karl Barth) gave a prominent place to the threefold office.

According to Schleiermacher, the threefold office is a necessary and adequate description of the achievements of Christ in the corporate life, that is, the church, founded by Christ.[8] As priest of active obedience who fulfills God's law, as priest of passive obedience who dies an atoning death, and as priest who intercedes for us with the Father, Christ assumes believers into the power of his God-consciousness for the sake of our redemption, and as priest Christ also assumes believers into the fellowship of his unclouded blessedness for the sake of our reconciliation. Christ's prophetic work consists of teaching, prophesying, and working miracles, and his kingly office entails that everything that we need for our salvation and well-being continually proceeds from him. Later in this essay we will

---

5. Ibid., 103.

6. Ibid., 104.

7. Ibid., 99–103. For a helpful contemporary discussion of Calvin's systematic use of the threefold office of Christ, see Edmondson, *Calvin's Christology*.

8. Wainwright, *For Our Salvation*, 101.

discuss a criticism of Schleiermacher's views as an example of some opposition to the notion of the threefold office.

Wainwright explains that after Calvin the notion of the threefold office was, amidst much suspicion, also used by some theologians in the Lutheran tradition (amongst others Helmut Thielicke and Edmund Schlink),[9] the Roman Catholic tradition[10] (Vatican II and amongst others Walter Kasper), to some extent by the Methodist tradition,[11] the Orthodox tradition (amongst others Alexander Schmemann)[12] and by the Anglican tradition (especially John Henry Newman when he was still an Anglican).

Wainwright argues in favor of a trinitarian understanding of the threefold office of Christ.[13] This office is Christocentric, but not Christomonistic. He refers to Calvin's view that it is the Father who anoints Christ with the Holy Spirit to be king, priest, and prophet.[14] Wainwright formulates this view as follows: "the Holy Spirit is the Father's gift by which Christ Himself, Christians, and the church and its ministers are all anointed."[15]

Wainwright's identification of five uses of the threefold office in the theological tradition of almost two millennia affirms this trinitarian framework of the threefold office.[16] The Christological and baptismal functions were predominant in the patristic period. The soteriological use received renewed emphasis during the Reformation. Since the nineteenth century the ministerial and ecclesiological functions enjoy predominance. The trinitarian framework of the threefold office describes Christ's Person and work in terms of their relatedness to the Persons and work of the Father and the Spirit, and in terms of their relatedness to the sacraments, salvation, ministry, and the church. The broad range in terms of how the Bible tells the story of God's redemptive dealings with human beings and the whole world, in and through his church, comes into the picture when we deal with the threefold office of Christ.

The Trinitarian framework also helps us to understand that all three offices are involved in both the state of humiliation and state of exaltation

9. Ibid., 105.

10. Ibid., 106–7, 118.

11. Ibid., 107–8.

12. Ibid., 113.

13. Ibid., 118–20.

14. Ibid., 99, 106.

15. Ibid., 118.

16. Ibid., 109–17.

of Christ, and in both his divine nature and his human nature. Wainwright opts for the exchange of properties (*communicatio idiomatum*) between Christ's divine and human natures in both states of humiliation and exaltation.[17] In the light of this unity in Christ we need not be too tense about the order in which to reflect upon the three offices.

It is especially Lutheran theologians who originally tabled various objections to the notion of the threefold office. Wainwright[18] mentions amongst others Wolfhart Pannenberg and J. E. Ernesti. Pannenberg cites some points of opposition to the threefold office.[19] Objections include that it describes the work of Christ inadequately and that it does not make room for other offices besides prophet, priest and king that were also recognized in the Old Testament. He doubts whether the name Christ can be linked to all three offices and questions the idea that the Spirit anointed Jesus for these offices. He is of the opinion that none of these three offices, except, to some extent, the priestly office, existed consistently in Israel's history. He also does not adhere to the idea described earlier that the three offices function in both the states of humiliation and exaltation of Christ. He feels the notion overemphasizes the earthly work of Christ.

The criticism of the notion of the threefold office from the perspective of postcolonial thinking is important, especially when we try to discern the significance of this office for contemporary complex public life.

American theologian Joerg Rieger, for example, offers some strong opposition to the continued use of the three offices of Christ in contemporary contexts. Rieger argues throughout his book that there is room for the continued use of the threefold office of Christ, on condition that Christian faith is liberated from the misuse of these offices to legitimize and support traditional and contemporary empires. Contemporary empires in postcolonial contexts need to be acknowledged, exposed and opposed.

Rieger describes the notion of empire clearly.[20] He identifies various features of the contemporary understanding of empire. Empire does not only refer to historical empires like the Hellenistic, Roman, Japanese, Spanish, Portuguese, English, and many other empires. Neither does it only refer to the United States, which is described in terms like power, superpower, and hyperpower in a so-called mono-polar world, which came into be-

17. Ibid., 118–19.

18. Ibid., 105.

19. Pannenberg, *Jesus*, 212–25.

20. Rieger, *Christ and Empire*, 1–3.

ing after the fall of the Soviet Union. Nor does empire only refer to the hyperpower of multinational corporations and the interests of the powerful nations of the G8 in today's globalizing world. For Rieger, empire

> has to do with massive concentrations of power that permeate all aspects of life and that cannot be controlled by any one actor alone. . . . Empire seeks to extend its control as far as possible; not only geographically, politically and economically—these factors are commonly recognized—but also intellectually, emotionally, psychologically, spiritually, culturally, and religiously.[21]

Rieger describes empire in terms of notions like control, as a dispersed reality that is embodied in various dependencies maintained through less visible ties, as primarily an economic reality that is tied to the growth of global capitalism, as a political power, as something that exerts power through cultural and intellectual webs that work in hidden ways.[22] With an appeal to Michael Hardt and Antonio Negri he describes power as biopower, that is, a form of power that regulates social life from its interior and that welds together economic, political, and cultural forces.

Rieger points to the writings of Schleiermacher as examples of using the notion of the threefold office that do not acknowledge how inter-related are faith and the growth of post-colonial oppression.[23] Rieger explains that Schleiermacher's portrayal of Christ as a prophet who teaches, offers social criticism, and performs miracles, is ambivalent. On the one hand it sounds like a criticism of all forms of oppression by empire. On the other hand Schleiermacher's so-called colonialist attitude is witnessed in his argument that the European nations need the prophetic work of miracle performing less than the people in the so-called European colonies. In Schleiermacher's thinking even the Jews need this miracle-work of Christ the prophet more than European Christians since these Christians are closer to God than the Jews are.

Schleiermacher's questionable employment of the notion of the three-fold office is, according to Rieger,[24] also clear in his exposition of the priestly office of Christ. This office proclaims that we share in Christ's perfection. It also communicates Christ's sympathy with the suffering and colonized

---

21. Ibid., 2–3.
22. Ibid., 3.
23. Ibid., 209–10.
24. Ibid., 210–12.

people of the world. In Rieger's opinion,[25] however, this suffering is described in too passive a spirit, and is devoid of an active spirit expressed in resistance and refusal to accept the colonialist status quo.

Rieger is skeptical about a second dimension of Schleiermacher's employment of the priestly office, namely that believers follow Christ in his role as universal mediator and reconciler of the world.[26] In Schleiermacher this crucial mediating role is limited to European Protestant Christians.

Moreover, Rieger argues that the idea of priestly dependence, vulnerability, relationality, and equality in the context of great asymmetry in power can obscure the reality of empire and provide a welcome cover-up.[27]

Rieger suggests that Schleiermacher's portrayal of the royal office of Christ is also ambivalent.[28] He acknowledges that Schleiermacher's Christ cannot be called a brutal colonist. He does not rule through coercion, but through attraction and love. Rieger, however, accuses Schleiermacher of viewing Christians as superior to Jews.

According to Rieger, Schleiermacher gives central salvation acts like resurrection, ascension, and judgement, as well as Christ's eternal involvement in creation, and also virgin birth, suffering and the cross, which are indispensable for the comprehensive salvation and liberation of people and the rest of creation, the status of *adiaphora* and non-essentials.[29]

Colonial Christians, Rieger[30] argues, are not criticized, challenged and transformed, but actually affirmed and strengthened by the way in which Schleiermacher and other theologians employ the notion of the threefold office.

Rieger is even skeptical about how Schleiermacher employs the love of Christ.[31] On the positive side, Schleiermacher views this love as universal and inclusive, but his use of the notion of Christ's love also runs the risk of making the colonizer appear in a positive light of legitimacy and mutuality. Love was used in the colonialist context to create boundaries, and call on some, that is, colonial races, to improve the colonized races.

25. Ibid., 210–11.
26. Ibid., 211–12.
27. Ibid., 15–16.
28. Ibid., 213–14.
29. Ibid., 215.
30. Ibid., 216.
31. Ibid., 225.

In the end, Rieger does not reject the notion of the threefold Christ, but he pleads for a use thereof that portrays Christ as a resisting and transforming Christ. We may not find his criticism of the Western theological employment of the threefold office completely convincing. But his plea to interpret the threefold notion in terms of its potential of resisting dehumanization, ecocide, injustice, and oppression, and in terms of its potential of actualizing dignity in the context of the integrity of creation, justice, and freedom, should be taken seriously.[32]

After this brief discussion of the confession of the threefold office of Christ we dedicate the last parts of this paper to some suggestions on the light that the threefold office sheds on contemporary understandings of the Person and work of Christ. This quest for a fresh understanding of the Person and work of Christ provides parameters for the way in which a public theology might serve the public role of churches.[33]

Because, as Wainwright has shown, we were baptized into Christ by the Spirit,[34] and since we are also anointed by the Spirit,[35] and because of our redemption and restoration in Christ,[36] we participate in the prophetic, priestly, and royal-servant work of Christ. Wainwright therefore suggests baptism into Christ, anointing by the Spirit, redemption and restoration in Christ as the pathway to our participation in the threefold office of Christ. Thereby he brings Christology, ecclesiology, and ethics together.

PUBLIC THEOLOGY AND THE PROPHETIC PUBLIC CALLING OF CHURCHES

The Heidelberg Catechism Question 31 describes the prophetic office of Christ as follows: ". . . our Prophet and Teacher who fully reveals to us the secret council and will of God concerning our redemption . . ."

---

32. John Caputo's short book, *What Would Jesus Deconstruct?*, also pleads for a fresh and liberating look at the Person and work of Christ.

33. In an interesting reflection on Christology and ethics, Reformed theological ethicist James Gustafson offers a description of the work of Christ that might illuminate our discussions on the public and ethical import of the threefold office of Christ. He portrays Christ as the Lord who is creator and redeemer, and as the sanctifier, justifier, pattern/example, and teacher. See Gustafson, *Christ and the Moral Life*.

34. Wainwright, *For Our Salvation*, 114.

35. Ibid., 99.

36. Ibid., 113.

In what he calls a contemporary hermeneutic, interpretation, and understanding of the prophetic office, Wainwright[37] argues that the ongoing discernment of the will of God might illuminate the quest in contemporary societies, which are experiencing an information explosion, to develop *sapientia*, wisdom, amidst so much *scientia* and information. And in a context of meaninglessness and purposelessness, the ongoing discernment of God's will provides *telos*, purpose, and meaning.

In the prophetic discourse of public theology in South Africa we might view our prophetic practices as witness about and participation in the life of Christ, the Prophet, who reveals the truth, the will of God, as a truth of our justification by Christ, and as a truth that entails our calling to seek justice in the world. The prophetic quest is therefore a quest for the truth of our justification and salvation in Christ, which is expressed in justice in the world, which is served by *sapientia* and discernment.

On the basis of this understanding of prophetic Christology, ecclesiology, and ethics one might venture to suggest five modes of prophetic speaking that might serve the prophetic calling of the church well.

Building upon, adjusting and appropriating the work of James Gustafson[38] about the public speaking of churches, I have constructed five interdependent and complementary modes of prophetic speaking. These are prophetic speaking as envisioning, criticism, storytelling, technical analysis, and participation in policymaking.

Envisioning entails the spelling out of the ideal picture of a new society. The vision informs a new and better reality. The vision also inspires a new lifestyle, new practices, and new habits and virtues. The vision of a new life transforms persons and systems, individuals and societies to reflect the values and the goods of a new society. A society of dignity that comes to expression in justice and freedom is the vision that South Africans from a variety of religious and secular backgrounds agree upon. This vision is expressed in the Bill of Rights of the 1996 South African Constitution.

Prophetic *criticism* refers first of all to self-criticism. Where churches fail to embody the vision of a new and transformed society, we offer

---

37. Ibid., 133–35.

38. Gustafson, *Varieties of Moral Discourse*. For an article in which Gustafson also discusses these discourses, see "An Analysis of Church and Society Social Ethical Writings." For an article in which Gustafson applies these discourses to medical questions, see "Moral Discourse about Medicine." For an application of Gustafson's theories to the question of justice, see Brady, *The Moral Bond of Community*. For an extensive discussion of these five modes of prophetic speaking, see Koopman, "Modes of Prophecy in a Democracy?"

self-criticism. Churches also offer courageous public criticism where individuals, leaders, and institutions betray this vision. Where the visionary task entails annunciation, the task of criticism entails denunciation. Where visionaries announce the liberating new, critics denounce the persistence of the oppressive old.

Prophetic *storytelling* refers to the telling of stories of pain and oppression. Storytellers give voice especially to the pain and cries of the marginalized, outcasts, and silenced people and creatures of society. Storytelling also brings to light the hopeful and inspiring stories of victory and liberation.

Technical analysis implies that, with the help of appropriate experts, thorough analyses are made of complex public problems and challenges. This technical discourse facilitates more credible and adequate responses by churches to complex and sophisticated public challenges.

Policy discourse refers to the participation of churches in the quest to make, implement and monitor policies that will enhance the plight of the most vulnerable in society. This discourse, however, implies that we need to move from merely offering broad visions for public life. We also should avoid providing blueprints for policies. But churches need to provide parameters for policymaking that are less broad than visions, and less specific than blueprints. The notion of middle axioms that was developed in 1937 by the Life and Work section of the later World Council of Churches might still prove helpful in this regard.[39]

PUBLIC THEOLOGY AND THE PRIESTLY PUBLIC CALLING OF CHURCHES

The Heidelberg Catechism Question 31 describes the priestly office of Christ as follows:

> ". . . our only High Priest, who by the one sacrifice of his body has redeemed us, and ever lives to make intercession for us with the Father . . ."

In his contemporary hermeneutic for the priestly office Wainwright argues that Christ the Priest replaces our pain and suffering, which are expressed in alienations, with reconciliation, and he replaces our sin and guilt, which are expressed in estrangement, with atonement. Christ restores us to divine

---

39. For a discussion of the potential of middle axioms, see Koopman, "Churches and Public Policy Discourses in South Africa."

communion and to communion with each other.[40] Wainwright spells out the concrete and public forms that cry out for this reconciliation, atonement and restored communion:

> . . . oppression is political alienation, for the disenfranchised are deprived of the privileges and responsibilities that go with the human vocation to live in society; poverty is economic alienation, for the impoverished are cut off from their share in the fruit of the earth that humankind is charged by God to cultivate; sickness is physical alienation, and a troubled mind is psychological alienation, and both remove the sufferers from the flourishing existence which God envisioned for his human creatures; slavery is alienation of identity, the profoundest infraction of the dignity of every child of God; bereavement displays death as the alienation of humankind from the life of communion for which it was made.[41]

Jesus Christ, the Public Priest, entered into this human condition of alienation and estrangement. This estranged humanity is the humanity that Christ assumed, and in the words of Hans Urs von Balthasar, "what had not been assumed would not have been healed."[42] For South African churches that seek to develop priestly public theologies, the recommendations offered by Wainwright might be very helpful in our context of so many manifestations of alienation and estrangement.

Public theology challenges, invites, and inspires churches to overcome political alienation. The young South Africa democracy has a good democratic vision and policy documents in place. We, however, need to work for social solidarity, social cohesion and the joint building of social capital. We have sound macroeconomic policies and practices in place, but the benefits do not reach the poor, and we still have the biggest gap between rich and poor in the world. Besides our noble human rights principles of access to basic necessities millions still are excluded from physical and mental health care. We still hurt each other on basis of racial, national, tribal, gender, and socioeconomic identities, and on basis of identity of sexual orientation, age and disability. We even hurt nature.

The priestly office calls us to work toward overcoming these alienations, hurts, and violations of dignity, and to work, therefore, for the

---

40. Wainwright, *For Our Salvation*, 150–53.

41. Ibid., 150.

42. Quoted by Wainwright, *For Our Salvation*, 151.

actualization of dignity, health, and healing, and for restitutive reconciliation and reconciling justice.

PUBLIC THEOLOGY AND THE ROYAL-SERVANT CALLING OF CHURCHES

The Heidelberg Catechism Question 31 describes the kingly office of Christ as follows: ". . . our eternal King, who governs us by his Word and Spirit, and defends and preserves us in the redemption obtained for us." Wainwright argues that the royal servant office teaches contemporary societies about authority, freedom, power, and hope. In a world that seeks autonomy and, in the process, aims to become deistic and eliminate any idea of divine action and rule, the plea is not to burn down the house of authority, and not to bring down the scriptures, creeds, liturgies and institutions of the admittedly imperfect historic church.[43]

In a society hungry for cultural freedom and an absolute right of self-expression, this office calls for recognition that my neighbor is, negatively put, the limit of my freedom, and, put positively, a personal call to service. He lastly mentions that this office assures us of ultimate hope in the exalted Lord and King.

In the South African context, this office might be employed to decontaminate imperialistic notions of power that seem to threaten the idea of servant power. That power is characteristic of the democratic vision with its central words like *minister*, which literally means servant, and the word *president*, which means the one who presides. This one serves as an example amongst the servants, the servant *par excellence*. More than that, the *Christocracy* tells of a Lord, a King who is Shepherd and the most humble of servants. Simultaneously this office calls disciples to fulfill their callings as citizens to public lives of respecting authority, and living responsibly, in the church and in all walks of life.

The royal-servant calling also entails that the life of freedom be defined as a life of freedom from bondage and freedom for a life of service. This view of freedom provides appropriate guidelines and parameters for developing a human rights culture, specifically to advance freedom and justice rights, and also to obey the call to freedom and justice responsibilities.

The royal-servant office also prompts a life of hope. Hope can be described in a threefold manner. Hope is realistic because it is founded in

43. Ibid., 169–71.

the biggest reality of all, namely the cross and resurrection, ascension and *parousia* of Jesus Christ, which is the fulfillment of the promises of God. Against this background hope is responsive hope. Hope therefore pays attention, functions proactively, and is expressed in concrete involvement in the matters of life. Hope is resilient. Despite the most difficult circumstances Christian hope perseveres with patience and fortitude.

And based on this calling, churches marked by authority and hope are moral communities for the formation of disciples and citizens of character and virtue. According to American theologians Bruce Birch and Larry Rasmussen,[44] an etymological study of the word *character* indicates that it has to do with the engraving of particular principles into a person. They refer to the Greek roots of the word that means engraving tool, and by extension the marks made by an engraving tool. Character, hence, has the notion of values that are engraved into a person, over time, so that they become assimilated, incarnated, and embodied in the person. Character, like the virtues, therefore develops over time in communion with God and other human beings.

The North American Christian ethicist J. Philip Wogaman offers a valuable description of virtue. He describes a virtue as "a disposition of the will towards a good end, as a tendency to think or behave in accordance with goodness, as a habit of the will to overcome a threat to our ultimate good."[45] A virtue is a predisposition, a tendency, an intuition to be and to act in a specific way without prior reflection. It almost happens instinctively. It to some extent has an element of unavoidability. The Greek word for virtue, *arète*, refers to the divine power that we do have to be and to act in accordance with goodness. Virtue also has the dimension of *habitus*. This implies that virtue is acquired in a process of consistent and collective habitual behavior. For David Cunningham virtues are dispositions that God has by nature, and in which we participate by grace. Virtues are characteristics of the triune God that are bestowed upon us freely.[46]

The Greek philosopher Aristotle has identified four so-called cardinal virtues. Cardinal is derived from the Latin word *cardo*, which refers to the hinge of a door. The four cardinal virtues are, therefore, the hinge on which all virtues turn. These virtues are justice, moderation/self-control, discernment/

---

44. Birch and Rasmussen, *Bible and Ethics*, 124.

45. Wogaman,*Christian Moral Judgment* 29.

46. Cunningham, *These Three are One*, 123.

wisdom, and courage/fortitude. Centuries later Thomas Aquinas added three theological virtues to these four, namely, faith, hope, and love.

Social and political scientists in various parts of the world argue that democracies with human rights cultures that serve the common good cannot become a reality without leaders and citizens of civic virtue and character. Societies hunger for people of public and civic virtue: public wisdom in contexts of complexity, ambiguity, tragedy, and *aporia* (dead end streets); public justice in context of inequalities and injustices on local and global levels; public temperance in context of greed and consumerism amidst poverty and alienation; public fortitude amidst situations of powerlessness and inertia; public faith amidst feelings of disorientation and rootlessness in contemporary societies; public hope amidst situations of despair and melancholy; public love in societies where public solidarity and compassion are absent.

CONCLUSION

As we seek to participate faithfully in the work of Christ, the threefold office not only provides a form or framework to discuss and understand afresh the Person and work of Christ, and the consequent public calling of churches. The threefold office also constitutes the redemptive contents of Christ's work, of this Christological work, this trinitarian work, which transforms us into people who seek to fulfil our calling faithfully. Alexander Schmemann[47] formulates it well:

> Redeemed and restored by Christ, we resume the original dignity and calling of humankind: to rule the earth as its benefactor and thus be free to enjoy it rather than exploit it; to sanctify the world by offering it to God rather than consuming it for ourselves; to discern the will of God and convey it to the world instead of seeking to possess the world in the absence of God.

Public theology might serve churches well if it reminds, informs, and inspires churches and the rest of humankind with regard to this original and exciting calling and dignity.

---

47. Quoted by Wainwright, *For Our Salvation*, 113.

Pastoral Theology

11

Members of One Another

Building a Restorative Church

–Deborah van Deusen Hunsinger

How is a community to heal when it learns of the sexual misconduct of its beloved pastor or of the treasurer's misappropriation of church funds? Or, where does a church turn for help when conflicts suddenly rage out of control? When shock, anger, or shame overwhelms a congregation, what steps will help the community regain its equilibrium? In the aftermath of churchwide trauma, how might congregational leaders sensitively open up communication about the painful ordeal?

Church communities are often crippled for years, at times even destroyed, when they face such a shock to the system. Mobilizing their resources of intelligence, faith, and imagination, they are nevertheless unable to meet the overwhelming needs clamoring for their attention. As anxiety rises to a higher and higher pitch, individuals react from a feeling of personal threat rather than respond from a place of communal strength. The overriding need *to act together* as members of a common body gets lost in the chaotic emotions that arise.

When the entire church is reeling in pain, it can be difficult to invent structures and processes that will restore its equilibrium. Those congregations that have a restorative framework for responding to harm already in place are best equipped to meet the challenges before them. This chapter seeks to introduce the concept of restorative practices as a promising avenue for responding to crisis, enduring conflict, harm, or community-wide trauma.

Restorative practices (RP) is a transdisciplinary field of study that has grown during the past thirty years in various cultural contexts in response to complex community needs.[1] Though Christian theology has been a significant generative force in shaping fundamental norms in both theory and practice,[2] a restorative framework is little known and seldom adopted as an overarching structure for its explicit relational practice in contemporary churches. I believe that if restorative practices were more widely known, and its structures and processes more widely put into place, churches would be far better equipped to deal with conflict, harm, or trauma in a healthy manner. They might even be able to avoid the kind of entrenched conflict that not only causes emotional turmoil but can also provoke a crisis of faith. If the gulf between the preaching of the gospel and the actual relational practice of the congregation grows too wide, people are in danger not merely of cognitive dissonance, but of disillusionment, cynicism, or even loss of faith.

WHAT IS RESTORATIVE PRACTICES (RP)?

The International Institute of Restorative Practices offers a succinct definition:

1. *Transdisciplinary studies* are "projects that . . . integrate academic researchers from different unrelated disciplines and non-academic participants . . . to research a common goal and create new knowledge and theory. Transdisciplinarity combines interdisciplinarity with a participatory approach." See definitions of *disciplinary, multidisciplinary, participatory, interdisciplinary* and *transdisciplinary* and *integrative* studies in Tress et al., *From Landscape Research*, 15–17.

2. Even in so-called secular venues, Christian values and norms are often either explicitly or implicitly present. See for example, Tutu, *No Future Without Forgiveness*, who describes the work of the Truth and Reconciliation Commission in South Africa. Howard Zehr, a practicing Mennonite, is one of the "founding fathers" of restorative justice worldwide. See Zehr, *The Little Book of Restorative Justice* and *Changing Lenses*, among others. See also the work of John Paul Lederach, a theorist and practitioner of transforming conflict at the level of international relations: *The Journey toward Reconciliation, The Little Book of Conflict Transformation*, and *The Moral Imagination*, among others.

The social science of restorative practices is an emerging field of study that enables people to restore and build community in an increasingly disconnected world. It offers a common thread to tie together theory, research and practice in seemingly disparate fields, such as education, counseling, criminal justice, social work and organizational management.

... Restorative practices is the study of building social capital and achieving social discipline through participatory learning and decision-making.[3]

The disparate fields engaged in this area of study approach it from a wide variety of theoretical perspectives, drawn from their own academic disciplines and the specific needs of their cultural and social contexts. What unites the various disciplines and experienced practitioners in this field of study is a commitment (developed both theoretically and practically) to working *with* people in order to deepen community ties instead of doing things *to* them or *for* them (or alternatively not to do anything at all). "The fundamental premise of restorative practices is that people are happier, more cooperative and productive, and more likely to make positive changes when those in authority do things *with* them, rather than *to* them or *for* them."[4]

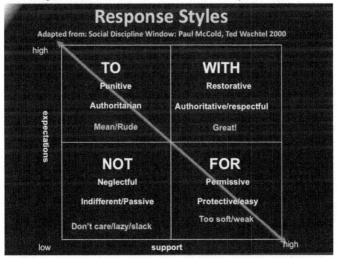

3. See http://www.iirp.edu/article_detail.php?article_id=399. Note the use of the term "restorative practices" (in the plural) in this definition. Some theorists prefer to speak of "restorative practice" (in the singular) to indicate their understanding that RP is not a set of techniques or processes but rather an overarching framework for understanding and strengthening relationship, a way of thinking and being. Within that framework, many kinds of processes or practices may be usefully employed. I am indebted to Mark Vander Vennen of FaithCARE for this point. See www.shalemnetwork.org.

4. See http://www.iirp.edu/whatisrp.php

Consider the above chart.[5] A restorative approach is portrayed in the upper right-hand quadrant as that relational stance that sets high expectations for behavior at the same time that it offers high levels of support. None of the other options (FOR, NOT, or TO) reinforce the kind of relational patterns that support people in taking responsibility for themselves. The upper right quadrant that features the word WITH describes a relational style that is respected by others because it is authoritative without being authoritarian. (The adjectives at the bottom of each quadrant reflect student evaluations of teachers whose relational styles are described there. Students are respectful toward those in authority who first of all respect *them* by taking their needs into account when making decisions that affect their lives). But the word WITH also entails an acknowledgment by those in authority that they genuinely *do not know* in any particular instance what is needed to restore a sense of well-being to the community. The community decides together how to live out its values. Those "in authority" do not own the process; rather the community as a whole owns it.

People need to be included in decisions that matter to them. They need to have their core values heard and their perspectives considered. As members of an interdependent society, all persons need avenues by which they can contribute to the community to which they belong.[6] This becomes even more significant when the community is in pain because of some harm done. In a healthy community, individuals are able to give of themselves and to perceive their impact on others as well as receive from others and gratefully acknowledge them in turn. A profound sense of mutuality is thus embedded in the single word, *with*.[7] At the heart of this transdisciplinary field, in both theory and practice, lies a commitment not to use one's power *over* others, but to engage as much as possible in relationships of mutuality

5. Social Discipline Window, created by Paul McCold and Ted Wachtel. See McCold and Wachtel, "In Pursuit of Paradigm," 1.

6. Marshall Rosenberg (*Nonviolent Communication*) argues that *contribution* and *belonging* are fundamental, universal human needs.

7. In his article "Reconceiving Practice," Craig Dykstra argues that a modern understanding of "practices" is ahistorical, individualistic, and technological, something done *to* and *for* others, undergirded by a utilitarian ethic. By contrast, he argues that the practices of the Christian faith are more adequately conceived as being cooperative and communal "complex traditions of interaction," something we do *with* others. We learn the practices of Christian faith by participating in them in the community, through mentoring relationships with others who are competent "practitioners." By entering into the practices of the faith, we develop new knowledge and insight that otherwise cannot be gained. See also Hunsinger, *Pray Without Ceasing*, xi.

for the sake of building interdependent community. Such a commitment can be challenging to sustain in the context of coercive structures that are intrinsic to many societal institutions.

MEMBERS OF ONE ANOTHER

Typical of contemporary discourse, what was once woven together as a seamless whole—one's theological assumptions, ethics, and practice—has now been fragmented into disparate avenues of inquiry. As members of a multicultural and multifaith society, we cannot suppose that others will share our theological assumptions. It is important, therefore, to differentiate two interdependent aims. I believe that as Christians, our deepest loyalty and most enduring commitment is to Jesus Christ and to all that we have received by faith in him. As we root and ground ourselves in Christ's love, we will seek to articulate a set of beliefs and engage in concrete practices that grow out of our calling to Christian discipleship. At the same time, as we pursue our mission in the wider world, we will seek ways to join forces with persons of other faiths (or no faith) who desire to build and restore community ties on the basis of fundamental shared values. As Glen Stassen comments,

> In public discourse, in a pluralistic society, we need *both* (1) an *explicitly Christian ethic* with a strong scriptural base and (2) a *public ethic* that appeals to reason, experience, and need and that cannot place the same emphasis on Scripture and prayer that an explicitly Christian ethic can.[8]

In community-wide conflicts or in tragedies of national or international significance, when we seek to join forces with those outside the church, we will appeal to shared values such as compassion and mutual respect or to universal norms such as justice and peace. But within the Christian community, in order to articulate our fundamental beliefs and values, we will seek to make explicit the scriptural base and theological norms by which we orient ourselves.

The church, though to the eye perhaps just as fragmented as the world around it, is known by faith to be a single body by virtue of each member's participation in Christ. Because all are members of Christ's body, we are also members of one another.

8. Stassen, *Just Peacemaking*, 93–94.

> For just as the body is one and has many members, and all the members of the body, though many, are one body, so it is with Christ. For in the one Spirit we were all baptized into one body—Jews or Greeks, slaves or free—and we were all made to drink of one Spirit. Indeed, the body does not consist of one member but of many. If the foot would say, "Because I am not a hand, I do not belong to the body," that would not make it any less a part of the body. And if the ear would say, "Because I am not an eye, I do not belong to the body," that would not make it any less a part of the body. If the whole body were an eye, where would the hearing be? If the whole body were hearing, where would the sense of smell be? But as it is, God arranged the members in the body, each one of them, as he chose. If all were a single member, where would the body be? As it is, there are many members, yet one body. The eye cannot say to the hand, "I have no need of you," nor again the head to the feet, "I have no need of you." On the contrary, the members of the body that seem to be weaker are indispensable. (1 Cor 12:12–22)

Is an eye of more importance to the functioning of the body than an ear? Doesn't a body function best when it has not only eyes, but also ears, not only a sense of smell, but also hands and feet? Even if the feet do their part, how can the body function without hands as well? Doesn't the body depend upon each member to bring its unique gifts and capacities to the whole? How could the body function if only one kind of faculty were present? Even the weakest member is indispensable.

Each one's essential indispensability is affirmed, as Paul sets forth his understanding of the radical interdependence of the members of the church. While the indispensability of some may not be obvious to general perception, those who walk by faith know that each person has a unique place of belonging by virtue of their participation in Christ. Moreover, because we internalize the context in which we live, what is outside of us is also inside each of us. We literally cannot cut ourselves off from the body to which we belong. "If one member suffers, all suffer together" (1 Cor 12:26). The suffering of one member, however seemingly marginal, does in fact affect the entire body.

The premise that the suffering of one brings suffering to the whole body functions, I believe, as a basic presupposition of restorative practices, though it is often cut loose from its moorings in Christian theology. Seldom made explicit, it is nevertheless crucial for understanding its core values.[9]

---

9. Various cultures and religions have their own conceptualization of the essential

CONFLICTS IN THE CHURCH

Conflicts in the church are hardly new. We have only to recall the Apostle Paul's intense frustration with the church at Corinth. Loyalties that divided the church into factions were intolerable. He reminded them repeatedly of their unity in Christ. "What I mean is that each of you says, 'I belong to Paul,' or 'I belong to Apollos,' or 'I belong to Cephas,' or 'I belong to Christ'" (1 Cor 1:12). Paul sees distorted theology at the root of such division—"Is Christ divided? Was Paul crucified for you? Or were you baptized in the name of Paul?" (1 Cor 1:13)—which he seeks to correct. The community's central identity as members of Christ's own body, and therefore as members one of another, is his basic presupposition. An appeal to our underlying unity in Christ perhaps remains the most persuasive argument which might still inspire a congregation to listen to one another with patience. The deeper a congregation's devotion to Christ, the greater will be its willingness to bear with one another, even in those situations when it is weary with conflict or stunned by crisis. What, apart from Jesus Christ himself, can inspire each member to reach toward those with whom she or he disagrees?

In recent years, contemporary students of congregational dynamics have been able to shed helpful light on the specific features of such a factionalized community.[10] In some conflicted churches, secrets distort information, creating alienation for some and a false sense of companionship for others, thereby raising the level of anxiety system-wide. Keeping secrets divides the community like an avalanche. Those who are "in" on the secret are able to communicate with one another far better than with anyone outside the group, "*about any issue*, not just about the secret."[11] The most important impact of secrets on the community's emotional well-being, however, is that "they exacerbate other pathological processes unrelated to the content of the particular secret, because secrets generally function to

---

interdependence of persons. Buddhist monk Thich Nhat Hanh, for instance, speaks eloquently of human "interbeing"; Bishop Desmond Tutu speaks of *ubuntu*; and many Christians understand *koinonia* with God and one another as the *telos* of human life: partnership, communion, or mutual indwelling. Consider this description of *ubuntu* by Tutu: "*Ubuntu* is very difficult to render into a Western language. It speaks of the very essence of being human. . . . It is to say, 'My humanity is caught up, is inextricably bound up, in yours.' We belong in a bundle of life. We say, 'A person is a person through other persons.' It is not, 'I think therefore I am.' It says rather: 'I am human because I belong. I participate. I share.'" Tutu, *No Future Without Forgiveness*, 31.

10. See Hunsinger and Latini, *Transforming Church Conflict*.

11. Friedman, *Generation to Generation*, 52.

keep anxiety at higher energy levels. . . . The formation of a . . . secret is always symptomatic of other things going on in the [community.]"[12] Other pathological processes include cut-offs by key members, whose departure from the community intensifies the anxiety of those who remain. Communication becomes indirect as attempts are made to avoid the emotional minefields created by taboo subjects. Congregational culture grows more conflict-avoidant. Triangles form. The anxiety arising between any two parties is absorbed by a third party who listens to both but is powerless to resolve their differences unless or until she finds a way to become a connecting bridge between them.[13] True impasses, in which members no longer recall the real issues, may evolve. The conflict ceases to be about the issues and begins to be about persons instead. Labeling, scapegoating, and diagnosing others prevail.[14] Power is no longer shared but is used by one group at the expense of another. Decision-making structures are altered to reinforce the power of the ruling faction.

The sense of alienation and hopelessness that typically grows out of long-term, unresolved conflict is among its most destructive fruit. As persons shrink back from engaging in overt conflict, it becomes more and more difficult to assess the complex dynamics at work. Typically, many disparate conflicts have arisen over time with various people involved. One person may see himself as the victim of another's hurtful action, while the other would identify *him* as the offender, focusing not on that action, but on the one immediately preceding it, to which she is simply responding. It is often challenging for church leaders to identify *a specific action* that might become the focus of a fruitful conversation. What is the conflict *about*? How might a particular focus be found that will open up channels of communication about what is at stake? If the aims of a restorative paradigm are mutual understanding, self-responsibility and fruitful action (and not mutual blame, self-justification, or finding a scapegoat), then in a certain sense it doesn't matter what the chosen focus is. What particular focus might best assist the church in reversing negative spirals toward isolation and help facilitate connection among its members?

12. Ibid., 53.

13. "When any two parts of a system become uncomfortable with one another, they will 'triangle in' or focus upon a third person, or issue, as a way of stabilizing their own relationship with one another" (ibid.). Friedman later reflects that "the most triangled person in any set of relationships is always the most vulnerable; when the laws of emotional triangles are understood . . . it tends to become the most powerful." Ibid., 35–39.

14. Lyon, "Scapegoating," 141–56.

Conflicts in a community are like mushrooms in the forest, which seem to sprout up at random. Though a professional mycologist would recognize these many mushrooms as a single rhizome (the horizontal root stem), the ordinary observer sees only a multitude of individual mushrooms. When persons are members of one another, as they are in the church, there is usually an underlying root conflict that is larger and more complex than any lone individual can perceive. How do the members of the community conceive of the overall shape of the rhizome hidden from view? The complex root system can be described adequately only through multiple perspectives. An intentional restorative process is designed to understand the *meaning* each person makes of the root conflict, and not to determine "what *really* happened."[15] Just as each of the four Gospel writers understood the meaning of Jesus' life, death, and resurrection differently, so every member of the community will make unique meaning out of the turmoil the church is experiencing.

In order to set up a churchwide restorative process, it is necessary to choose only a single manifestation of the complex underlying conflict, trusting that any entry point will lead to the root. With the careful listening of those who gather for a restorative circle, any particular focus would enable a sustained meditation on the interrelated parts of a single conflict, in both its unity and its complexity. By intentionally choosing a single focus, in other words, the intricately woven interdependence of the community will be disclosed. Though the whole is hidden in any part (i.e., any particular mushroom will lead one to the hidden root system), it is helpful to choose a specific focus that will likely be significant for the community as a whole.

Churches that embrace a restorative paradigm understand that healthy open conflict is far less destructive than denied or suppressed conflict; in fact, open conflict can bring a community new vitality:

> Productive conflict can include a feeling of change, expansion, joy. It may at times have to involve anguish and pain too; but even these are different from the feelings involved in destructive or blocked conflict. Destructive conflict calls forth the conviction that one cannot possibly "win" or, more accurately, that nothing can really change or enlarge. It often involves a feeling that one must move away from one's deeply felt motives, that one is losing

15. The single rhizome of the mushroom plant as an extended metaphor to describe conflict in community was developed by Dominic Barter in his workshop on the theme "Building Compassionate Justice for the 21st Century," University of St. Thomas, St. Paul, Minnesota, October 2008.

> the connection with one's most importantly held desires and needs. . . . Adults have been well-schooled in suppressing conflict but not in conducting constructive conflict. Adults don't seem to know how to enter into it with integrity and respect and with some degree of confidence and hope.[16]

Churches that adopt a restorative practice framework will not be conflict avoidant. These churches will teach their members how to initiate constructive conflict with some degree of confidence and hope.[17] As more and more members have the experience of working through conflicts successfully, they will increase not only their skill level but also their trust in the process.

Conflicts of many kinds and at various levels of intensity need a sensitive, differentiated response. Consider this continuum of increasing levels of conflict:

Parish Restorative Practice Continuum[18]

Low level matters < _____ > Serious

Informal < _____ > Formal

Restorative Conversation	Impromptu Restorative Conversation	Circle Processes for Decision-Making	Large Group Incorporating Restorative Processes	Formal Restorative Conference

When hurt occurs in the context of a solid relationship of trust, it can usually be addressed by simple affective statements (at the far left of the continuum). An example might be the following: (*Parishioner to Pastor*): "I felt hurt that you didn't return my phone call last week when you heard that my daughter was seriously ill. I especially needed your support at such a stressful time." Such an honest expression of one's feelings and needs would likely evoke a response that would help restore trust and contribute to mutual understanding.[19] As we move toward the right of the continuum, we find

---

16. Miller, *Toward a New Psychology*, 129.

17. Interpersonal skills in nonviolent communication can be and are being taught in a variety of contexts, including Christian churches. See Rosenberg, *Nonviolent Communication*, and Hunsinger and Latini, *Transforming Church Conflict*.

18. IIRP (International Institute for Restorative Practices) Canada, developed by Bruce Schenk, presented at the IIRP International Conference, Bethlehem, Pennsylvania, October 2010.

19. Nonviolent communication teaches that expressing one's feelings and needs, instead of judgments, evaluations, or diagnoses, helps restore connection among

conflicts of a more serious nature that require more stable structures.[20] An impromptu restorative conversation might be undertaken by two or three people who understand that the purpose of the conversation is to promote mutual understanding. Those who have been instructed by Matthew 18 will recognize the progression: first, try to work things out directly with the other person involved. If you are unable to resolve matters at that (lowest) level, then ask one or two others to join you.

> If another member of the church sins against you, go and point out the fault when the two of you are alone. If the member *listens to you*, you have regained that one. But if you are *not listened to*, take one or two others along with you, so that every word may be confirmed by the evidence of two or three witnesses. If the member *refuses to listen to them*, tell it to the church; and if the offender *refuses to listen* even to the church, let such a one be to you as a Gentile and a tax collector. Truly I tell you, whatever you bind on earth will be bound in heaven, and whatever you loose on earth will be loosed in heaven. Again, truly I tell you, if two of you agree on earth about anything you ask, it will be done for you by my Father in heaven. For where two or three are gathered in my name, I am there among them. (Matt 18:15–20, italics added)

Congregations need instruction in resolving harm at these lower levels in order to prevent conflicts from escalating. At this level, participants who have been trained to listen—*note the key skill of listening* repeated four times—will generally have the trust that though the conversation may be difficult, it will be worthwhile in the end. Those churches that have held circles for a wide variety of purposes will have all the mechanisms in place, as well as a considerable fund of trust, for tackling the more difficult large-group or churchwide restorative circles.

Circles for decision-making are quite different—both in intent and in process—from a typical church meeting in which the pros and cons of a possible course of action are debated and a "majority rules" vote is taken. Restorative circles are not designed to be forums for winning proponents, persuading others to one's point of view, or making an opposing party look bad. Such tactics only increase ill feeling and lend themselves to polarization. A restorative approach *wants* to hear those with whom the majority disagrees, not so that they can be defeated, but so that their needs can be

---

individuals and groups. See Rosenberg, *Nonviolent Communication*.

20. See the Social Discipline Window, developed by Paul McCold and Ted Wachtel, earlier in this chapter.

fully heard and taken to heart. A restorative church knows that if it operates within a win/lose paradigm, the whole church will lose. Just as in a marriage where only win/win arguments enable the couple to flourish, so also in a church, members are careful *not* to try to "win" at someone else's expense. As we move further toward the far right-hand column to large-group restorative processes or to a churchwide formal restorative conference, clear structures and processes need to be in place that will provide safety for more challenging conversations. Though these conversations can sometimes be painful, they often issue in newfound energy and even joy. As members speak of their deepest convictions, they grow in respect and understanding of one another. Their unity in Christ becomes more visible as they see that those with whom they disagree are taking their views to heart and considering them in a new light.

At the formal conference end of the continuum, it can be helpful to invite an outside facilitator to oversee the process.[21] Many situations arise in the church where a pastor needs to be an active participant in the circle, and not the facilitator. Including the pastor as a member of the circle enables members to understand him or her as a human being with feelings and needs and not simply as the person in authority. Dominic Barter tells the story of a kindergartener who requested a restorative circle over an upsetting event at her school. The principal participated in the circle as an equal partner to help restore harmony.

It is worth noting that it is in the context of community conflict—when one member of the church is sinning against another and *refuses to hear* the impact it has on others—that Jesus explicitly promises to be in their midst. The promise of Jesus' presence is given to us precisely in those situations in which we feel most threatened, when we have been hurt and find ourselves unable to make our voice heard. When one who "has sinned against us" *refuses* to listen to us, we are instructed to ask one or two others to go with us to find a way to restore trust (impromptu restorative conversation). Skill in listening is essential for such a conversation to succeed. If the person refuses to hear the impact of his actions on others, conversations that include still others may need to take place. Because any particular offense is nested in larger complex processes, the perspective of others will widen the scope, helping to shed light on the overarching context. When the community's clear intent is one of mutual understanding

21. FaithCARE in Hamilton, Canada, for example, provides consultation for churches in crisis, using a restorative practice framework. See www.shalemnetwork.org.

and not blaming or scapegoating, the circle process can be liberating and exciting. New information will emerge; hearts closed down and hardened will soften; and creative new directions will spring up.

What if the person who has brought suffering to the body refuses to listen to the whole church? Jesus says that he or she is to be treated as a Gentile or tax collector. Churches through the ages have taken Jesus to mean that such a person is to be utterly rejected, perhaps even cast out from the community. Yet here we must ask about Jesus' own practice toward Gentiles and tax collectors. Does he refuse to have anything to do with them? *No, he seeks deepened fellowship with them.*[22] He invites himself into the home of Zaccheus, the despised tax collector, for example, and engages in serious theological conversation with the woman from Samaria.[23] Against all the customs of his culture, Jesus *listens to* those whom others consider sinful and unworthy. Even at the formal conference end of the continuum, when clear harm has been done, the goal is not to cast out those who have harmed others, but to deepen fellowship with them so that a true communion of mutual understanding can grow.

Guiding Principles of Restorative Practice

When strife or trauma has come to the community, the fundamental questions informing a restorative approach would be the following:

1. Who has been hurt?

2. What are their needs?

3. Whose obligations are these?

4. Who has a stake in this situation?

5. What is the appropriate process [in which] to involve stakeholders in an effort to put things right?[24]

The focus of the work is to identify and address the needs of every person impacted by the incident, *including* the needs of those who have caused harm. Recognizing our own need for mercy, we are to extend mercy toward any who acknowledge their responsibility for their choices. If a clear

22. Lederach, *Journey toward Reconciliation*, 134.

23. Though Samaritans were not technically Gentiles, "Jews have no dealings with Samaritans" (John 4:9).

24. Zehr, *Little Book of Restorative Justice*, 38.

restorative process has already been established in the church, parishioners will expect a restorative circle to be called, so that the matter can be discussed in a safe and productive manner. It is of crucial significance that the person who has brought harm to the community needs to acknowledge the *fact* of her actions. The *meaning* of the action for her, as well as for others, will come out in the restorative circle. Not only will others come to understand her motivations for acting as she did, but she will have an opportunity to hear the impact her choices had on other members of the community.

Guiding principles at work in a restorative paradigm are listed below:

1. The conflict or difficulty, whatever its dimensions, belongs to the community in which it takes place. It needs to be owned by the community and not taken over by outside agents (e.g., the criminal justice system, social workers, lawyers or other authorities, professionals, or agencies attempting to offer support).[25]

2. Its purpose (and central focus) is to restore and heal relationships through face-to-face participation of those affected.

3. It is a voluntary process for everyone involved. No coercion of any kind is used. People are invited to participate, not mandated to do so.

4. Trained facilitators from within the community coordinate the restorative processes.

5. Each person participating will have equal access to the processes developed as well as informed consent upon which to make a decision whether to participate or not.

6. Restorative circles end on an Action Plan to which everyone agrees. Those directly affected together determine the outcome.

7. No observers are included in the process, only participants who have a vital stake in the outcome.

8. Everyone present is given a chance to speak and be heard.

9. The greater the alignment with these principles, the more restorative the outcome.[26]

---

25. Nils Christie argues this thesis in his groundbreaking article "Conflict as Property": "My suspicion is that criminology to some extent has amplified a process where conflicts have been taken away from the parties directly involved and thereby have either disappeared or become other people's property. In both cases a deplorable outcome" (1).

26. These principles represent my understanding of the teachings of Dominic Barter

Those persons who participate in the circle decide what strategies might best serve the needs of the whole by discovering which specific actions will be done, by whom, and by what date. Persons then make requests of one another or offer constructive actions that either directly meet the identified needs or symbolically connect to them in a meaningful way.

Choosing a Planning Team

In any serious conflict in the church, it is important to create a planning team or "reference committee."[27] Such a team is made up of lay leaders who are familiar not only with the issues the congregation is facing but also the history of some of its longstanding interpersonal impasses. These leaders need to be sanctioned by the church governing body and widely respected by the congregation. If church factions are polarized, it is important to have proponents of each faction on the team. It would be unwise, however, to choose extreme representatives of one party or another. Instead, it is best to choose those more moderate in their opinions, especially if they are skilled in listening to those with whom they disagree. Their success in offering effective leadership will depend in large part on their ability to work together as a team. The quality of their dialogue "tends to affect the quality of the overall dialogue within the congregation. . . . Their essential job is to advocate a fair process and not a particular outcome."[28]

The planning team will oversee a process that has three segments: a *pre-circle* to support clarity about the specific act that will serve as the focal point for conversation and to explain the whole process to all those who need to be included; a *restorative circle* that aims toward mutual understanding, self-responsibility, and effective action; and a *post-circle* to help the community assess the level of satisfaction with the steps taken. Restorative circles can function at varying degrees of complexity and levels of emotional intensity. In each case, only those people directly or indirectly impacted by the act should be involved. Because of the complex interdependent nature of a church community or in the event of a serious crisis, situations may arise in which a churchwide restorative circle needs to take place. This kind of circle is represented on the restorative practice

---

at the New York Intensive Residential Training in Nonviolent Communication in Binghamton, New York, August 2008.

27. Brubaker, *Promise and Peril*, 147–50.

28. Ibid., 149.

continuum at the far right of the continuum: *Formal Restorative Conference*. If the church is familiar with a restorative approach, having worked frequently at much lower levels of conflict or crisis, the planning team can go into immediate action.

Churches dealing with any specific action that has diminished the community's sense of well-being gather to talk about the harm that has impacted them, by answering a series of prepared questions (that will be contextualized for the specific situation). At the most generalized level, each person will be asked to reflect on three questions:

- What do you want others to know about how you are now in relation to [what happened]? What impact has this event had on you? (*Grounding in the present—which seeks to support mutual understanding.*)

- What do you want others to know about what you were looking for when you acted (or responded) as you did to the event? (*Investigating the past which seeks to support self-responsibility.*)

- What would you like to see happen next? Is there a specific request or offer you want to make that would address the needs of the community as you understand them? (*Agreeing to future action that seeks to support effective movement forward.*)[29]

Each person in the circle will have an opportunity to speak and to be heard. Questions that first ground the participants in the present help build bridges of mutual understanding. Questions that investigate the reasons people chose to respond as they did help each person to take responsibility for his or her choices. And requests or offers of support that are concrete and doable help promote effective action. Situations that interface with legal processes (such as the sexual misconduct of the pastor or the treasurer's

---

29. The form of these questions is based on my understanding of Dominic Barter's creative work with restorative circles in Brazil. It should be noted that formal restorative conferences (or circles) take on different shapes depending on their institutional context and their specific purpose. For example, family group conferencing might occur in the context of making foster-care decisions in family and youth social services. The criminal justice system has formal procedures for helping courts determine sentences based on victim-impact statements developed by communities who have been harmed. Schools hold restorative conferences to deal with delinquencies and disruptions in classes, either in a particular classroom or, if the whole school has been impacted, schoolwide. In each instance, the questions asked and considered by the participants will vary according to the specific needs of those involved, but it is important to address the present, the past, and the future, giving everyone a chance to be heard.

misappropriation of church funds) will need clear guidelines that respect the rights of the alleged offender and victims, but at the same time attend to the congregation's needs for healing and connection at a time of potentially overwhelming stress.

Structuring a Churchwide Restorative Circle

A churchwide restorative circle can transform conflict in completely un-expected ways.[30] There is a natural flow to conflict that needs assistance in reaching its full potential. A facilitator (or ideally, a pair of co-facilitators) helps the group establish clear guidelines and keeps the process on track. The facilitators' tasks are

- to help the community come to an agreement about guidelines for the dialogue by explaining the overall aims of the restorative circle;
- to check whether each person who speaks is heard to his or her own satisfaction;
- to prepare each participant in a pre-circle process before the circle meets (pre-circles will be explained below);
- to schedule the date and time of the restorative circle;
- to care for the space by choosing a quiet and symbolically meaningful place, and by having drinks, tissues, pens, and paper available;
- to set forth the process clearly for all participants;
- to greet all persons as they enter the space, initiate a simple process for introductions to be made, and offer a clear opening sentence that reminds them of the intention that brought them all there.[31]

The group's first task will be to develop process guidelines. These typi-cally include showing respect for each person by agreeing to keep what is said within the group (agreement regarding confidentiality), and by having only one person speak at a time (agreement regarding respect and

30. For practical ideas and useful suggestions for setting up such circles, see Kraybill, *The Little Book of Cool Tools*.

31. I am drawing here on my understanding of the key elements required of facilita-tors as presented by Barter in his workshop "Building Compassionate Justice for the 21st Century" (see note 15).

fairness)—sometimes facilitated by the use of a "talking piece" or symbolic object that is held by the person who is speaking.[32]

Setting chairs in a circle communicates a commitment to valuing every person's voice. As Kay Pranis comments, a circle communicates by its very shape that "no person is more important than anyone else."[33] The particular focus of the conversation is described in the form of a neutral observation in order to avoid attributing blame to any particular person(s). Whatever happened is an event that cries out for understanding. The aim of calling a circle is to facilitate a greater sense of connection among the members of the community, giving each member a keen sense of belonging. If a harmful event involves an actual crime, necessary legal processes might need to occur concomitantly to the circle process. It is crucial in such cases to distinguish between such procedures and the congregation's urgent need for care and healing. Fears about legal ramifications will sometimes muzzle a congregation at the very time it most needs to hear from one another. If discord has arisen in the body, it is of fundamental importance to have a safe way to come together and process the emotions that are having an impact.

In order to facilitate connection among its members, the core aims of a restorative circle are: mutual understanding, self-responsibility, and an action plan.[34] Mutual understanding is supported when each person has an opportunity to be heard about the *significance* of a particular event, the meaning that it holds for him or her now. After each person speaks, the facilitator asks one of the members of the circle, "What did you hear is important to her?" That member replies with a summary of the essence of what he heard. Then the facilitator turns to the person and asks, "Is that what you wanted understood?" By adding this simple step, everyone in the circle receives immediate feedback about how she has been heard. This gives each person an opportunity to restate what she wants to be known by others until she is heard completely to her satisfaction. This back and forth

32. "The use of a talking piece allows for full expression of emotions, deeper listening, thoughtful reflection, and an unhurried pace." Pranis, *Little Book of Circle Processes*, 12.

33. Ibid., 8.

34. I am indebted to Dominic Barter's oral presentations in which he teaches the processes, principles, and structures of restorative circles. Barter, a certified trainer in nonviolent communication, is an internationally recognized facilitator and teacher of restorative practices. See his website for information on his work in Brazil and his teaching throughout the world: http://www.restorativecircles.org/. My understandings of his teachings have been contextualized specifically for the church.

process between speaker and listener only seems to slow down the process. In the end, it brings much more ease to the process because little facilitates mutual understanding more readily than the experience of being heard as one hopes to be heard.

The intention of this process is to focus on the people present and how they see and understand one another, in order to reestablish a sense of connection. The facilitation helps the participants to gain trust in the process as well as insight into the other members of the community who are affected by an important event in the church's life. Sometimes, it might be a gathering of the entire community and several circles may need to be held. Hearing from others in this way helps to build bridges of mutual understanding as each person begins to hear the others' humanity.

Self-responsibility takes place when each person in the community acknowledges and owns the choices he or she has made in reference to the act or event in question, by engaging this question: "What do you want others to know about what you were looking for when you acted as you did?" Every member of the congregation has contributed to the *ethos* of the community by his or her actions (or inaction). Each person is encouraged to reflect on what in particular he or she was seeking in relation to the act. As each person hears from others, he may be able to give more articulate voice to his own motivations (i.e., what needs he was trying to meet through his particular choices). Naming these before the community helps persons to take responsibility for their own needs, a process that at once decreases blame and increases a sense of empowerment.

Because the process is slow and reflective, giving people the time and space to process their emotions and taking the time for full reflective listening, a sturdy bridge among the participants is built. Only after the interpersonal bridge is securely in place do the facilitators move the process to the third step: toward the creation of an action plan. With restorative circles, churches can avoid the common mistake of rushing into action. After a trauma or tragedy, many people will offer some version of the advice that was a popular slogan in the 1960s: "Don't mourn, organize!" While taking action often brings with it a wonderful sense of empowerment, it will not accomplish a fraction of what it is meant to accomplish if the step of *mourning together* is sidestepped. When the members of the community are reconnected with each other from the heart, a palpable shift can be felt in the room. At that point, the third question can be asked: "What would you like to see happen next? Is there a specific request—or offer—that you want to make that would address the needs of the community, as you understand them?"

At this point in the conversation, creative strategies usually begin to flow, sometimes to overflow. The group is energized by the hard work it has done in steps one and two and is eager to move forward together in a constructive way. Any offering or request needs to be concrete, specific, and doable within a particular time frame. The action plan aims to take into consideration *all* the needs that have been expressed. Here an exciting sense of collaboration often grows palpably. A plan is agreed upon by all members of the circle and is to be carried out within a specific period of time. At the end of the whole process (*after* the action plan has been implemented) a post-circle will be called to assess whether the action plan did in fact meet the needs of the community as it had hoped. If not, a new action plan can be created.

It is not the responsibility of the facilitators to resolve the conflict; this is the work of the entire community. The facilitators enter the circle process along with everyone else, *not knowing* how things will go. They do not have a specific end in mind. Holding fast to the fundamental principles of the practice, facilitators work throughout the entire process *with* the community, and in many instances are themselves members of the community. They do not enter the circle holding on to roles of authority but join the circle simply as those members who will guard the integrity of the process and assist the group in adhering to the agreed-upon principles. Because restorative circles are completely voluntary, the persons who commit themselves to the circle process are those willing to take responsibility for the next steps. Anyone who does not wish to take part is free to decline. In that case, however, the facilitators make it clear that the circle will proceed without them. In this way, no one has the power to sabotage the healing of the community by his or her choice not to participate.

Pre-circles

As mentioned, there are three distinct phases to the overall process for a churchwide restorative conference: pre-circles; the restorative circle itself; and the post-circle. The facilitators meet with each group (or each individual, depending on the scope and the particulars of the event to be discussed) represented in a pre-circle meeting. That is to say, the facilitators meet with those who are the authors of the act, those who are the direct recipients, and those who are part of the larger community (those indirectly impacted) in three different pre-circles. The facilitators' goals in these pre-circles are to forge an empathic connection with each person involved; to gain clarity about the precise nature of the act by asking each person "what happened" as he or she sees it; to ask who needs to be involved in order to resolve the conflict; and to gain each individual's informed consent. It is at this point that the facilitators explain the purpose of the circle, the precise questions that will be asked, and the underlying principles that will be adhered to. The overall process is explained.

The facilitators end the pre-circles by asking each person whether or not he or she would like to participate. Their aim is to adapt the form to the local context and culture as much as possible so that it will truly serve the people involved. As they help the congregants to articulate what really matters to them about the incident, the facilitators show forth a collaborative spirit that helps to form a sturdy bond of trust. As more people decide to participate, the more promising it becomes that the circle(s) will reach its restorative aim.

Post-circles

A post-circle is called by the facilitators at an agreed-upon time set by the action plan. An agreement will have been made by all the participants in the restorative circle to take certain actions that they believe will bring about healing, harmony, or ease, help make amends, or provide occasions for mutual support. In the post-circle, the community gathers to assess its level of satisfaction with the actions taken. Every person has an opportunity to acknowledge the contributions of the others and to express gratitude. At the same time, each person assesses whether or not anything further is needed to bring about the agreed-upon aims of the circle. What further actions might be taken that would contribute to the healing, peace, or reconciliation of the community?

Perhaps the actions they took did not meet their needs in the ways that they had anticipated. Now they can propose new actions based on newly discovered needs. When the meaning these actions hold for each participant is explored, community connections are further deepened. Each participant has an opportunity to delve deeper into the meaning the proposed actions carry for him personally, as he is now newly aware of them. Is there something further that can be done that would capture the essence of what is at stake? Are there new circumstances that have arisen that now need to be considered?

If the agreed-upon actions were not in fact carried out, the post-circle offers an opportunity to explore what needs were met by *not* following through on those actions. That is to say, what are the reasons for anyone choosing not to follow through on the action plan? What needs would not have been met by undertaking the action? The post-circle provides an opportunity to fine-tune the action plan, in other words, not to blame or shame those who did not follow through on the agreement. Newly discovered needs may then lead to a new action plan within a new time frame.[35]

As before, the facilitator will check with each speaker whether or not she has been heard to her own satisfaction by asking another to repeat the essence of what is important to the one who just spoke. This step continues to be important because it closes the communication loop. Trust in the process is deepened as people discover that what matters to them has been fully heard.

Churches that are not in the midst of crisis are wise to consider the principles of restorative practice and agree to create a restorative system in which to nest any particular restorative circle. A church doesn't have to be in the midst of conflict to become a restorative congregation. Indeed, proactive circles that are not responding to crisis can be established in order to deepen relational ties. Circles can be developed as the church's normal way of doing business. For example, a church council meeting could be conducted, not according to *Robert's Rules of Order*, but rather according to a circle process. Youth in youth groups might agree to check in with each other (with a talking piece) by describing the highs and lows of their week. An upcoming issue that is not contentious could be discussed in church-wide circle processes. By these means the church would model in all of its practices that everyone's voice matters, that processes are invitational, not coerced, and that the power structures of the community are not seeking to assert power over others but want to empower all members to participate in the crucial decisions of the community. Decisions will still be made by those responsible to make them (e.g., staff, council, pastors, etc.) but members will grow in trust that their voices are heard about issues that matter to them. Restorative circles are inscribed as a way of life for the community.

---

35. The aims and procedures of both pre- and post-circles represent my understanding of Barter's teachings as presented in "Building Compassionate Justice for the 21st Century" (see note 15).

When institutional agreements are in place for how conflicts are to be approached, a community is more readily prepared to use any given conflict as an opportunity for growth. Physical space needs to be set aside where circles can be undertaken. Members of the community need to be trained to facilitate circles at the lower end of conflict intensity. The process for requesting a restorative circle needs to be made accessible to all members, so that all persons are equally empowered.[36]

CONCLUSION

The purpose of this chapter has been to introduce the field of restorative practices to the contemporary church as a way to promote mutual understanding, self-responsibility, and effective action in communities torn apart by conflict or shocked by trauma. While restorative processes are deeply embedded in the theology and history of the church—especially in the so-called historic "peace" communions—they are rarely given the place they deserve, at least in mainline denominations in the United States. Yet, because forgiveness and reconciliation lie at the core of the gospel, the church, for the sake of its basic integrity, needs to be tireless in aligning its relational practices with its beliefs.

In his book *The Tacit Dimension*, Michael Polanyi writes,

> To rely on a theory for understanding nature is to interiorize it. For we are attending from the theory to things seen in its light, and we are aware of the theory, while thus using it, in terms of the spectacle that it serves to explain. This is why mathematical theory can be learned only by practicing its application: its true knowledge lies in our ability to use it. . . . A true knowledge of a theory can be established only after it has been interiorized and extensively used to interpret experience.[37]

Conceptual models, such as the one presented here, become tools for knowing only when we indwell both the model and the situation at hand. Does the model illuminate the situation? How? Does it fail to account for

---

36. The importance of creating a community-wide agreement to a restorative system is a major point of emphasis in Barter's teaching. Without this institutional understanding and agreement in place, any restorative circle would have little impact on the congregational culture as a whole.

37. Polanyi, *Tacit Dimension*, 17–21.

certain factors? In what way? Does it open up new avenues for further investigation?

I believe that restorative practices have a great deal to offer churches who are struggling with entrenched conflict or reeling from traumatic events in the life of the community. The model also offers clear and simple guidelines for reaching across any of the normal barriers that separate human beings in community. When differences become barriers to understanding, restorative circles have much to commend them. Whether the differences are racial, cultural, political, or religious does not seem to matter. Circles such as those described here will facilitate mutual understanding, self-responsibility and new creative action. That is perhaps why they are used increasingly in a wide variety of venues: in education, criminal justice, and social service agencies. Once the basic principles and practices are understood, circles can be adopted in an even wider variety of contexts. Individual families might use these simple guidelines to deepen relational ties among their members. Those trained in facilitation in their churches will have these uncomplicated skills they can use wherever they go, skills that will contribute substantively to any community of which they are a part.

Those churches that have decided to adopt restorative practices for their community provide opportunities for their members to learn more honest and caring ways to communicate. They give visible shape to the church's commitment to speak the truth in love, not as an abstract ideal to strive for but rather as a growing skill that will empower the community to take responsibility for its own conflicts. Working through interpersonal pain is one way of trusting in God's grace. In honoring the interdependent needs of every member, in facilitating mutual understanding, and in offering opportunities for real accountability, the gospel of Jesus Christ can be lived out.

These practices have the potential to develop each member's capacity to see the human beings with whom they are in conflict as precious members of the body of Christ, brothers and sisters made in the image of God, not as opponents to be controlled or conquered. The circle process enables each person to participate as a fully equal and valued member of the community. All members are given an opportunity to co-create constructive solutions. In the process, every member who participates will learn crucial skills in how to undertake dialogue in a respectful way.

Every voice is valued as the whole body together seeks God's kingdom. "Again, truly I tell you, if two of you agree on earth about anything you ask, it will be done for you by my Father in heaven. For where two or three are gathered in my name, I am there among them" (Matt 18:19–20). The fundamental interdependence of the members of the body is essential to this understanding. Emphasis is squarely placed on the unity of the body of Christ, even though each member plays a unique, indispensable role. We are members of one another and "if one member suffers, all suffer together with it" (1 Cor 12:26). Jesus reminds his disciples over and again that even "the least of these" matter in the kingdom of God. Restorative circles offer a structure in which the members of the church can experience the truth that everyone does in fact matter.

The Apostle Paul reminds the church that we are to "bear one another's burdens" (Gal 6:2) as a way of fulfilling the law of Christ. At the same time, we are admonished to take responsibility for our own actions: "For all must carry their own loads" (Gal 6:5). Restorative circles highlight the fact that all our choices are made in the context of mutual accountability. As we listen to one another, we gain a wider vision of how our words and actions have affected others in the community. If we regret our choices, we are given an opportunity to make amends. Since all members are treated with basic respect, it is not a matter of humiliation to acknowledge regret. On the contrary, to do so is a sign of the Holy Spirit's work in our midst.

As churches offer safe places to strengthen frayed bonds of trust, and as they call upon God to minister to the community in its pain, they give opportunities for each person to express what has wounded her most. Restorative circles offer a safe structure, a clear process, and a healing intention for members of the body to hear one another's stories in a public forum. Now the hurting parties can be heard respectfully. It takes time to heal. Even more importantly, it takes willingness. No one can make another willing to begin such a healing journey, but without clear processes in place, no healing journey can ever be begun. Such circles offer the church concrete practices for working through churchwide impasses where mutual understanding, genuine accountability, and basic trust are the core needs of the community. Out of such honestly faced conflict, new life and hope will, by the grace of God, spring up.

12

A Post-secular Theology of Compassion

The Moral-Spiritual[1] and Psychological
Underpinnings of "Good Care"

−Hetty Zock

THEOLOGY AND SPIRITUAL CARE
IN A POST-SECULAR AGE

"**D**O YOU TEACH THE students to pray, at the theological department?" a colleague in the medical department recently asked
me a bit teasingly, yet with a serious undertone. It is not easy to be a theologian in the contemporary postmodern world, especially not in a highly
secularized country such as the Netherlands. Christian believers are often
encountered with suspicion and the churches have increasingly less influence. Theologians are a marginalized group, faced with the task of explaining the relevance of their discipline for contemporary social, political, and

1. In this chapter, I use the adjective "moral-spiritual" to indicate that moral and
spiritual perspectives go together in the search for a meaningful life. This is in line with
Charles Taylor (*Sources of the Self*), who takes the moral as an intrinsic part of the spiritual domain. In his view, the term *moral* points to "hyper-goods," that is, constitutive values
that make life worthwhile and provide moral guidance.

ethical issues. Moreover, Christian theology itself becomes as diverse and fragmented as the many other available philosophies of life.[2] As a result of the plurality of worldviews, cultural diversity and the dynamics of globalization processes, the individual faces the task of establishing his/her own identity and worldview, with the help of many cultural perspectives offered. It is argued that "small narratives" have become more important than a grand, overarching master-narrative (or even have replaced it).[3] Because the focus is on the individual search for meaning, personal appropriation of traditions has become more important. Traditions are only viable when they are realized, "lived," in the life-story. One could mention here the "turn to the subject"[4] and "the anthropological turn" in practical theology[5] (i.e., the interest in "lived religion"). Furthermore, there is a great interest in spirituality outside the borders of established religious traditions and institutions, such as management and health care. It has become fashionable to use the term *spirituality* in this encompassing way.[6] This postmodern situation with respect to worldview and spirituality may be characterized as "post-secular": we see the re-emergence of the religious in other forms in secular domains.[7]

In the master's program in spiritual care at the University of Groningen, we train students to become non-denominationally bound spiritual caregivers (chaplains) in health care settings. Thus, they are at the heart of the search for meaning in a post-secular context, in existential situations where it really counts. When people are confronted with death, illness, and suffering, and when they have to make difficult ethical choices, they are thrown back on their (more or less implicit) philosophies of life and spiritual resources, to which they often no longer have access through lack of use. So spiritual caregivers in the Netherlands have to counsel clients who

2. See Molendijk, "Theology Unbound," chapter 3 in this volume.

3. The classic book here is, of course, Lyotard, *The Postmodern Condition*. I have absolutely no pretension to give an adequate description of the complex theorizing on "postmodernity" here. For the sake of this paper, it may suffice to indicate some of its major elements: plurality, fragmentation, cultural diversity, individualization, and processes of globalization. Cf. Zock, "Voicing the Self in Postsecular Society" and "The Prophetic Voice."

4. Taylor, *Sources of the Self.*

5. Streib et al., *Lived Religion*; McGuire, *Lived Religion*; Gräb and Charbonnier, *Secularization Theories.*

6. Belzen, "Studying the Specificity of Spirituality," and Westerink, "Spirituality in Psychology of Religion."

7. Molendijk et al., *Exploring the Postsecular*, x and 20.

hold widely different beliefs and who are often not familiar with specific spiritual practices. It is telling in this respect that only about 33 percent of the Dutch still have an affiliation with a religious institution.

A new development is that the spiritual caregivers themselves are often not linked to a specific religious tradition or institution. The number of non-denominational chaplains in the Netherlands is rapidly increasing. Elsewhere, I explained this by pointing to the fact that the Dutch spiritual caregiver is no longer primarily a religious office holder fulfilling ecclesiastical functions. S/he has turned more and more into an existential counselor, focusing on the search for meaning and life-orientation of all the clients/patients/residents, irrespective of their religion or philosophy of life.[8] This requires a new view on the professional identity of spiritual care. The spiritual caregiver's own philosophy of life and spirituality remains his or her main instrument, but it is no longer the focal point in administering spiritual care. Now the focus is how philosophy of life and spirituality may contribute to the quality of care as a whole and to the well-being of patients in particular. It is about the function of philosophy of life rather than about its content. Moreover, the question arises as to what the specific contribution of spiritual care consists of in comparison with other care disciplines, since spirituality is no longer confined to the domain of spiritual care only.

It is precisely in this context that the term *compassion* plays a crucial role. I will show that, in the present pluralized context, there is a common philosophy of life that binds Dutch spiritual caregivers, which may be characterized as *passion for and compassion with people*. This "philosophy of compassion" is shared with other health care professionals. Compassion is seen nowadays as an important factor regarding the quality of care and the work satisfaction of care professionals. For instance, Christina Puchalski, the leading figure in the palliative care movement, states that "spiritual or compassionate care involves serving the whole person—the physical, emotional, social, and spiritual. Such service is inherently a spiritual activity."[9] So she considers spirituality as a dimension of all forms of care.

In this chapter, I will critically analyze the emerging philosophy of compassion in health care. I will argue that *compassion* is a useful post-secular crossover term that serves both as a moral-spiritual[10] and as a psy-

---

8. Zock, "The Split Professional Identity of the Chaplain" and "The Spiritual Caregiver as a Liaison Officer."

9. Puchalski, "The Role of Spirituality in Health Care."

10. See note 1.

chological underpinning for what makes for "good care." The term is heard in both religious and secular circles. It is used by spiritual caregivers, care professionals, and researchers in the field of health and spirituality alike. Thus, the term *compassion* has the capacity to connect not only diverse philosophies of life (religious and non-religious ones), diverse domains (religious and secular), and diverse care disciplines, but also diverse perspectives: "good" refers not only to the moral-spiritual dimension of care but also to the possible effects of compassion on the quality of care and the well-being of patients.

This enterprise is not a systematic-theological one, aiming at the construction of a theology of compassion. Rather, this is a hermeneutical endeavor with a practical-theological edge. My aim is to highlight the possibilities of cooperation between spiritual caregivers and other care professionals, and thus to improve the spiritual dimension of care.

COMPASSION: A POST-SECULAR CROSSOVER TERM

The term *compassion* is suddenly heard all over the place. It has religious origins, though.

Compassion—charity, caring for those who suffer—is considered to be a crucial value in all the great religious and spiritual traditions: it is propagated by Jesus, Muhammad, and the Buddha alike. It is linked to the "Great Commandment" in the Christian tradition (e.g., Matt 22:37–40: "Love God and love your neighbor as yourself"). To give a short working definition: compassion is unselfish love, "centered on the good of the other."[11] Yet it is frequently argued that being compassionate is "good" for the love-giver too.

Public religious figures with different backgrounds find each other in the field of compassion. The present Dalai Lama, for instance, wrote a short piece in *The New York Times* titled "Many Faiths, One Truth."[12] He tells about Thomas Merton and himself discovering compassion as the core of both the Christian and the Buddhist message. He has worked out this idea in his *Toward a True Kinship of Faiths.*[13] Here we see that the concept of compassion is used in an interreligious dialogue, crossing the boundaries between religious traditions—often with an open eye to the dangers

11. Oman, "Compassionate Love," 945.

12. Gyatzo, "Many Faiths, One Truth," *The New York Times*, May 24, 2010.

13. Gyatzo, *Toward a True Kinship of Faiths.*

of religiously motivated intolerance and violence. It is especially (liberal) Christian and Buddhist groups that are inspired by the Dalai Lama, but he is often quoted in humanist and new spirituality circles, too.

In a similar and still broader vein, human solidarity and loving one's neighbor is promoted in the Charter for Compassion, initiated by Karen Armstrong. The principle of compassion, the Charter states,

> Lies at the heart of all religious, ethical and spiritual traditions, calling us always to treat all others as we wish to be treated our- selves. Compassion impels us to work tirelessly to alleviate the suffering of our fellow creatures, to dethrone ourselves from the centre of our world and put another there, and to honour the in- violable sanctity of every single human being, treating everybody, without exception, with absolute justice, equity and respect.[14]

Here we have the great commandment in a "secularized" translation ("treat all others as you wish to be treated yourself"), encompassing humanists, atheists—and all other "people of good faith." From a theological point of view, one may criticize the Charter for its uniform view on religions, its predominantly liberal-theological position, and for a schematic view on compassion, which is not fleshed out. Yet it is telling that Karen Armstrong and her work appeal to big audiences.

The term *compassion* is also heard in the political domain. In 2011, the Christian Democratic Party (CDA) in the Netherlands was thinking about taking "compassion" as a key element in its political program. It should be kept in mind, however, that this is something quite different from the "compassionate conservatism" promoted by George Bush, or the "modern compassion" promoted by the British Prime Minister David Cameron. In American conservative eyes, the Dutch Christian Demo- crats must seem a rather liberal and progressive movement, appealing to Christians and non-Christians alike. In that sense, it fits into the Charter of Compassion movement.

A different field where the term *compassion* is popular these days is what I call the "health and happiness industry." Here the religious roots of compassion are much more at the background. The main message is that "compassion is good for you." In *Ode*, a magazine for "intelligent opti- mists," I found an article about "the compassion instinct."[15] The Dalai Lama is quoted here too: "If you want others to be happy, practice compassion.

14. http://charterforcompassion.org/the-charter/#charter-for-compassion.

15. Gallagher, "The Compassion Instinct." Cf. Keltner et al., *The Compassionate Instinct*.

If you want to be happy, practice compassion."[16] *Ode* refers in this respect to research outcomes and to present-day psychological health gurus (e.g., David Servan-Schreiber) who argue that it is good for you to be compassionate. Also, the journal pays attention to the various kinds of meditative therapeutic practices, such as "compassion meditation," and the popular mindfulness-based therapies, in which self-compassion—being mild to yourself—is a key principle.[17]

These therapeutic practices of compassion are based on research in neuroscience, evolutionary psychology, and positive psychology that shows that caring for others has good effects on the caregivers too. We may mention here the Center for Compassion and Altruism Research and Education (CCARE) at Stanford University—financially sponsored by the Dalai Lama, by the way—and the research on Compassionate Love sponsored by the Fetzer Institute.[18] Later I will focus on this research.

How do we explain this booming interest in compassion across the boundaries of diverse worldviews and societal domains? One might argue that it fits the present experience-driven society (*Erlebnisgesellschaft*),[19] where emotions and personal experience are valued more highly than rationality and functionality. It fits into the modern turn towards the subject, as Taylor has noted. It may also be understood as a reaction to the dominant rational-economical, market-oriented way of "managing" public domains, which is now causing havoc as the financial and economic crisis deepens.

In the following section, I will focus on the use of the term *compassion* in health care. I propose to look at it as a post-secular crossover term, connecting the religious domain of spiritual caregivers to the domains of other health care professionals. I take the term *crossover* from Cloke and Beaumont, who use Habermas's idea[20] about "the possibility of distinct crossover narratives between the secular and the religious" in their analysis of how religious and non-religious organizations in cities work together to improve care, welfare, and justice. This demonstrates new ways of "how the assimilation and mutually reflexive transformation of secular and theological ideas may represent

16. One might argue that this statement of the Dalai Lama is taken out of context. Yet on the very day I was writing this paper, I found the following tweet, by the office of the Dalai Lama, on Twitter: "Compassion is the ultimate source of success."

17. Examples are MBCT (Meditation-Based Cognitive Therapy), developed by Jon Kabat Zinn, and ACT (Acceptance and Commitment Therapy).

18. See http://www.fetzer.org/resources/compassionate-love-research.

19. Schulze, *Die Erlebnisgesellschaft.*

20. Habermas et al., *An Awareness of What Is Missing.*

crossover narratives around which post-secular partnerships can converge around particular ethical precepts and practical needs."[21]

COMPASSION IN HEALTH CARE

There is a lot of talk about compassion in the domain of health care.[22] A compassionate attitude is considered to be an essential aspect of caregiving that is often felt as missing in the market-oriented care sector, where effectiveness and efficiency are leading norms. In this section, I will first present the spiritual caregivers' view on compassion. Second, I will go into compassion as the moral foundation of professional care as such. Third, I will discuss psychological research on the effects of compassionate love in health care.

Compassion as a Connecting Narrative in Spiritual Care

As pointed out earlier, a denominational background has become less important for the professional identity and work of spiritual caregivers—at least in the Netherlands. A group of spiritual caregivers will be very heterogeneous in terms of philosophy of life, denominational affiliation and spiritual resources. Yet most of them recognize the heart of the profession in a common, unwritten philosophy, which has the following elements:[23]

A focus on the client (patient, resident, etc.) as an individual subject. Spiritual caregivers want to approach their client as a fellow human being, as one who is valuable and unique, and thus who deserves respect. (Cf. the Christian/religious/humanist idea that everyone matters to God—think of the parable of the lost sheep.) Therefore, the point of departure in counseling is the client's point of view, experience, and worldview. A point of debate among spiritual caregivers is whether this attitude is contrary to the dominant approach to clients as "objects" of the other health care professionals. The identity of spiritual care would then be a counter-identity, depending

21. Cloke and Beaumont, "Geographies of Postsecular Rapprochement."

22. E.g., Puchalski, "The Role of Spirituality in Health Care," and Volpintesta, "Compassion." For an illustration of a spiritual care program for health care professionals about compassion and presence, see http://www.spcare.org/nl/st-prog/act-int.html. See also http://www.compassionforcare.com/en/.

23. This is based on an analysis of the Dutch *Journal for Spiritual Care* (*Tijdschrift Geestelijke Verzorging*) and of the topics discussed at the yearly meetings of the Dutch Association of Spiritual Counselors in Care Institutions (VGVZ).

on a societal critical view of technocratic health care, representing something which is lacking in the other health care professions. At any rate, all spiritual caregivers, including those who do not agree with this polemical view, would agree that their approach is primarily person-oriented, and not problem- and symptom-oriented. This is why spiritual caregivers favor work on the micro-level: counseling individual clients.[24]

A holistic view of human beings. Spiritual caregivers argue that bodily, psychic, social, and spiritual aspects cannot be separated and are in constant interaction. They have "a passion for wholeness and healing."[25] This is clearly reminiscent of Christian language, as the Dutch words for *heal* and *whole* have the same root as the Dutch word for *salvation* and *holy*.[26]

A relational view of human beings. Spiritual caregivers have a relational view of human beings.[27] The spiritual caregiver and the client, as human beings, are seen as interdependent and share the search for meaning and existential questions. Therefore, the professional relationship between client and spiritual caregiver should be a subject-subject relationship.

"How precious is a vulnerable human being." This line from a poem by the Dutch theologian Okke Jager will be endorsed by almost every spiritual caregiver. Human solidarity—being engaged in the suffering and well-being of their clients—is a central motivation. Again, we hear reminiscences of the Christian heritage: the focus on mercy, charity, and the alleviating of suffering (and also, albeit less, on letting others flourish). This is about having "passion" for human beings and being "compassionate," based on the realization that we are all vulnerable, limited, yet intrinsically valuable persons.

This philosophy of compassion, shared by Dutch spiritual caregivers with different backgrounds, is a multi-interpretable frame that can be filled in a specific way, either religiously or non-religiously. It is, of course, only part of the professional identity of spiritual care,[28] but as an ideological frame it can connect spiritual caregivers and other care professionals, constructing together what "good care" is about.

24. Smeets, *Spiritual Care in a Hospital Setting.*

25. Veltkamp, "In de Ontmoeting Geboren."

26. The relevant Dutch words are *helen, heel, heil,* and *heilig.*

27. Zock, "The Spiritual Caregiver as a Liaison Officer."

28. See the Professional Standard of the Dutch Association of Spiritual Counselors in Care Institutions (VGVZ). This standard elaborates the core tasks of the profession and offers quality criteria for attitude, skills, and knowledge.

Compassion as the Ethical Underpinning of Health Care

A brief Web search shows that the term *vocation* figures a lot in stories told by health care professionals about their motivation and inspiration. It is precisely the passion for and compassion with people that proves to be the main motivational factor in choosing a profession in health care. This may explain the big interest in "intrinsic motivation" in circles of counselors and Human Resource departments.[29]

Two major Dutch ethicists/theologians have published recently on the ethical underpinning of care relationships. Both emphasize other-centered love and human solidarity as the basic motivation of care professionals. Let me briefly sketch their views.

The Roman-Catholic Annelies van Heijst argues in *Professional Loving Care*[30] that professional care consists of two aspects: "craftsmanship" (competence, skills) and "professional love." Professional love involves two values. First, human dignity: every person is unique and valuable in him/herself, and this requires a respectful attitude. It is important to let the other know: "you are important, it matters that you exist." The second value is compassion, human solidarity: being touched by the suffering of others, willing to alleviate suffering, and enjoying the caring itself. These two aspects together lead to what van Heijst calls *a compassionate attitude*—a caring, respectful involvement in patients, as the moral counterpart of all competent and knowledgeable professional care interventions (i.e., craftsmanship). With such an attitude of professional love, one sees the other primarily as a fellow human being. This involves a mutual relationship between caregiver and care recipient, as both are human beings who deserve respect and compassion. Yet one person in the relationship is given priority. The needs of the care recipient have priority in that his or her distress needs to be taken care of; and this need evokes a caring response. However, the caregivers themselves are valuable and unique human beings, too. That is why self-care is a must, and why van Heijst warns against too much self-sacrifice and self-denial. On the other hand, one must be aware of the danger of hidden motives of self-interest. She warns not to get lost in emotional involvement—critical, rational discernment is needed for craftsmanship and for an equitable distribution of care.

---

29. Deci and Ryan, *Intrinsic Motivation and Self-Determination*; Deci and Ryan, "Self-Determination Theory."

30. Van Heijst, *Professional Loving Care*.

The Protestant Frits de Lange develops a similar view in *In the Hand of the Others.*[31] He defines professional care as "the continuation of old-fashioned charity organized with modern means."[32] Professional care is based on the interdependency of caregiver and care recipient, which presupposes a tacit sense of mutual trust.[33] De Lange develops an ethics of compassion (also meant for the political sphere—he was involved as an expert in writing the new party program of the CDA), out of biblically oriented Christian charity. De Lange mentions four pitfalls for professional caregivers: sentimentalizing, self-sacrifice, arbitrariness (compassion should be linked to justice), and paternalism. He distinguishes three environments (*Lebenswelten*) the professional caregiver is engaged in: that of the *metier* (craftsmanship), that of the person (the existential world of subjectivity and personal relationships), and that of the institutional world (concerning the political, economic, and administrative organization of care). Compassion is linked to the personal world. Here the two poles of "career and *caritas*" come together. As van Heijst does, de Lange emphasizes the joy and pleasure in the act of caring (he speaks about "the flow of goodness" (my translation), and departs from a relational view of human beings. Caregiver and care recipient are mutually dependent; they are "in the hands of the other." His theological guide is the Danish theologian Knud E. Løgstrup, who argues that trust is a key feature of care relations: caring appeals to trust, but may also be betrayed. In the ethical theory of care he develops, De Lange makes a plea not only for respecting the other while administering care, but also for stimulating the care recipient's autonomy and responsibility. His view is based on the humanist and Christian principle that people are unique beings, and have both the capacity and the mission to design their uniqueness. But to do this, they need other human beings.

In sum, both van Heijst and de Lange have developed an ethical underpinning of what constitutes "good care." Anchored in the Christian tradition, both authors explicitly aim at a more general moral-philosophical underpinning of care.[34]

---

31. De Lange, *In Andermans Handen.*

32. Ibid., 8 (my translation).

33. He is inspired here by the Danish theologian Knud E. Løgstrup.

34. It would be interesting to examine if and to what extent their ideas are taken up in health care organizations with non-Christian backgrounds.

Psychological Research on Compassionate Love

Being able to give a moral-philosophical underpinning of care will not suffice for contemporary care managers. The laws of economic rationality require that they also consider the effectiveness. What are the effects of a compassionate attitude? In what way does it influence the well-being of caregivers and care recipients and the quality of care? I will present here the new research field that has emerged in the last decade, centered on the concept of "compassionate love."[35]

Social scientific research on aspects of other-centered love, such as empathy, altruism, and forgiveness, is not new. "Agape" (altruistic love), for instance, is considered as one of six romantic love styles. Many love scales include aspects such as altruism, compassion, and sacrifice.[36] The research on "compassionate love" further elaborates on this research. The concept was constructed in a World Health Organization (WHO) project to develop instruments to measure the Quality of Life (WHOQOL), to be used in diverse cultural contexts and countries.[37] One of the working groups had to develop an instrument to assess quality of life for the domain of spirituality and religion (Spirituality, Religiousness, and Personal Beliefs).[38] The group consisted of social scientists and health professionals with diverse religious and nonreligious backgrounds, from all over the world. One of the facets of the domain was "love for others," or "loving-kindness." After considerable discussion, the term *compassionate love* came up as a compromise term for this facet: the Buddhists preferred the term *compassion*; the Muslims preferred the term *love*, to emphasize the affective component. (The second best term all agreed on was *altruistic love*.) So the term *compassionate love* emerged from multifaith conversations. All participants agreed that compassionate love encompasses two aspects: "addressing human suffering and encouraging human flourishing."[39] By the way, this double meaning is explained with a reference to the Christian term *passio*, which can mean "suffering" (*cum-passio*: to suffer with) but also "being passionate," or having passion for something or someone.

Fehr and Sprecher argue on the basis of research of laypeople's understanding of the term that the concept cannot be rendered in a classical

---

35. Fehr et al., *Science of Compassionate Love*; Oman, "Compassionate Love."

36. Fehr and Sprecher, "Compassionate Love."

37. Underwood, "Compassionate Love," 8–9.

38. WHOQOL-SRPB Group 2012; cf. Underwood, "Compassionate Love."

39. Underwood, "Compassionate Love," 9.

definition.[40] Rather, it is a prototype concept, that is: a cloud of characteristics which can be distinguished, of which some may be more central to the concept than others. Besides, this may vary from culture to culture. Fehr and Sprecher conclude that although the term *compassionate love* as such is not heard often, laypeople have a coherent understanding of what the concept is about. It is clearly related to real-life experiences. The concept as used by experts (researchers) differs in some respect from this real-life prototype concept.

Lynn Underwood[41] further developed the concept of compassionate love, distinguishing the following characteristics:

1. Valuing the other at a fundamental level. "Some degree of respect for the other person is necessary . . . rather than pity. . . . To be pitied does not elevate us as human beings."[42]

2. Free choice for the other. Compassionate love reflects a free choice to love, rather than being primarily instinctually driven (or, of course, something coerced).

3. Cognitively accurate understanding, to at least some degree, of the situation. This includes understanding "something of the needs and feelings of the person to be loved, and what might be appropriate to truly enhance the other's well-being."[43]

4. Response of the heart. "Some sort of emotional engagement and understanding [seems] to be needed to love fully in an integrated way."[44]

5. Openness and receptivity. An open attitude "allows one to see opportunities for the expression of compassionate love in specific situations."[45] "Specifically religious inspiration is not a necessary component . . . [but] the definition needs to leave room for this kind of divine input or open receptive quality."[46]

---

40. Fehr and Sprecher, "Prototype Analysis," 344.

41. Underwood, "Compassionate Love" and "The Human Experience of Compassionate Love."

42. Underwood, "Compassionate Love," 7.

43. Ibid.

44. Ibid., 8.

45. Underwood, "Human Experience of Compassionate Love," 73.

46. Underwood "Compassionate Love," 8, quoted in Oman, "Compassionate Love," 946–47.

Thus defined, compassionate love is clearly distinguishable from previously well-researched constructs such as empathy, altruism, and forgiveness. Underwood further develops a working model to do research on compassionate love. She distinguishes three aspects.[47] First, there is the "substrate"—the individual in his/her context: compassionate love involves emotional, physical, and cognitive life-dimensions, and takes place in a specific sociocultural environment. Therefore, one has to look at the specific situation in which compassion is researched (urgent or non-urgent needs; appeal or no appeal; close others or strangers; professional or private context, etc.). Second, it is important to consider motivation and discernment in compassionate behavior. And, third, one has to look at the results: attitudes, actions, and scores on scales of well-being.

For the theme of this paper, I want to draw attention to the second aspect of Underwood's working model, that of motivation and discernment. In compassionate love, both are necessary. Here we see similar observations to those of Van Heijst and De Lange. The motivation in compassionate love, Underwood argues, is always mixed: self-centered motives are always there and can get in the way of good care. Therefore, it is more appropriate to define compassionate love as "*centered on* the good of the other" instead of as a *completely altruistic* attitude (italics mine). The aspect of discernment, on the other hand, is very important in weighing matters cognitively: a critical, analytical attitude is necessary for compassionate love. It is not enough to have good intentions, to be affected by the needs of the other, and to want to help. One must be able to weigh self-interest versus the interests of others (i.e., putting on one's own oxygen mask first). One must also consider short-term and long-term effects and conflicting demands (for instance between close and distant others). Moreover, one must be aware of the power balance (giving versus receiving) and of the tension between justice and mercy (e.g., altruistic punishment: being strict for the good of the other).[48]

A lot of research has been done using this concept of compassionate love. On the whole, the research suggests that compassionate love is indeed "good for you"—both when you are on the receiving and on the giving end of care. Recently, Oman has evaluated the research on

47. Underwood, "Compassionate Love," 10.

48. A point of discussion is in how far "automatic" heroic and altruistic behavior go. New research in neurobiology, evolutionary psychology, and ethnology shows that empathy and altruistic behavior are rooted in deep parts of the brain, although they are primary in the neocortex, where cognitive capacities for discernment reside. Cf. Waal, *The Age of Empathy.*

compassionate love sponsored by the Fetzer Institute.[49] He concludes that a lot of work still needs to be done regarding methodical issues, such as the measurement tools and the operationalization of concepts. Further, there are only a few research projects that encompass all the aspects of the concept of compassionate love. Projects were concerned, for instance, with the motivation of caregivers, the experiences of care recipients, and the correlations between compassionate love, on the one hand, and stress reduction, burnout, and self-efficacy of caregivers, on the other. A general conclusion is that compassionate love reduces the risk of burnout of caregivers, leads to less stress and to better mental health, physical, and psychosocial well-being. On the side of patients, compassion-oriented meditation may have a positive effect on pain and coping.

CONCLUSION

In the previous section, we saw that there is a shared philosophy of compassion emerging in health care. The concept of compassion as professed by Dutch spiritual caregivers closely resembles that of the two presented Christian ethicists and the concept of compassionate love as it is developed by the WHO researchers. Both the ethicists and the researchers make a distinction between two indispensable aspects of care: human compassion and professional craftmanship. Both groups emphasize the necessity of self-care and the danger of power imbalance—issues which are dealt with in handbooks of spiritual care and the Professional Standard of the VGVZ (the Dutch Association of Spiritual Counselors in Care Institutions). Thus, we may conclude that at present the moral-spiritual language of compassion is a dominant narrative in health care, indicating the motivation and inspiration that should be inherent in all care practices. Compassion is considered to be the indispensable companion of competent and effective care interventions; and this goes for every care discipline, spiritual care included.

Although this shared narrative of compassion may not be a "grand" narrative in the old sense of the word, it definitely has a connecting, cross-over function in our post-secular age. It captures a dimension of human life in general and of care practices in particular, that succeeds in transcending different worldviews and cultural contexts, and that can connect diverse

49. Oman, "Compassionate Love."

health care professionals in administering "good care."[50] The importance of compassion is demonstrated by way of ethical and theological-philosophical reasoning, and by way of research on its effectiveness. We can speak of "good care" when care practices have both a sound moral-spiritual underpinning and good effects.

I conclude by mentioning two challenges this shared narrative of compassion in health care brings for theologians and for spiritual caregivers. First, a thorough interdisciplinary discussion between theology and psychology is required. Theologians should take seriously the outcomes of psychological research, and consider the possibility that what we take as morally or theologically "good" may not have good effects at all. But what if that is the case? Can we simply argue that the moral-spiritual and the psychological perspectives are incompatible? In my view, a dialogical view is more productive than such either/or thinking. The outcomes of research could and should inform theological and moral discussions, while the moral-spiritual dimension could and should be taken into account in psychological research. Yet an important issue for theological reflection remains that of the intrinsic versus the extrinsic function of compassion. Is the instrumental use of compassion detrimental to compassion as an intrinsic value? We can learn here from a similar discussion taking place about mindfulness-based therapies. What does it mean that these are loosened from their religious roots, and are used purely in the service of health gains, such as the reduction of depressive symptoms? I think that, *sub specie aeternitatis*, it is a theological task to take different angles, to warn against being swayed by the issues of the day, and to guard against a one-dimensional approach to human beings.

Second, spiritual caregivers are faced with the task of underpinning their profession in a new way. In the post-secular context, it is no longer sufficient to refer to a specific philosophy of life, either religious or non-religious, as the core of their profession. Nor is the philosophy of compassion an adequate alternative here, as this is shared with other care professionals. Rather, spiritual caregivers should focus on what their contribution to care as a whole consists of. In short, they are experts in the spiritual dimension of human functioning. As experts in existential issues, ethical dilemmas and choices, and philosophies of life, they assist people in the search for

---

50. The narrative of compassion may also have a crossover function in other societal domains, such as social services and politics. One could consider, for instance, the cooperation between FBOs (faith-based organizations) and non-FBOs.

meaning with the help of cultural resources. Their task is to show how the spiritual dimension is inextricably linked with the bodily, psychic, and social dimensions. This requires not only having one's own philosophy of life available as an instrument in the service of others, but also a solid hermeneutical, ethical, and psychological training, and knowledge of different worldviews. Moreover, I argue that an important theological task is to take the lead in developing a shared philosophy of compassion. Instead of claiming "compassion" as their core business only, spiritual caregivers must use the emerging philosophy of compassion as a post-secular narrative to work together with other health care professionals, aiming at "good care." Let us face the challenge!

13

A Call to Confession

Or What Protestant Christians May Learn from Orthodox and Roman Catholic Christians[1]

–Allan Hugh Cole Jr.

Confession is a conversion and a call to discipleship . . . Genuine community is not established until confession takes place.

—DIETRICH BONHOEFFER[2]

BROACHING THE PRACTICE OF CONFESSION

Protestant Christians do well to reclaim a practice of private confession, along with acts of public confession in the context of worship, as they seek to be faithful to God and to experience healing, reconciliation, and peace as concerns personal transgressions.

A few years ago, I began trying to test the aforementioned claim. I sent a questionnaire to 169 people exploring questions of confession. By

---

1. A version of this essay was published previously in *Insights: The Faculty Journal of Austin Seminary* (Spring 2010). Used by permission.

2. Bonhoeffer, *Spiritual Care*, 63.

confession I mean disclosing personal pain, and especially that associated with one's own transgressions, to God *and* to other persons. I asked recipients to respond to six sets of questions related to "disclosing something of significance to you—and something that was private, personal, awkward, or embarrassing—to another person (or persons)." The first question called for them to identify and explain what they disclosed. In subsequent questions I asked about the act of disclosing. Among other details, I wanted to know to whom people disclosed and also how it felt, at the time and later, to have made the disclosure. Using an online research tool to distribute the survey, respondents' identities were unknown to me. They could be as honest and forthright as they wanted without feeling awkward about my linking particular disclosures to them.

I posed these questions to test a long-held belief. I believe that most people want and even need to disclose their personal pain, and especially their transgressions. To use biblical language, we have the desire and need to confess our sins, not only to God but also to other persons; and not confessing them proves painful and destructive. Perhaps we recognize the wisdom of Proverbs even if we do not always heed it, that "one who conceals one's sins does not prosper, but whoever confesses and renounces them finds mercy" (Prov 28:13). To state it differently, we live with a desire and need to "come clean" and to aim differently in life when we have "missed the mark," the literal meaning of the word *sin*. Our desire and need persist even amid the most hurtful and egregious of our transgressions. When we confess our sins, whether to God or others, we experience relief, healing, grace, and gratefulness. As a result, we live less burdened lives, but we also experience a greater sense of accountability (to God and to other people) and a greater spiritual maturity. All of these observations inform one facet of the long-held belief that I wanted to test—that we have a need to confess our sins to other persons, and that doing so brings "God's benefits" (Ps 103:2).

On the other hand (and this gets us to a second facet of my belief), to the extent that they disclose personal pain and especially personal transgressions to others, many professing Christians do so more readily and frequently with their spouses, family members, close friends, or therapists, and less readily and frequently with their ministers or fellow church members. Furthermore, clergy rarely disclose to their colleagues, mentors, or judicatory-level spiritual advisors (e.g., bishops, district superintendents, or executive presbyters).

In my survey I intentionally did not ask directly about "confessing" or "confession." I wanted to see what types of responses would be offered to a more general request that did not come with particularly religious over-tones.[3] I *was* interested, however, in learning whether any respondents, in identifying a particular disclosure, would use the language of "confess" or "confession," or the language of "sin." Whether they used any of this language or not, I wanted to know what informed their acts of disclosure, how it made them feel to make these disclosures, and, as significant as any of this, to *whom* they disclosed and why they chose the person or persons.

HOW WE CONFESS

Whereas some respondents reported the transgressions of others and how these had caused personal pain, more respondents identified their own transgressions and described the pain that these had caused themselves and others. Thus, the majority of respondents identified a personal sin that they confessed to another person and then described that experience.

I did not assume all responses would meet a definition of confession, but most responses did meet my definition and a large number of responses also included language of "confessing" or "confession." Only a few respons-es, however, included language of sin. Moreover, almost everyone who reported and reflected on a personal transgression also noted that the act of sharing helped them feel better, live differently, and move forward less burdened than they had been prior to making their confession. Most re-spondents also said that they would make the disclosure again to the same person in a similar manner. Several added that they only wished they had done so sooner. Confession proves helpful to many people.

At the same time, almost all respondents (82 percent) disclosed to a spouse, close friend, family member, or therapist. A relative few reported making disclosures to a minister (10 percent) or to a member of their faith community (6 percent). Note that "minister" here refers not only to one's pastor but also to one's clergy colleagues and supervisors, whether in local congregations or in institutional settings such as hospitals, and also to one's spiritual director, which respondents defined in various ways. When we narrow the term *minister* to apply only to one's pastor, barely 3 percent re-ported making their disclosure to him or her. As I expected, whereas many people reported disclosing their sins to other people and finding benefits

3. The large majority of recipients and respondents to the questionnaire identify as professing Christians, and most identify as Protestants.

with this, a relative few reported making disclosures to their pastors or siblings in faith.[4]

While people may confess to close associates, it has become a popular practice to "confess" anonymously at various websites. These include Daily Confession.com, Group Hug (http://www.jfry.co/grouphug/), and Secret Confessions (http://www.secret-confessions.com). It has also become popular to "confess" through postings on various social networks like Facebook or Twitter—or, in the case of celebrities, to confess through mass media via the use of their publicists. All of these approaches point to the fact that people want and need to confess. But these methods for maintaining anonymity remove some of the hard work and pain of confessing face-to-face to another human being and, consequently, remove some of the healing and character-building potential found in more personal acts of confession.

A CALL TO CONFESSION

I am advocating for a broad-based approach to confession that includes *private* confession as well as corporate confession. This approach requires intentional efforts toward confessing our sins not only to God and not merely in the context of public worship, essential as these practices remain and which numerous Christian traditions rightfully embrace. We must also confess to other Christians, including our ministers, in both liturgical settings *and* in more intimate and even private venues. For instance, we need confession in public worship, when many traditions of Christianity include corporate prayers of confession that worshippers recite together and then receive words of assurance that God has forgiven them their sins. We also need confession in one-on-one, face-to-face, encounters between Christians, where liturgical forms (confessional acts, prayers, words of assurance) may or may not be included. The latter practice is sometimes referred to as "private confession." Although less common in the Roman Catholic tradition since Vatican II, private confession, or, more properly, confession that occurs in the Sacrament of Reconciliation, continues to be practiced. Moreover, the act of confessing to a priest, which occurs in the Sacrament

---

4. It is possible, of course, that spouses, family members, and close friends would be siblings in faith (fellow church members), but presumably the determining factor in choosing to make a disclosure to these people was familial or filial relationships, not one's status as a fellow church member, Christian, or believer. Respondents indicated that this is an accurate interpretation when detailing why they chose their particular confessors.

of Penance, continues to be normative in Orthodox Christian traditions. Rarely, however, do Protestant Christians embrace the practice of private confession, as suggested by responses to my survey.

Reformers such as Martin Luther and John Calvin, and more contemporary theologians such as Dietrich Bonhoeffer, recognized the importance of so-called private confession along with public confession, and each urged that all Christians embrace and practice both forms. Calvin states beautifully the benefits of confessing with and to our fellow Christians when he writes, "We should lay our burdens on one another's breasts, to receive among ourselves mutual counsel, mutual compassion, and mutual consolation," and we should follow these efforts with prayer for one another.[5] With Calvin's words in mind, I write particularly for Protestant Christians, a group to which I belong, to encourage us to embrace what he, Luther, Bonhoeffer, and others have recognized as benefits for the faithful life, namely, the regular practice of confession broadly conceived.

Calvin advocated for both public and private confession, but he explicitly ties the latter to "the cure of souls." He notes that scripture "approves two forms of private confession."[6] The first is confession "made for our own sake," as referred to in the Letter of James: "Therefore confess your sins to one another, and pray for one another, so that you may be healed. The prayer of the righteous is powerful and effective" (Jas 5:16). The second form of confession aims to assist our neighbor, "to appease him and to reconcile him to us if through fault of ours he has been in any way injured."

Calvin also advocated for Christians making particular appeals to their pastors to serve as confessors and for pastors to welcome this privilege. He writes, "We must also preferably choose pastors inasmuch as they should be judged especially qualified above the rest. Now I say that they are better fitted than the others because the Lord has appointed them by the very calling of the ministry to instruct us by word of mouth to overcome and correct our sins, and also to give us consolations through the assurance of pardon [Matt 16:19; 18:18; John 20:23]."[7] Making an even stronger appeal, Calvin adds: "Let every believer remember that, if he be privately troubled and afflicted with a sense of sins, so that without outside help he is unable to free himself from them, it is a part of his duty not to neglect what the Lord has offered to him by way of remedy. Namely, that, for his

5. Calvin, *Institutes*, 1:630.

6. Ibid., 1:636–37.

8. Ibid., 1:636.

relief, he should use private confession to his own pastor; and for his solace, he should beg the private help of him whose duty it is, both publicly and privately, to comfort the people of God by the gospel teaching."[8]

For Calvin, private confession takes on the status of a duty. Christians have a duty to respond faithfully to what God has offered them—namely, the opportunity to confess to one another but also to hear one another's confessions, and to dispense comfort to one another by appealing to the gospel's promise of God's forgiveness. All Christians have these duties and responsibilities. However, pastors hold particular responsibilities in this regard by virtue of their calling and office to which "the Lord has appointed them." Calvin refers to pastors as "ordained witnesses and sponsors of [divine mercy] to assure our consciences of forgiveness of sins."[9] To be sure, Calvin has a high view of the pastoral office—one that approaches the status of sacramental—and high expectations for pastors as curers of souls. In my estimate, his view warrants the church's reclaiming, particularly in the present age, and not simply for the purposes of confession but for the purposes of ministry more broadly conceived.

Calvin's thinking about confession may be traced to Luther, who suggested that Christians should confess three ways: in daily prayers to God, in public worship, and also in more intimate conversations with other Christians.[10] Dietrich Bonhoeffer largely concurred with Luther's and Calvin's thinking, referring to confession as "the heart of spiritual care." Bonhoeffer especially supported the practice of personal confession offered to other Christians, including pastors and fellow church members, recalling Luther's well-known statement from the *Large Catechism*: "When I exhort people to confession, I am exhorting them to be Christians."[11]

Luther, Calvin, and Bonhoeffer each recognized that scripture pays a good deal of attention to the act of confession, which indicates its significance for people of faith. As the psalmist declares, "For day and night your hand was heavy upon me; my strength was dried up as by the heat of summer. Then I acknowledged my sin to you, and I did not hide my iniquity; I said, 'I will confess my transgressions to the Lord,' and you forgave the guilt of my sin. Therefore let all who are faithful offer prayer to you; at a time of distress, the rush of mighty waters shall not reach them" (Ps

8. Ibid., 1:636–37.

9. Ibid., 1:636.

10. Bonhoeffer, *Spiritual Care*, 60.

11. Ibid., 61.

32:4–6). Similarly, as the First Letter of John points out, "If we confess our sins, he who is faithful and just will forgive us our sins and cleanse us from all unrighteousness" (1 John 1:9). Whereas Protestant Christians regularly confess their sins publicly in Sunday worship, they do so less regularly in more private or intimate settings. Yet the Bible tells us that the practice of confessing fulfills one's responsibility toward God, but that it also serves to ease one's burdens when one shares them with other people of faith: "Confess your sins to one another, and pray for one another, so that you may be healed" (Jas 5:16).

PRIVATE CONFESSION OFFERS BENEFITS

How exactly does private confession ease burdens?[12] Confessing our sins aloud to another person helps us identify those sins with directness and honesty. This practice also encourages us to take greater ownership of our sins and greater responsibility for their effects precisely because we have shared them with others who may hold us accountable.

Several additional benefits may follow. As Bonhoeffer suggests, these benefits include deepened and new relationships, or what he calls "breakthroughs."[13] These include *breakthroughs with the community of faith*, which we recognize as a community of sinners in need of redemption but also of people like ourselves who will hear our confessions, which we value more than ever; *breakthroughs with the cross of Christ*, which involves a deeper sharing in Christ's suffering and humiliation because we recognize our own complicity in sin as well as the complicity of others; *breakthroughs in our new life in Christ*, our discipleship, as we turn from a sinful past to follow Jesus (Bonhoeffer calls this conversion); and also *breakthroughs relating to the profound assurance of our status as forgiven by God*, which comes with certitude of God's love and which Christians may dispense to one another generously. Moreover, by helping us understand our experience of sin more deeply and authentically, confession made to other Christians fosters the *breakthrough of learning to accept responsibility for our transgressions* more readily by strengthening our resolve to go forward living differently than before; that is, in a different relationship to the sin or burden. This kind of resolve may lead to yet another benefit, namely, that our struggle holds less power in our life.

12. For a fuller discussion of the power of confession, see Cole, *Be Not Anxious*, 210–13.

13. Bonhoeffer, *Life Together; Prayerbook of the Bible*, 108–18.

Openly acknowledging burdens (including sins) fosters courage. When we confess, we discover that although our struggles or transgressions may be significant and enduring, we can acknowledge them without being consumed by them. Acknowledging transgressions, especially to another person, often serves to remove the "suffering in suffering" that comes with denial or secrecy, both of which can lead to the assumption that we alone struggle *and* that we struggle alone.[14]

In light of these benefits, we need to reclaim private confession with a minister *and* with siblings in faith. We must also engage the more common practice of corporate confession in worship, perhaps as we continue confessing to spouses, close friends, family members, therapists, and other close associates, too. Yet private confession should hold a central place in our lives of discipleship.

The basis for private confession lies *not* in the need to have a pastor or priest intercede for us before God or absolve our sins. Luther was correct in recognizing the theological error informing such a view of intercession. Rather, confessing verbally to another human being, and especially one who represents the Christian faith, involves a kind of intimacy and truth-telling that occurs against the backdrop of God's promises in Jesus Christ, which offer forgiveness, redemption, and peace.

Having our own truth-telling met by these promises enriches our relationships with God and the faith community, and it also changes our relationship to our sins. Specifically, this practice serves efforts to "bear one another's burdens" (Gal 6:2) in ways that scripture calls for, so that we no longer carry our sins alone. This practice also serves efforts to "externalize" what has been confessed.[15] By "externalize" I mean that we can, in a sense, objectify our sins by taking them out of us, examining them and relating to them in different, less destructive ways. In turn, we may recognize our sin as something that was once "in us" and destructive for us, but now is "outside us" (external to us) and holds less power over us. Similarly, we may view our sin as not essential to who we are—as not being definitive in our lives—but rather as a problem, burden, struggle, or evil that has affected us.

14. "Suffering in suffering" is Jürgen Moltmann's phrase. See Moltmann, *Crucified God*, 46.

15. Here I appeal to a concept of narrative therapy, "externalizing the problem," that was identified and first developed by Michael White and David Epston in the 1980s and early 1990s and was influenced by the thought of Michel Foucault. See White and Epston, *Narrative Means to Therapeutic Ends*; Parry and Doan, *Story Re-visions*; and White, *Maps of Narrative Practice*.

Although this problem could affect us again, we see that it need not affect us in the same way, if it affects us at all.

This act of externalizing our sin (our problem) allows us also to work with it, and live with it, in new and presumably more faithful ways. One may learn to engage in an externalizing process through self-talk, meaning without speaking with another person. However, externalization proves most effective when utilized in interpersonal conversations because others hear us, receive us in our brokenness, and yet hold us accountable as we seek to "sin no more." Christians benefit from regularly conducting these conversations with one another against the backdrop of God's promises for forgiveness and redemption in Jesus Christ, which includes assurances of reconciliation.

The practice of confession is underutilized in Protestant faith communities. Although many traditions include a corporate prayer of confession in worship services, this alone proves insufficient for meeting many people's needs to disclose sin and other personal pain. Further evidence for this underutilization may be found in the fact that many Protestant Christians look easily and regularly to therapists and counselors to serve as their confessors. This phenomenon certainly confirms the common need for one to disclose one's struggles to another person, and I heartily endorse this practice. At the same time, this phenomenon raises questions regarding why comparatively few Protestant Christians think of their ministers or fellow church members as primary persons to whom personal pain, including sinfulness, may be disclosed.

WHAT GETS IN THE WAY OF CONFESSION?

If disclosing our personal transgressions (sins) privately to our siblings in faith and especially to our ministers is both faithful and helpful, and yet proves difficult for many of us, especially as compared to reciting corporate prayers of confession during public worship services, then we do well to inquire further about some reasons for this difficulty. I want to mention a few that may hold a particularly powerful influence and to suggest how we may move beyond their effects to embrace confession and its benefit in our lives.

First, people feel ashamed to disclose their transgressions to "church folks."[16] This shame tends to link with assumptions, whether implicit or explicit, that one must be good, pure, or otherwise "have it all together" to go to church and take part in the faith community. These assumptions may prove especially influential when one's experience in the church has been marked by hurtful criticism or judgment coming from church members or leaders. This is true when such criticism is aimed toward oneself, but also when it is aimed toward others. In other words, when members of a faith community openly criticize, judge, or otherwise speak harshly of those who fall short of expectations for the Christian life—for those who commit sins—this criticism may make any who hear it more reluctant to share their own burdens tied to personal transgressions.

In this same vein, my own experiences, as minister and church member, tell me that even the best intentioned congregations may not create as inviting an environment as they could create to receive people with messy lives. As Bonhoeffer notes, "Many Christians would be unimaginably horrified if a real sinner were suddenly to turn up among the pious. So we remain alone with our sin, trapped in lies and hypocrisy, for we are in fact sinners."[17] At the same time, however, as Bonhoeffer reminds us, "the grace of the gospel, which is so hard for the pious to comprehend, confronts us with the truth. It says to us, you are a sinner, a great, unholy sinner. Now come, as the sinner you are, to your God who loves you. For God wants you as you are, not desiring anything from you—a sacrifice, a good deed—but rather desiring you alone."

With regard to creating a different congregational environment, one that recognizes and even prizes the grace of the gospel, I have in mind an environment that invites people to "come as you are, *especially* as you struggle with imperfections and continue toward becoming the person God desires you to be." In faith communities where such invitations remain absent or less obvious, people participate in church life most fully when they have it

16. I especially have in mind here church experiences informed by what Donald Capps has termed "shame-based theologies." These fail to distinguish between feelings of guilt linked to "what we have done or not done," which are more easily dealt with, and feelings of shame linked to "who I am," which often prove more difficult and even destructive. Shame-based theologies inform and perpetuate experiences of self-estrangement, self-deficiency, and self-depletion. See Capps, *The Depleted Self*.

17. Bonhoeffer, *Life Together; Prayerbook of the Bible*, 108.

more or less "together," a status that waxes and wanes for all of us, and these same people feel less inclined to share their struggles with messiness (sin).

How might we do better in this regard? It takes concerted efforts by church leaders and church members alike to cultivate an ethos of hospitality toward sinners. By that I mean an ethos of "come as you are"—namely, as a sinner in need of redemption. Fostering this ethos becomes especially difficult when one views it as possible only by not taking sin and its effects seriously. Congregations that seek to promote inclusiveness often get dubbed as endorsing an "anything goes" creed. But faith communities can take sin seriously, by which I mean recognizing its destruction and working with a commitment to condemn it and curb it, without becoming exclusive of those with messy lives (and we all have messy lives). We need look no further than to Jesus for our cue here. He is the one who said to the woman caught in adultery, "Go your way, and from now on do not sin again" (John 8:11), but also the one who said to those who wished to stone this woman, "Let anyone among you who is without sin be the first to throw a stone at her" (John 8:7). Jesus made a similar observation to those who faulted him for eating with sinners and tax collectors, who represent in scripture people with the messiest of lives: "Those who are well have no need of a physician, but those who are sick; I have come to call not the righteous but sinners" (Mark 2:17; see also Matt 9:12 and Luke 5:31–32). Jesus took sin seriously and condemned it even as he continued to welcome sinners with open arms. Congregations that make this kind of hospitality explicit in their shared lives invite people of faith to confess their sins with the confidence that they do so among kindred souls, all of whom stand in need of the assurance of God's forgiveness and redemption as promised by the gospel.

Ministers and other leaders may also foster a congregational ethos marked by Jesus' example of hospitality as they have the courage to admit publicly their own mistakes, transgressions, struggles, or life's messiness in appropriate ways. I say "appropriate" ways in that a line exists between sharing one's shortcomings as an invitation for others to do the same while pointing to the grace and mercies of God, and sharing one's shortcomings as a way merely to draw attention to oneself or one's situation. I am advocating the former approach, for when ministers or other leaders become too much the focus of the sermon, the lesson, or another aspect of congregational life in which they disclose their transgressions, their disclosures draw attention away from others in the group and thereby carry less redemptive possibilities for them. As I often put it in class, "Better to bleed a little during an occasional Sunday's sermon than to hemorrhage from the pulpit week after week."

An ethos of hospitality also arises from ministers and church members squelching their own harsh judgments of "sinners" and as they challenge persons in their communities making similar judgments. It's one thing to recognize sin and to condemn it. It's something much different to further humiliate or exclude those who have missed the mark, especially "since all have sinned and fall short of the glory of God" (Rom 3:23).

An ethos of hospitality also follows from congregations engaging ministries with individuals and groups of persons who have identified publicly that they don't have it all together, that they have messy lives. Of course, if we attune ourselves to those we sit beside in our pews, or if we look into our mirrors, we'll recognize messy lives there, too. But what I have in mind here includes ministry beyond one's church doors, to persons who note their struggles with sins related to such things as addictions, poverty, racism, sexuality, mental illness, excess, or greed, all of which may be our own sins, too. I have in mind, further, ministries that entail more than simply financial support. I mean ministries that call us to sit face-to-face and arm-in-arm with those living messy lives, which we may discover resemble our own lives in certain ways. These ministries reflect faithfulness to Jesus' example and calling upon those who follow him. These ministries also serve to give us permission, and even courage, to address our own messes more directly and to be more inclined to journey with others through theirs, all of which may foster a greater propensity to share these messes with others in our faith communities. Extending hospitality encourages Christians to face our transgressions more intentionally and in solidarity precisely because we recognize that "*all* have sinned and fall short of the glory of God" (Rom 3:23).

There is nothing novel in what I suggest here. We find ample evidence in both scripture and tradition for hospitality, particularly toward sinners, marking a faithful approach to following Jesus. Furthermore, many congregations already practice this kind of faithfulness to Jesus' example. Yet given the current attractions that large groups of Christians have to a gospel of success or the prosperity gospel, which perpetuates the idea that with God's love and favor come various forms of inevitable success—financial, relational, spiritual, physical, or other—we need to hear louder, clearer, and more informed voices among those who understand and embrace a different approach to the Christian life because they hold to a different Good News.

Another reason for difficulty with private confession relates to ministers and church members not keeping sensitive information in their confidences, especially when this failure leads to destructive gossip. I have known ministers and church folks who have difficulties with this practice of keeping confidences. A result is that people feel reluctant to disclose their most personal experiences, particularly awkward or embarrassing ones, because they fear that these may become more widely known and also that others in the community may judge or criticize them. I have known ministers who were excellent preachers, teachers, and administrators, but their pastoral ministry was inevitably compromised because people in their care did not trust them to keep appropriate confidences. The same could be said about other people I have known in congregational life, and in seminary life, too. Perhaps this essay will prompt readers to consider their own practices with keeping appropriate confidences and not engaging in destructive gossip.

So convinced am I that many of us need improvement with this practice of keeping confidences, that in my pastoral care courses I speak of it directly and repetitively. I underscore my belief that at the end of the day ministers (whether ordained or not) maintain their integrity by holding what others share with them as sacrosanct, which means that we view it as privileged information and that it does not become fodder for destructive gossip or other unnecessary discussion. Unfortunately, many church members perceive that sensitive information they share with others might not remain undisclosed.

A few simple practices encourage us to do better in this regard. One entails reminding ourselves of the privilege and responsibility tied to listening to another person with pastoral ears. When someone opens his or her life to us, inviting us to share in its intimate details, we may simply say to ourselves (and maybe to the one who opens up to us) something like this: "I will treat this information as sacred and I am honored that you would entrust me with it." And repeating this several times, at least to ourselves, may serve to help us internalize this practice. Another approach involves conveying this same value to the curious in our midst—clergy colleagues, church members, family members (whether our own or others') who want to know the "scoop"—such that we indicate that we take our duties and responsibilities as "confessors" seriously because we recognize that these come from God. If we embrace a high view of the pastoral office, or a high view of the life of discipleship, we cannot discount the role of keeping confidences for maintaining Christian integrity and faithfulness.

HOW WE MAY CONFESS

One's approach to confessing with a minister or with siblings in faith may vary, and several approaches may prove fruitful. We may choose to meet informally with these persons and simply share from the heart what we need to share, such that no particular method is required. I encourage this approach, and some may feel most drawn to it, especially if they identify most closely and comfortably with a less liturgically centered Christian tradition. Here, however, I want to suggest a way to practice private *and* corporate confession more intentionally while incorporating liturgical aids.[18] Specifically, I want to mention three rich examples of what may be termed "Confessional Liturgies" and to include one of these liturgies for closer consideration. Space will not allow comment on them, but I offer them in hopes that readers will consider making use of them in their confessional practices.

The first liturgy, a rite called "The Reconciliation of a Penitent," is found in the *Book of Common Prayer* of the Episcopal Church, in the section "Pastoral Offices."[19] The second liturgy, called "Individual Confession and Forgiveness," is found in the Evangelical Lutheran Church in America's *Lutheran Book of Worship*.[20]

A third liturgy, found in the Presbyterian Church (USA)'s *Book of Common Worship*, is called "A Service of Repentance and Forgiveness for Use with a Penitent Individual."[21] It has a rather cumbersome title but it offers a sound approach to confession with one's minister and one's siblings in faith. Here is the order of service:

A Service of Repentance and Forgiveness for

18. I have written more extensively about the benefits of incorporating liturgical resources for the life of prayer, and similar benefits apply to the practice of confession. See Cole, *Life of Prayer*, esp. 101–11.

19 An online version may be found at http://www.bcponline.org. See also *Book of Common Prayer*, 446–52.

20. *Lutheran Book of Worship*, 322–23.

21. In a separate survey, I asked one hundred people, most of whom identify as members of the Presbyterian Church (USA) (57 percent), about their familiarity with this particular service. Although 30 percent of respondents were familiar with the service, only 5 percent had participated in one (this includes all the Presbyterians who responded). However, with regard to "services of wholeness and healing," 87 percent of respondents were familiar with these, and 84 percent had participated in one. Thirty-five percent of respondents had participated in such a service ten times or more.

Use with a Penitent Individual[22]

Outline
Invitation to Confession
Prayer of Confession
Declaration of Forgiveness
The Peace

Invitation to Confession
The minister . . . or other member of the Christian community invites their confession of sin together, saying:

If we confess our sins, God who is faithful and just will forgive us our sins and cleanse us from all unrighteousness (1 John 1:9).

God, be merciful to me, a sinner.

N., join me in a prayer of confession.

Prayer of Confession (prayed in unison)
Merciful God, we confess that we have sinned against you in thought, word, and deed, by what we have done, and by what we have left undone. We have not loved you with our whole heart and mind and strength; we have not loved our neighbors as ourselves. In your mercy forgive what we have been, help us amend what we are, and direct what we shall be, so that we may delight in your will and walk in your ways, to the glory of your holy name.

Declaration of Forgiveness
The assurance of God's forgiving grace is declared to the penitent in these or similar words:

The mercy of the Lord is from everlasting to everlasting. I declare to you, in the name of Jesus Christ, you are forgiven. May the God of mercy, who forgives all your sins, strengthen you in all goodness, and by the power of the Holy Spirit keep you in eternal life. Amen.

The Peace
May the peace of God, which passes all understanding, keep your heart and your mind in Christ Jesus. ***Amen.***

A sign of peace may be shared here.

---

22. *Book of Common Worship*. Note that "A Service for Wholeness for Use with an Individual" may be utilized in conjunction with the "Service for Repentance and Forgiveness." See 1018–22.

SERVING ONE ANOTHER THROUGH CONFESSION

Above my desk in my office at Austin Seminary hangs a painting titled *Divine Servant*.[23] It depicts a scene from what we call Maundy Thursday, when Jesus met with his disciples on the night before he was killed and demonstrated his love and care for them through the humble act of washing their feet. While washing Peter's feet and hearing his objections to this act, Jesus' words to his disciples were: "If I, your Lord and Teacher, have washed your feet, you also ought to wash one another's feet. For I have set you an example, that you also should do as I have done to you" (John 13:14–15).

While gazing upon that image, I realize that daring to confess our sins to one another, and holding this privilege as both sacred and beautiful, is to become divine servants. As is the case with foot washing, in an act of confessing and serving as confessor for others, we humbly demonstrate our love, care, and trust for one another, and our trust that God somehow takes part. We do so, moreover, as we journey *together*, fellow pilgrims in faith, seeking to serve God, one another, and the world in Jesus Christ, and to serve in all the togetherness *and* messiness joined to our journeys. Both of these acts, washing feet and offering and hearing confessions, are sacred in that they foster what Calvin wanted for us and what I believe Jesus would want, too—namely, that "we should lay our burdens on one another's breasts, to receive among ourselves mutual counsel, mutual compassion, and mutual consolation," and we should follow these efforts with prayer for one another.[24]

Much is at stake when we broach the act of confession in ways that I have advocated. As Jesus taught, "From everyone to whom much is given, much will be required; and from the one to whom much has been entrusted, even more will be demanded" (Luke 12:48b.). Confessing sins and serving as confessors requires courage, trust, responsibility, and fidelity, to God and to one another. These confessional acts also require that we not misuse the power that persons inevitably give us when becoming vulnerable by disclosing their pain. And yet, a richer confessional life offers God's benefits (Ps 103:2). It fosters eagerness to serve one another in ways that the Gospel invites. It helps us relinquish some of the burdens that come with hiding our transgressions, so that we change our relationship to our sins, and our relationships with those they affect, in faithful ways. With a richer confessional life we may grow more and more into the hope, joy, and grace

---

23. The work of this Texas artist, Max Greiner Jr., encompasses religious themes.

24. Calvin, *Institutes*, 1:630.

that is ours precisely because God has forgiven us and we may forgive one another in the name of Christ.

Bibliography

Adams, Nicholas. "Rahner's Reception in Twentieth Century Protestant Theology." In *The Cambridge Companion to Karl Rahner*, edited by Declan Marmion and Mary E. Hines, 211–24. New York: Cambridge University Press, 2005.

Alison, James. "Sacrifice, Law and the Catholic Faith: Is Secularity Really the Enemy?" The 2006 *Tablet* Lecture. Online: www.jamesalison.co.uk/texts/eng36.html.

Alston, William. *Beyond "Justification": Dimensions of Epistemic Valuation*. Ithaca: Cornell University Press, 2005.

"American Piety in the 21st Century: New Insights to the Depth and Complexity of Religion in the United States." Selected findings from the Baylor Religion Survey, September 2006. Online: http://www.baylor.edu/content/services/document.php/33304.pdf.

Anonymous. "Pleidooi voor herwaardering dogmatiek." *Reformatorisch Dagblad*, July 4, 2008. Online: http://www.refdag.nl/kerkplein/kerknieuws/pleidooi_voor_herwaardering_dogmatiek_1_265643.

Antonova, Clemena. "On the Problem of 'Reverse Perspective': Definitions East and West." *Leonardo* 43 (2010) 464–69.

———. *Space, Time, and Presence in the Icon: Seeing the World with the Eyes of God*. Farnham, UK: Ashgate, 2010.

Audi, Robert. *Rationality and Religious Commitment*. Oxford: Oxford University Press, 2011.

Babcock, Linda, and George Loewenstein. "Explaining Bargaining Impasse: The Role of Self-Serving Biases." *Journal of Economic Perspectives* 11 (1997) 109–26.

Baptism, Eucharist, and Ministry. Faith and Order Paper 111. Geneva: World Council of Churches, 1982.

Barnes, Patrick. "The Church Is Visible and One: A Critique of Protestant Ecclesiology." Online: http://orthodoxinfo.com/inquirers/church.pdf.

Barstow, Anne Llewellyn, ed. *War's Dirty Secret: Rape, Prostitution and Other Crimes against Women*. Cleveland: Pilgrim, 2000.

Barth, Karl. "Church and Theology." In *Theology and Church: Shorter Writings, 1920–1928*, translated by Louise P. Smith, 286–306. New York: Harper & Row, 1962.

———. *Church Dogmatics*. Edited by Geoffrey Bromiley and T. F. Torrance. 4 vols. Edinburgh: T. & T. Clark, 1956–1976.

———. *The Epistle to the Romans*. Translated by Edwyn C. Hoskyns. Oxford: Oxford University Press, 1968.

———. *Evangelical Theology*. Translated by Grover Foley. Grand Rapids: Eerdmans, 1992.

———. *Prayer and Preaching*. London: SCM, 1964.

Basu, Moni. "A Symbol of Defiance in Gadhafi's Libya, Eman al-Obeidi Just Wants to Be Left Alone." *CNN*, April 9, 2012. Online: http://edition.cnn.com/2012/04/08/us/colorado-libyan-rape-victim/index.html.

Belzen, Jacob A. "Studying the Specificity of Spirituality: Lessons from the Psychology of Religion." *Mental Health, Religion and Culture* 12 (2009) 205–22.

Benjamin, Walter. *Reflections: Essays, Aphorisms, Autobiographical Writings*. Edited by Peter Demetz. New York: Harcourt Brace Jovanovich, 1978.

Berger, Peter L. *Between Relativism and Fundamentalism: Religious Resources for a Middle Position*. Grand Rapids: Eerdmans, 2010.

Berger, Peter L., and Anton C. Zijderveld. *In Praise of Doubt: How to Have Convictions without Becoming Fanatic*. New York: HarperCollins, 2009.

Bergmann, Michael. "Rational Disagreement after Full Disclosure." *Episteme* 6 (2009) 336–53.

Berkhof, Heinrik. *Christelijk Geloof: Een inleiding tot de geloofsleer*. Nijkerk: Callenbach, 1973. English translation: *Christian Faith: An Introduction to the Study of the Faith*. Grand Rapids: Eerdmans, 1979.

Berscheid, Ellen. "Love in the Fourth Dimension." *Annual Review of Psychology* 61 (2010) 1–25.

Birch, Bruce, and Larry Rasmussen. *Bible and Ethics in the Christian Life*. Minneapolis: Augsburg, 1989.

Birkner, Hans-Joachim. "Glaubenslehre und Modernitätserfahrung: Ernst Troeltsch als Dogmatiker." In *Umstrittene Moderne: Die Zukunft der Neuzeit im Urteil der Epoche Ernst Troeltschs*, edited by Horst Renz and Friedrich Wilhelm Graf, 325–37. Gütersloh: Gerd Mohn, 1987.

Bonhoeffer, Dietrich. *Life Together; Prayerbook of the Bible*. Dietrich Bonhoeffer Works 5. Edited by Geffrey B. Kelly. Translated by Daniel W. Bloesch and James H. Burtness. Minneapolis: Fortress, 2005.

———. *Spiritual Care*. Translated by Jay C. Rochelle. Minneapolis: Fortress, 1985.

Book of Common Prayer. N.p.: Seabury, 1979.

Book of Common Worship. Presbyterian Church (USA). Louisville: Westminster John Knox, 1993.

Book of Confessions. Louisville: Office of the General Assembly, Presbyterian Church (USA), 1996.

Bowcott, Owen. "Libya Mass Rape Claims: Using Viagra Would Be a Horrific First." *The Guardian*, June 10, 2011. Online: http://www.theguardian.com/world/2011/jun/09/libya-mass-rape-viagra-claim.

Brady, Bernard V. *The Moral Bond of Community: Justice and Discourse in Christian Morality*. Washington, DC: Georgetown University Press, 1998.

Brownmiller, Susan. *Against Our Will: Men, Women, and Rape*. New York: Simon and Schuster, 1975.

Brubaker, David R. *Promise and Peril: Understanding and Managing Change and Conflict in Congregations*. Herndon, VA: Alban Institute, 2009.

Bullens, Lottie, et al. "Keeping One's Options Open: The Detrimental Consequences of Decision Reversibility." *Journal of Experimental Social Psychology* 47 (2011) 800–805.

Bullinger, Heinrich. *Second Helvetic Confession* (1566). *The Book of Confessions*, The Constitution of the Presbyterian Church (USA), Part I. Louisville: Office of the General Assembly, 2004.

Busch, Eberhard. "Reformed Strength in Its Denominational Weakness." In *Reformed Theology: Identity and Ecumenicity*, edited by Wallace Alston and Michael Welker, 20–33. Grand Rapids: Eerdmans, 2003.

Calvin, John. *Commentary on the Gospel of John*. Calvin's Commentaries. Grand Rapids: Baker, 2009.

———. *Institutes of the Christian Religion*. Edited by John T. McNeill. Translated by Ford Lewis Battles. 2 vols. Philadelphia: Westminster, 1960.

Capps, Donald. *The Depleted Self: Sin in a Narcissistic Age*. Minneapolis: Fortress, 1993.

Caputo, John D. *What Would Jesus Deconstruct? The Good News of Postmodernism for the Church*. Grand Rapids: Baker Academic, 2007.

Chopp, Rebecca. *The Power to Speak: Feminism, Language, God*. New York: Crossroad, 1991.

Christie, Nils. "Conflicts as Property." *The British Journal of Criminology* 17 (1977) 1–15.

Chulov, Martin. "Gaddafi Killer Faces Prosecution, Says Libyan Interim Government." *The Guardian*, October 28, 2011. Online: http://www.theguardian.com/world/2011/oct/27/gaddafi-killers-face-prosecution-libya.

Cloke, Paul, and Justin Beaumont. "Geographies of Postsecular Rapprochement in the City." *Progress in Human Geography*, April 18, 2012. Online: http://phg.sagepub.com/content/37/1/27.full.pdf+html.

Cole, Allan Hugh, Jr. *Be Not Anxious: Pastoral Care of Disquieted Souls*. Grand Rapids: Eerdmans, 2008.

———. *The Life of Prayer: Mind, Body, and Soul*. Louisville: Westminster John Knox, 2009.

Collins, Randall. *The Sociology of Philosophies: A Global Theory of Intellectual Change*. Cambridge, MA: Belknap, 1998.

Conee, Earl. "Peerage." *Episteme* 6 (2009) 313–23.

Cottingham, John. *The Spiritual Dimension: Religion, Philosophy, and Human Value*. Cambridge: Cambridge University Press, 2005.

Cunningham, David S. *These Three Are One: The Practice of Trinitarian Theology*. Oxford: Blackwell, 1998.

Daniel, Lillian. "Spiritual but Not Religious? Please Stop Boring Me." *Huffington Post*, September 13, 2011. Online: http://www.huffingtonpost.com/lillian-daniel/spiritual-but-not-religio_b_959216.html.

Dawkins, Richard. *The God Delusion*. New York: Mariner, 2008.

Deci, Edward L., and Richard M. Ryan. *Intrinsic Motivation and Self-Determination in Human Behavior*. New York: Plenum, 1985.

———. "Self-Determination Theory and the Facilitation of Intrinsic Motivation, Social Development, and Well-Being." *American Psychologist* 55 (2000) 68–78.

"Decoding a Death: What Happened to Muammar Gaddafi?" *Global Post*. Online: http://www.globalpost.com/dispatch/news/regions/africa/111021/gaddafi-news-globalpost-videos-photos-dispatches.

De Lange, Frits. *In Andermans Handen: Over Flow en Grenzen in de Zorg*. Zoetermeer: Meinema, 2011.

Ditmanson, Harold. "A Response to the Fries-Rahner Proposal for Church Unity." *Lutheran Quarterly* 1 (1987) 375–91.

D'Onofrio, Giulio. "The *Concordia* of Augustine and Dionysius: Toward a Hermeneutic of the Disagreement of Patristic Sources in John the Scot's *Periphyseon.*" In *Eriugena: East and West*, edited by Bernard McGinn and Willemien Otten, 115–40. Notre Dame: Notre Dame University Press, 1994.

Dykstra, Craig. "Reconceiving Practices." In *Shifting Boundaries: Contextual Approaches to the Structure of Theological Education*, edited by Barbara Wheeler and Edward Farley, 35–66. Louisville: Westminster John Knox, 1991.

Edmondson, Stephen. *Calvin's Christology*. Cambridge: Cambridge University Press, 2004.

Elders, Leo. "Thomas Aquinas and the Fathers of the Church." In *The Reception of the Church Fathers in the West*, edited by Irena Backus, 337–66. Leiden: Brill, 1997.

Elgin, Catherine. "Persistent Disagreement." In *Disagreement*, edited by Richard Feldman and Ted A. Warfield, 53–68. Oxford: Oxford University Press, 2010.

Elwell, Walter A., ed. *Evangelical Dictionary of Theology*. Grand Rapids: Baker, 2001.

Emery, Gilles. "A Note on St. Thomas and the Eastern Fathers. 2 vols." In *Trinity, Church, and the Human Person: Thomistic Essays*, 193–207. Naples, FL: Sapientia Press of Ave Maria University, 2007.

Fehr, B., and S. Sprecher. "Compassionate Love: Conceptual, Measurement, and Relational Issues." In *The Science of Compassionate Love: Theory, Research, and Applications*, edited by Beverly Fehr et al., 27–52. Malden, MA: Wiley-Blackwell, 2008.

———. "Prototype Analysis of the Concept of Compassionate Love." *Personal Relationships* 16 (2009) 343–64.

Fehr, Beverly, et al. *The Science of Compassionate Love: Theory, Research, and Applications*. Malden, MA: Wiley-Blackwell, 2009.

Feldman, Richard, and Ted A. Warfield. *Disagreement*. Oxford: Oxford University Press, 2010.

Flannery, Austin, ed. *Vatican II: The Conciliar and Post-Conciliar Documents*. New rev. ed. Northport, NY: Costello, 1975.

Florovsky, Georges. "Patristic Theology and the Ethos of the Orthodox Church." In *Aspects of Church History*, 11–30. Collected Works of Georges Florovsky 4. Belmont, MA: Nordland, 1975.

Friedman, Edwin. *Generation to Generation: Family Process in Church and Synagogue*. New York: Guilford, 1985.

Fries, Heinrich, and Karl Rahner. *Unity of the Churches: An Actual Possibility*. Translated by Ruth C. L. Gritsch and Eric W. Gritsch. 1985. Reprint, Eugene, OR: Wipf & Stock, 2008.

Gaillardetz, Richard A., ed. *When the Magisterium Intervenes*. Collegeville, MN: Liturgical, 2012.

Gallagher, Larry. "The Compassion Instinct." *Ode* 133 (2011). Online: http://odewire.com/118151/the-compassion-instinct.html.

Ghellinck, Joseph de. *Le Mouvement Théologique du XIIe Siècle*. 2nd ed. Bruges: Éditions "De Tempel," 1948.

Gräb, Wilhelm, and Lars Charbonnier. *Secularization Theories, Religious Identity and Practical Theology: Developing International Practical Theology for the 21st Century*. Conference of the International Academy of Practical Theology 8. Berlin: LIT, 2009.

Graber, D. R., and M. D. Mitcham. "Compassionate Clinicians: Take Patient Care beyond the Ordinary." *Holistic Nursing Practice* 18 (2004) 87–94.

Graf, Friedrich Wilhelm. *Moses Vermächtnis: Über göttliche und menschliche Gesetze.* Munich: C. H. Beck, 2006.

Gramsci, Antonio. *Selections from the Prison Notebooks.* Edited by Quintin Hoare and Geoffrey Nowell Smith. New York: International, 1971.

Gustafson, James. "An Analysis of Church and Society Social Ethical Writings." *Ecumenical Review* 40 (1988) 267–78.

———. *Christ and the Moral Life.* Chicago: University of Chicago Press, 1968.

———. "Moral Discourse about Medicine: A Variety of Forms." *Journal of Medicine and Philosophy* 15 (1990) 125–42.

———. *Varieties of Moral Discourse: Prophetic, Narrative, Ethical, and Policy.* Stob Lectures of Calvin College and Seminary. Grand Rapids: Calvin College and Seminary, 1988.

Gutiérrez, Gustavo. *A Theology of Liberation: History, Politics and Salvation.* Fifteenth anniversary ed. Maryknoll, NY: Orbis, 1988.

Gutting, Gary. *What Philosophers Know: Case Studies in Recent Analytic Philosophy.* Cambridge: Cambridge University Press, 2009.

Gyatzo, Tenzin. "Many Faiths, One Truth." *The New York Times,* May 24, 2010. Online: http://www.nytimes.com/2010/05/25/opinion/25gyatso.html.

———. *Toward a True Kinship of Faiths: How the World's Religions Can Come Together.* New York: Three Rivers, 2010.

Habermas, Jürgen, et al. *An Awareness of What Is Missing: Faith and Reason in a Postsecular Age.* Cambridge: Polity, 2010.

Hahnenberg, Edward P. *Awakening Vocation: A Theology of Christian Call.* Collegeville, MN: Liturgical, 2010.

Haight, Roger. *Christian Community in History.* 3 vols. New York: Continuum, 2004–2008.

———. "Preface." In *Comparative Ecclesiology,* edited by Gerald Mannion, xix–xxi. London: T. & T. Clark, 2008.

Hankey, Katherine, and William Fischer. "I Love to Tell the Story." Online: http://www.hymnsite.com/lyrics/umh156.sht.

Harman, Gilbert. "Practical Aspects of Theoretical Reasoning." In *The Oxford Handbook of Rationality,* edited by Alfred E. Mele and Piers Rawling, 45–56. Oxford: Oxford University Press, 2004.

Hartley, L. P. *The Go-Between.* London: Hamish Hamilton, 1953.

Healy, Nicholas M. *Church, World and the Christian Life: Practical-Prophetic Ecclesiology.* New York: Cambridge University Press, 2000.

Hedgepeth, Sonja M., and Rochelle G. Saidel, eds. *Sexual Violence against Jewish Women during the Holocaust.* Waltham, MA: Brandeis University Press, 2010.

Heijst, Annelies van. *Professional Loving Care: An Ethical View of the Health Care Sector.* Leuven: Peeters, 2011.

Hunsinger, Deborah van Deusen. *Pray Without Ceasing: Revitalizing Pastoral Care.* Grand Rapids: Eerdmans, 1995.

Hunsinger, Deborah van Deusen, and Theresa F. Latini. *Transforming Church Conflict: Compassionate Leadership in Action.* Louisville: Westminster John Knox, 2013.

Hunsinger, George. *The Eucharist and Ecumenism: Let Us Keep the Feast.* Cambridge: Cambridge University Press, 2008.

Irvin, Dale. *Christian Histories, Christian Traditioning: Rendering Accounts.* Maryknoll, NY: Orbis, 1998.

Isasi-Diaz, Maria. *En la Lucha: A Hispanic Women's Liberation Theology.* Minneapolis: Fortress, 1993.

Jackson, Eric. "The Top Ten Lessons Steve Jobs Can Teach Us—If We'll Listen." *Forbes,* October 5, 2011. Online: http://www.forbes.com/sites/ericjackson/2011/09/19/the-top-ten-lessons-steve-jobs-can-teach-us-if-well-listen/.

Johnson-Laird, Philip. *How We Reason.* Oxford: Oxford University Press, 2006.

Josephus, Flavius. *Jewish Antiquities.* Books 5–8. Translated by Henry Saint John Thackeray and Ralph Marcus. Cambridge, MA: Harvard University Press, 1935.

———. *The Works of Flavius Josephus.* Translated by William Whiston. Auburn, NY: John E. Beardsley, 1895.

Kahneman, Daniel. *Thinking, Fast and Slow.* London: Allen Lane, 2011.

Kant, Immanuel. *Religion Within the Limits of Reason Alone.* New York: Harper, 1960.

Keltner, Dacher, et al. *The Compassionate Instinct: The Science of Human Goodness.* New York: Norton, 2010.

Kirkpatrick, David D. "Court in Egypt Says Rights of Women Were Violated." *The New York Times,* December 28, 2011. Online: http://www.nytimes.com/2011/12/28/world/africa/egyptian-court-says-virginity-tests-violated-womens-rights.html.

———. "Mass March by Cairo Women in Protest Over Abuse by Soldiers." *The New York Times,* December 21, 2011. Online: http://www.nytimes.com/2011/12/21/world/middleeast/violence-enters-5th-day-as-egyptian-general-blames-protesters.html?pagewanted=all.

Kirkpatrick, David D., and Rod Nordland. "Waves of Disinformation and Confusion Swamp the Truth in Libya." *The New York Times,* August 24, 2011. Online: http://www.nytimes.com/2011/08/24/world/africa/24fog.html?pagewanted=all.

Koopman, Nico. "Churches and Public Policy Discourses in South Africa." *Journal of Theology for Southern Africa* 136 (2010) 41–56.

———. "Modes of Prophecy in a Democracy?" In *Prophetic Witness: An Appropriate Contemporary Mode of Public Discourse? Theology in the Public Square/Theologie in der Öffenlichkeit,* edited by Heinrich Bedford-Strohm and Étienne de Villiers, 181–92. Berlin: LIT, 2011.

Kraybill, Ron. *The Little Book of Cool Tools for Hot Topics: Group Tools to Facilitate Meetings when Things Are Hot.* Intercourse, PA: Good Books, 2007.

Kuitert, H. M. *Het Algemeen Betwijfeld Christelijk Geloof: Een Herziening.* Baarn: Ten Have, 1992.

Lafont, Ghislain. *Imagining the Catholic Church: Structured Communion in the Spirit.* Collegeville, MN: Liturgical, 2000.

Lakeland, Paul. *The Church: Living Communion.* Collegeville, MN: Liturgical, 2009.

Larrick, Richard P. "Debiasing." In *Blackwell Handbook of Judgment and Decision Making,* edited by Derek Koehler and Nigel Harvey, 316–37. Oxford: Blackwell, 2004.

Leas, Speed. *Moving Your Church through Conflict.* Bethesda, MD: Alban Institute, 1985.

Lederach, John Paul. *The Journey toward Reconciliation.* Scottdale, PA: Herald, 1999.

———. *The Little Book of Conflict Transformation.* Intercourse, PA: Good Books, 2003.

———. *The Moral Imagination: The Art and Soul of Building Peace.* New York: Oxford University Press, 2005.

Lehmann, Paul. *Forgiveness: A Decisive Issue in Protestant Thought.* Ann Arbor, MI: University Microfilms, 1941.

Lonergan, Bernard. *A Second Collection: Papers.* Edited by William F. J. Ryan and Bernard J. Tyrrell. Toronto: University of Toronto Press, 1974.

Lorentzen, Lois Ann, and Jennifer Turpin, eds. *The Women and War Reader.* New York: New York University Press, 1998.

Lutheran Book of Worship, Minister's Edition. 1978. Reprint, Philadelphia: Board of Publication, Lutheran Church in America, 2001.

Lyon, K. Brynolf. "Scapegoating in Congregational and Group Life: Practical Theological Reflections on the Unbearable." In *Healing Wisdom: Depth Psychology and the Pastoral Ministry,* edited by Kathleen Greider, Deborah van Deusen Hunsinger, and Felicity Brock Kelcourse, 141–56. Grand Rapids: Eerdmans, 2010.

Lyotard, Jean-François. *The Postmodern Condition: A Report on Knowledge.* Translated by Geoff Bennington and Brian Massumi. Minneapolis: University of Minnesota Press, 1999.

Mannion, Gerard, ed. *Comparative Ecclesiology.* London: T. & T. Clark, 2008.

———. *Ecclesiology and Postmodernity: Questions for Our Time.* Collegeville, MN: Liturgical, 2007.

Marler, J. C. "Dialectical Use of Authority in the *Periphyseon.*" In *Eriugena: East and West,* edited by Bernard McGinn and Willemien Otten, 95–113. Notre Dame: Notre Dame University Press, 1994.

Martin, James. *Between Heaven and Mirth: Why Joy, Humor and Laughter Are at the Heart of the Spiritual Life.* New York: HarperCollins, 2011.

Massingale, Bryan. "See, I Am Doing Something New!" Online: http://www.jknirp.com/massin.htm.

McCold, Paul, and Ted Wachtel. "In Pursuit of Paradigm: A Theory of Restorative Justice." Paper presented at the 13th World Congress of Criminology, Rio de Janeiro, August 10–15, 2003. Online: http://www.iirp.edu/pdf/paradigm.pdf.

McGilchrist, Iain. *The Master and His Emissary.* New Haven: Yale University Press, 2009.

McGuire, Danielle. *At the Dark End of the Street: Black Women, Rape and Resistance—a New History of the Civil Rights Movement from Rosa Parks to Black Power.* New York: Knopf, 2010.

McGuire, M. B. *Lived Religion: Faith and Practice in Everyday Life.* Oxford: Oxford University Press, 2008.

Mersch, Emile. *The Whole Christ: The Historical Development of the Doctrine of the Mystical Body in Scripture and Tradition.* 1938. Reprint, Eugene, OR: Wipf & Stock, 2011.

Miller, Jean Baker. *Toward a New Psychology of Women.* Boston: Beacon, 1976.

Molendijk, Arie L. "Abschied vom Christentum: Der Fall Allard Pierson." In *Post-Theism: Reframing the Judeo-Christian Tradition,* edited by Henri Krop, Arie L. Molendijk, and Hent de Vries, 141–57. Leuven: Peeters, 2000.

———. *The Emergence of Science of Religion in the Netherlands.* Leiden: Brill, 2005.

———. "'Non-Binding Talk': The Fate of Schleiermacher's Concept of Historical-Empirical Dogmatics." In *Schleiermacher, the Study of Religion, and the Future of Theology: A Transatlantic Dialogue,* edited by Brent Sockness and Wilhelm Gräb, 203–13. Berlin: de Gruyter, 2010.

———. *Zwischen Theologie und Soziologie: Ernst Troeltschs Typen der Christlichen Gemeinschaftsbildung: Kirche, Sekte, Mystik.* Gütersloh: Gerd Mohn, 1996.

Molendijk, Arie L., et al. *Exploring the Postsecular: The Religious, the Political, the Urban.* Leiden: Brill, 2010.

Moltmann, Jürgen. *The Crucified God.* 1974. Reprint, Minneapolis: Fortress, 1993.

Murray, Paul D., ed. *Receptive Ecumenism and the Call to Catholic Learning.* Oxford: Oxford University Press, 2008.

Nieman, James R. "The Theological Work of Denominations." In *Church, Identity, and Change: Theology and Denominational Structures in Unsettled Times*, edited by David A. Roozen and James R. Nieman, 625–53. Grand Rapids: Eerdmans, 2005.

Norris, Richard A., Jr., ed. and trans. *The Christological Controversy.* Sources of Early Christian Thought. Minneapolis: Fortress, 1980.

Oakley, Francis, and Bruce Russett, eds. *Governance, Accountability, and the Future of the Catholic Church.* New York: Continuum, 2004.

Oman, D. "Compassionate Love: Accomplishments and Challenges in an Emerging Scientific/Spiritual Research Field." *Mental Health, Religion and Culture* 14 (2011) 945–81.

Oppy, Graham. "Disagreement." *International Journal of Philosophy of Religion* 68 (2010) 183–99.

Palmer, Jason. "Religion May Become Extinct in Nine Nations." *BBC News*, March 24, 2011. Online: http://www.bbc.co.uk/news/science-environment-12811197.

Pannenberg, Wolfhart. *Jesus: God and Man.* 1968. Reprint, Philadelphia: Westminster, 1977.

Parry, Alan, and Robert E. Doan. *Story Re-visions: Narrative Therapy in the Postmodern World.* New York: Guilford, 1994.

Pauw, Amy Plantinga. "Presbyterianism and Denomination." In *Denomination: Assessing an Ecclesiological Category*, edited by Paul Collins and Barry Ensign-George, 133–46. London: T. & T. Clark, 2011.

Pierson, Allard. "Heidelberg" (1888). In *Uit de verspreide geschriften van Allard Pierson: Feuilletons verschenen in 1858–1889*, 85–91. The Hague: Martinus Nijhoff, 1906.

———. "Ter Uitvaart." *De Gids* 40 (1876) 185–249, 434–500.

Plested, Marcus. *Orthodox Readings of Aquinas.* Oxford: Oxford University Press, 2012.

———. "The Patristic Hermeneutic of the Council of Aachen: Towards a Theory of Iconic Reception." In *Die Filioque-Kontroverse*, edited by Michael Böhnke et al., 130–37. Freiburg im Breisgau: Herder, 2011.

Plous, Scott. *The Psychology of Judgment and Decision Making.* New York: McGraw-Hill, 1993.

Polanyi, Michael. *The Tacit Dimension.* Garden City, NY: Anchor, 1967.

Pranis, Kay. *The Little Book of Circle Processes.* Intercourse, PA: Good Books, 2005.

Professional Standard of the Association of Spiritual Counselors in Care Institutions (VGVZ). Online: http://www.vgvz.nl/userfiles/files/Algemene_teksten_website/beroepsstandaard.pdf.

Puchalski, C. M. "The Role of Spirituality in Health Care." *Proceedings* (Baylor University Medical Center) 14 (2001) 352–57.

Puchalski, C. M., et al. "Improving the Quality of Spiritual Care as a Dimension of Palliative Care: The Report of the Consensus Conference." *Journal of Palliative Medicine* 12 (2009) 885–904.

Rahner, Karl. *Foundations of Christian Faith: An Introduction to the Idea of Christianity.* Translated by William V. Dych. New York: Crossroad, 1978.

Rasmussen, Larry. "Shaping Communities." In *Practicing Our Faith*, edited by Dorothy Bass, 117–30. San Francisco: Jossey-Bass, 1997.

Richey, Russell E. "Denominations and Denominationalism: An American Morphology." In *Reimagining Denominationalism: Interpretive Essays*, edited by Robert Bruce Mullin and Russell E. Richey, 74–98. Oxford: Oxford University Press, 1994.

Rieger, Joerg. *Christ and Empire: From Rome to Postcolonial Times*. Minneapolis: Fortress, 2007.

Rigby, Cynthia L. "Beautiful Playing: Moltmann, Barth, and the Work of the Christian." In *Theology as Conversation: The Significance of Dialogue in Historical and Contemporary Theology*, edited by Bruce L. McCormack and Kimlyn J. Bender, 101–16. Grand Rapids: Eerdmans, 2009.

Robinson, Marilynne. *The Death of Adam: Essays on Modern Thought*. New York: Picador, 2005.

Rosenberg, Marshall. *Nonviolent Communication: A Language of Life*. Encinitas, CA: Puddledancer, 2003.

Ryan, Richard M., et al. "Living Well: A Self-Determination Theory Perspective on Eudaimonia." *Journal of Happiness Studies* 9 (2008) 139–70.

Saxena, Shekhar, et al. "A Commentary: Cross-Cultural Quality-of-Life Assessment at the End of Life." *The Gerontologist* 42 (2002) 81–85.

Schafer, Mark, and Scott Crichlow. *Groupthink versus High-Quality Decision Making in International Relations*. New York: Columbia University Press, 2010.

Schleiermacher, Friedrich. *Kurze Darstellung des theologischen Studiums* (2nd rev. ed., 1830). In vol. I/6 of *Kritische Gesamtausgabe*, edited by Dirk Schmid, 317–446. Berlin: de Gruyter, 1998.

———. *Der christliche Glaube nach den Grundsätzen der evangelischen Kirche im Zusammenhange dargestellt* (2nd rev. ed., 1830–31). In volume I/13 of *Kritische Gesamtausgabe*, edited by Rolf Schäfer. Berlin: de Gruyter, 2003.

Schulze, Gerhard. *Die Erlebnisgesellschaft: Kultursoziologie der Gegenwart*. Frankfurt am Main: Campus, 2005.

"The Second Helvetic Confession." In *The Constitution of the Presbyterian Church (USA): Part I, Book of Confessions*. Louisville: Office of the General Assembly, Presbyterian Church (USA), 1996.

Sinkewicz, Robert. *Saint Gregory Palamas: The One Hundred and Fifty Chapters*. Studies and Texts 83. Toronto: Pontifical Institute of Mediaeval Studies, 1988.

Smeets, Wim. *Spiritual Care in a Hospital Setting: An Empirical-Theological Exploration*. Leiden: Brill, 2006.

Stassen, Glen H. *Just Peacemaking: Transforming Initiatives for Justice and Peace*. Louisville: Westminster John Knox, 1992.

Stoppelenburg, Eric, et al. *Mindfulness: Spirituele Traditie of Therapeutische Techniek?* Tilburg: KSGV, 2009.

Streib, Heinz, et al. *Lived Religion: Conceptual, Empirical and Practical-Theological Approaches; Essays in Honor of Hans-Günter Heimbrock*. Leiden: Brill, 2008.

Taylor, Charles. *A Secular Age*. Cambridge, MA: Belknap, 2007.

———. *Sources of the Self: The Making of the Modern Identity*. Cambridge, MA: Harvard University Press, 1989.

Thiele, Leslie Paul. *The Heart of Judgment: Practical Wisdom, Neuroscience and Narrative*. Cambridge: Cambridge University Press, 2006.

Thomassin, Louis. *Dogmatum theologicorum*. Vol. 1. Paris: Francis Muguet, 1684.

Thune, Michael. "'Partial Defeaters' and the Epistemology of Disagreement." *The Philosophical Quarterly* 60 (2010) 355–72.

Bibliography

Tierney, Brian. "Church Law and Alternative Structures." In *Governance, Accountability, and the Future of the Catholic Church*, edited by Francis Oakley and Bruce Russett, 49–61. New York: Continuum, 2004.

Todd, Margo. "Bishops in the Kirk: William Cowper of Galloway and the Puritan Episcopacy of Scotland." *Scottish Journal of Theology* 57 (2004) 300–312.

Tombs, David. "Crucifixion, State Terror and Sexual Abuse." *Union Seminary Quarterly Review* 53 (1999) 89–108.

———. "Gaddafi Sexually Abused on Capture." BBC Radio Ulster, *Sunday Sequence*, October 25, 2011.

———. "Prisoner Abuse: From Abu Ghraib to *The Passion of the Christ*." In *Religions and the Politics of Peace and Conflict*, edited by Linda Hogan and Dylan Lehrke, 179–205. Eugene, OR: Pickwick, 2008.

Tress, Bärbel, et al., eds. *From Landscape Research to Landscape Planning: Aspects of Integration, Education and Application*. Dordrecht: Springer, 2006.

Troeltsch, Ernst. "The Dogmatics of the History-of-Religions School" (1913). In *Religion in History*, edited by James Luther Adams, 87–108. Minneapolis: Fortress, 1991.

———. *Glaubenslehre*. Munich: Duncker & Humblot, 1925.

———. "Half a Century of Theology: A Review" (1908). In *Writings on Theology and Religion*, translated and edited by Robert Morgan and Michael Pye, 53–81. London: Duckworth, 1977.

Tutu, Desmond. *No Future Without Forgiveness*. New York: Doubleday, 1999.

Underwood, Lynn G. "Compassionate Love: A Framework for Research." In *The Science of Compassionate Love: Theory, Research, and Applications*, edited by B. A. Fehr et al., 3–25. Malden, MA: Blackwell, 2008.

———. "The Human Experience of Compassionate Love: Conceptual Mapping and Data from Selected Studies." In *Altruism and Altruistic Love: Science, Philosophy, and Religion in Dialogue*, edited by Stephen Garrard Post et al., 72–88. New York: Oxford University Press, 2002.

Van Huyssteen, Wentzel. *Theology and the Justification of Faith: Constructing Theories in Systematic Theology*. Grand Rapids: Eerdmans, 1989.

Van Inwagen, Peter. "It Is Wrong, Always, Everywhere, and for Anyone, to Believe Anything, Upon Insufficient Evidence." In *Faith, Freedom, and Rationality*, edited by Jeff Jordan and Daniel Howard-Snyder, 137–54. Lanham, MD: Rowman & Littlefield, 1996.

Veltkamp, J. "In de Ontmoeting Geboren: Pastorale Identiteit op het Raakvlak van Religieuze Biografie en Theologische Existentie." *Tijdschrift Geestelijke Verzorging* 39 (2006) 27–35.

Volpintesta, Edward J. "Compassion." *The Hastings Center Report* 41 (2011) 7–8.

Waal, Frans B. M. de. *The Age of Empathy: Nature's Lessons for a Kinder Society*. New York: Harmony, 2009.

Wainwright, Geoffrey. *For Our Salvation: Two Approaches to the Work of Christ*. Grand Rapids: Eerdmans, 1997.

Webster, John. "The Visible Attests the Invisible." In *The Community of the Word: Toward an Evangelical Ecclesiology*, edited by Daniel Treier and Mark Husbands, 96–113. Downers Grove, IL: IVP Academic, 2005.

Weiner, Eric. "Americans: Undecided about God?" *The New York Times*, December 10, 2011. Online: http://www.nytimes.com/2011/12/11/opinion/sunday/americans-and-god.html?_r=0.

———. *Man Seeks God: My Flirtations with the Divine*. New York: Hachette, 2011.

Westerink, Herman. "Spirituality in Psychology of Religion: A Concept in Search of Its Meaning." *Archive for the Psychology of Religion* 34 (2012) 3–15.

White, Michael. *Maps of Narrative Practice*. New York: Norton, 2007.

White, Michael, and David Epston. *Narrative Means to Therapeutic Ends*. New York: Norton, 1990.

WHOQOL-SRPB. World Health Organization Quality of Life Assessment—Spirituality, Religiousness, and Personal Beliefs, 2012. Online: http://www.who.int/mental_health/media/en/622.pdf.

Williams, Rowan. "Saving Time: Thoughts on Practice, Patience and Vision." *New Blackfriars* 73 (1992) 319–26.

Wogaman, J. Philip. *Christian Moral Judgment*. Louisville: Westminster John Knox, 1989.

Wolfe, Lauren. "Gloria Steinem on Rape in War, Its Causes, and How to Stop it." *The Atlantic*, February 2012. Online: http://www.theatlantic.com/international/archive/2012/02/gloria-steinem-on-rape-in-war-its-causes-and-how-to-stop-it/252470/.

Wolterstorff, Nicholas. *Reason within the Bounds of Religion*. Grand Rapids: Eerdmans, 1976.

Wyman, Walter E., Jr. *The Concept of Glaubenslehre: Ernst Troeltsch and the Theological Heritage of Schleiermacher*. Chico, CA: Scholars, 1983.

Zahn-Harnack, Agnes von. *Adolf von Harnack*. Berlin: Hans Bot, 1936.

Zehr, Howard. *Changing Lenses: A New Focus on Crime and Justice*. Scottdale, PA: Herald, 2005.

———. *The Little Book of Restorative Justice*. Intercourse, PA: Good Books, 2002.

Zock, Hetty. "The Prophetic Voice in a Culture of Multiplicity. A Perspective from Psychological Identity Theory." In *Prophetic Witness in World Christianities: Rethinking Pastoral Care and Counseling*, edited by Annemie Dillen et al., 97–114. International Practical Theology 13. Münster: LIT, 2011.

———. "The Spiritual Caregiver as a Liaison Officer: Relational Experiences, Spirituality and the Search for Meaning." *Counseling and Spirituality* 29 (2010) 65–84.

———. "The Split Professional Identity of the Chaplain as a Spiritual Caregiver in Contemporary Dutch Health Care." *The Journal of Pastoral Care & Counseling* 62:1–2 (2008) 137–39.

———. "Voicing the Self in Postsecular Society: A Psychological Perspective on Meaning-Making and Collective Identities." In *Exploring the Postsecular: The Religious, the Political, the Urban*, edited by Arie L. Molendijk et al., 131–44. Leiden: Brill, 2010.

Printed in Great Britain
by Amazon

10084182R10139